The Moral Significance of Class

The Moral Significance of Class analyses the moral aspects of people's experience of class inequalities. Class affects not only our material wealth but our access to things, relationships and practices which we have reason to value, including the esteem or respect of others and hence our sense of self-worth. It shapes the kind of people we become and our chances of living a fulfilling life. Yet contemporary culture is increasingly 'in denial' about class, finding it embarrassing to acknowledge, even though it can often be blatantly obvious. By drawing upon concepts from moral philosophy and social theory and applying them to empirical studies of class, this fascinating and accessible study shows how people are valued in a context in which their life-chances and achievements are objectively affected by the lottery of birth class, and by forces which have little to do with their moral qualities or other merits.

ANDREW SAYER is Professor of Social Theory and Political Economy at the Department of Sociology, Lancaster University. His publications include *Microcircuits of Capital* (1988, with K. J. Morgan), *Method in Social Science* (1992), *The New Social Economy* (1992, with R. A. Walker), *Radical Political Economy: A Critique* (1995), and *Realism and Social Science* (2000), and over eighty articles.

The Moral Significance
of Class

Andrew Sayer

CAMBRIDGE
UNIVERSITY PRESS

CAMBRIDGE UNIVERSITY PRESS
Cambridge, New York, Melbourne, Madrid, Cape Town, Singapore, São Paulo

Cambridge University Press
The Edinburgh Building, Cambridge CB2 2RU, UK

Published in the United States of America by Cambridge University Press, New York

www.cambridge.org
Information on this title: www.cambridge.org/9780521850894

© Andrew Sayer 2005

First published 2005

Printed in the United Kingdom at the University Press, Cambridge

A catalogue record for this book is available from the British Library

ISBN 0 521 85089 4 hardback
ISBN 0 521 61640 9 paperback

Contents

Preface and acknowledgements

I was tempted to call this book 'Think You're Better Than Us, Do You?', as that challenge, real or imagined, gets to the heart of the moral significance of class in everyday life. Class is not a reflection of moral worth or needs, and its relationship to merit is zero in childhood and more cause than effect later. Yet since class fundamentally affects the kind and quality of life we can lead its legitimacy is in question. This is what gives class its moral significance, not simply as a matter for moral and political philosophers to consider, but for our daily lived experience, in terms of how people treat and value one another. For all the many books on class in social science, remarkably few of them analyse the moral dimension of class. This is because of the wider problem, particularly in sociology, of what Axel Honneth terms 'anti-normativism', which renders opaque the evaluative character of our relationship to the world. In particular our concerns – the things that matter to us for our well-being, the things which we value and care about – are either ignored or dealt with in an alienated and alienating way which fails to identify why they matter so much.

Although this book is very much about the moral texture of everyday, lay, experience, I shall use concepts and analyses from philosophical literature on ethics – much of it normative – as well as sociology, to interpret lay responses to class. This is an unusual combination – indeed it is an experiment – but I hope to convince readers of its value primarily by example. At the same time I shall use and refer to many concepts which are simple and indeed familiar in everyday life, but my belief is that such is their familiarity that they are taken for granted instead of analysed. When we do examine them, we frequently find that they are rich in explanatory resources and normative implications.

This book was completed with the support of an ESRC fellowship, and sabbatical leave from Lancaster University.

Intellectually the book is most indebted first to the work of the late Pierre Bourdieu, whose untimely death in 2002 lost social science an outstanding theorist and its most perceptive analyst and enemy of class, and secondly to that widely misunderstood figure of the Scottish Enlightenment, Adam Smith.

Closer to home, I would like to thank John O'Neill for his generosity and clarity in discussing philosophical matters. For suggestions, feedback and generally provoking further thought, my thanks and appreciation to Margaret Archer, Jo Armstrong, John Baker, Rosemary Crompton, Norman Fairclough, Steve Fleetwood, Bob Jessop, Tony Lawson, Kathleen Lynch, Maureen McNeil, Jamie Morgan, Diane Reay, Garrath Williams, and Majid Yar, and likewise to Beverley Skeggs, Alan Warde, Nick Crossley and the other members of the Manchester Sociology Bourdieu group. For supporting research and sanity in academic life, I would like to thank Bob McKinlay, and Bob Jessop and my other sociology colleagues at Lancaster. For making the department run smoothly and happily, my thanks to Claire O'Donnell, Karen Gammon, Cath Gorton, Pennie Drinkall, and Joann Bowker. For musical sustenance I would particularly like to thank the VSBs, Richard Light, Gillian Welch and David Rawlings, and the late, incomparable, Kathleen Ferrier. My love and thanks to Eric Clark, Bridget Graham, Steve Fleetwood, Helle Fischer, Costis Hadjimichalis, Frank Hansen, Richard Light, Kevin Morgan, Caroline New, Wendy Olsen, John O'Neill, Lizzie Sayer, Beverley Skeggs, Dina Vaiou, Linda Woodhead and Karin Zotzmann for friendship and support, and special thanks and good wishes to Abby Day. The book is dedicated to my late mother, Mary Sayer, 29.9.1910–18.10.2003.

1 Introduction

Class is an embarrassing and unsettling subject. In many social situations it would be considered insensitive to refer to class, particularly to the class of someone to whom we are talking or who is within earshot. Unless they happen to be sociologists it is rare for people to ask others what class they are, not merely because it's usually obvious, but because it can seem rude to do so. It is significant that when we do mention it we generally use the euphemisms of 'working' class for lower class and 'middle' to include upper class. The embarrassment reflects the morally problematic nature of class, deriving from the fact that people's life-chances and who they become are strongly influenced by the accident of their natal class and the inequalities which follow from this. While we may want to say that class should not be seen as having anything to do with worth, this only makes the existence of class inequalities more troubling: how is it that our life-prospects, be they bleak or bright, have so little to do with what we need or deserve? Such questions are posed by the everyday experience of class, especially our relations with others of different classes.

Class matters to us not only because of differences in material wealth and economic security, but also because it affects our access to things, relationships, experiences and practices which we have reason to value, and hence our chances of living a fulfilling life. At the same time it affects how others value us and respond to us, which in turn affects our sense of self-worth. We are evaluative beings, continually monitoring and assessing our behaviour and that of others, needing their approval and respect, but in contemporary society this takes place in the context of inequalities such as those of class, gender and 'race' which affect both what we are able to do and how we are judged. Condescension, deference, shame, guilt, envy, resentment, arrogance, contempt, fear and mistrust, or simply mutual incomprehension and avoidance, typify relations between people of different classes. Some people may be, or want to be, respectful, considerate and warm to individuals from other classes, but the inequalities themselves are likely to frustrate their attempts by tainting them with suspicions of condescension, disrespect or unwanted familiarity. In responding in more or less subtle ways to others' class we are of course reacting to circumstances largely beyond their control, indeed to the accident of birth. To the extent that people are aware of this fact it can hardly fail to colour their feelings about class. All these things account for the common embarrassment and evasion that surrounds its discussion. Like it or not, class raises issues of how people are valued in a context in which their life-chances and achievements are objectively affected by factors which have little to do with their moral qualities or other merits.

In this book I attempt to analyse and explain the often-suppressed moral dimension of the subjective experience of class, and why it is significant. This dimension is implicit in many studies of this topic by sociologists, but is often overshadowed by emphases on the habitual character of behaviour, the pursuit of self-interest and power, and the influence of prevailing discourses. While all these are important, I want both to highlight the moral dimensions of actors' behaviour and struggles, and to analyse the lay normative ideas and sentiments that lie behind them in terms of their rationales. This is an analysis of how class inequalities influence people's commitments and their valuation and pursuit of goods, their ethical dispositions and their treatment of others, and how these in turn influence the reproduction or transformation of those inequalities. These are not simply mere facts about people; they clearly *matter* to them a great deal. They are things that they care about, and which make a difference to their well-being, indeed they are crucial to their identity or self-hood.

To analyse them I shall draw not only on existing work in sociology and social theory but on moral philosophy. This is an unusual combination but one that I feel is warranted by the complementarities in their strengths and weaknesses: insofar as sociology takes an interest in lay normative thought and feelings ('lay normativity', for short) it tends to be more interested in their social coordinates and in their implications for social order than in their actual rationales; on the other hand, in focusing on these rationales, moral philosophy tends to abstract moral concepts and sentiments from their social context, producing an individualistic analysis which imputes more responsibility to individuals than they can reasonably be expected to exercise. (Ironically, in view of the difference in degree of abstraction, this tendency to exaggerate the responsibility of individuals is common in lay thought too.) By these means, I hope not only to deepen understanding of class but to improve social theory's ability to illuminate lay normativity.

People's normative concerns in relation to class go beyond the unequal distribution of material goods and recognition and respect, to questions of just what is good in terms of ways of life, practices, objects, behaviours and types of character that people see as desirable. According to their class, gender, 'race', ethnicity and other social divisions, some may feel that they are achieving these goods, others that they lie beyond their reach. Actors compete and struggle both *for* such goods, that is compete for things which are agreed to be worthwhile, and over the definition of what *is* valuable or worthwhile. Some may want mainly the goods that the dominant groups monopolise, others may care most about different kinds of goods. I shall argue that we cannot understand these struggles purely in terms of a Hobbesian pursuit of advantage in terms of economic, cultural and social capital, as argued by Pierre Bourdieu (Bourdieu, 1984). Although achieving these goods may bring power, recognition and perhaps envy, actors may pursue them for their own value too. The struggles are not merely for power and status but are about how to live.

People experience class in relation to others partly via moral and immoral sentiments or emotions such as benevolence, respect, compassion, pride and envy, contempt and shame. Such emotions should not be seen as counterposed to reason: as many philosophers have argued, they are about something; they are embodied evaluative judgements of matters influencing people's well-being and that of others. Thus a feeling of shame may reflect awareness of our lack of something that we and others value, which causes those who do have it to regard us as inferior. Compassion is a response to someone's undeserved suffering. Different moral sentiments have different normative structures and analysing these can tell us something about the situations in which they are produced. Moreover, insofar as moral sentiments are a response to people's circumstances and how they are treated, we can expect them to vary in their distribution roughly according to individuals' position in the social field. One of my main objectives is to suggest how this works out, though it would be too much to say that there is a 'logic' to this. While there might be some pattern to such feelings, reflecting common forms of reasoning, the sentiments and reasoning are as likely to involve slippages, blockages, non-sequiturs and wishful thinking, as logical inferences supported by evidence. For example, where there is a desire on the part of those in subordinate positions to be generous in spirit and to avoid the discontent that accompanies resentment, it may prompt a refusal to regard the advantages of the dominant as undeserved, no matter how strong the evidence to the contrary. As Bourdieu recognised, in the face of deeply embedded undeserved inequalities, resistance may be more painful and less rewarding than compliance and deference; practical pressures may obstruct the following of reason (Bourdieu, 1984).

However, nonconformity and resistance are not unusual; actors may be able to think beyond their own social position and self-interest, and moral ideas are one of the main resources in enabling them to do this. Insofar as our moral education, both formal and informal, encourages us to treat others with respect and as of equal moral worth, we confront a society in which people are manifestly not treated equally at the level either of distribution of resources or of recognition. Thus, class differences, like gender differences, conflict with moral principles and dispositions supporting equal recognition and respect. Of course, lay morality is itself inconsistent and often supports unjustified inequalities, wrongly imagining them, as in the case of gender inequality, to be naturally based. But scarcely anyone supposes that class differences have a natural basis.

There is a tension running throughout the book. It results from focusing on the moral significance of class while insisting on class's non-moral determinants. But I shall argue that this tension is generated by the nature of class itself and underpins popular unease and ambivalence about class. Class lacks a moral justification, but people of different classes are likely to feel obliged to justify their differences. This is problematic for them, because of the huge influence of natal class and the mechanisms of class reproduction and symbolic domination – neither of which reflects moral differences. They may seek to make sense of this either by ignoring these mechanisms and imagining class differences to reflect differences in moral worth or other kinds of merit, or by facing up to their own moral luck and acknowledging the undeserved nature of their advantages or disadvantages. Often, actors appeal to a mixture of both kinds of argument, and experience varying degrees of discomfort, embarrassment, resentment, shame and guilt about it, though some may feel proud of their class position. Some may see themselves as equals rather than inferior or superior, and want to be seen as such. Some may seek advantages over others. Some may assertively demand respect while others may deferentially seek respectability. Many may attempt to distinguish themselves from others through moral boundary drawing, claiming virtues for themselves and imputing vices to their others.

In their more reflective moments people may call upon and develop 'folk sociologies' to explain the behaviour and characteristics of others, particularly the behaviour of members of other classes which they find problematic. They may simply attribute it to class position, perhaps on the basis of simple stereotyping, but they sometimes take into account the effects of moral luck in terms of class position, so that they can judge others either to have done well or badly because of their class advantages or disadvantages, or well or badly despite them. While they may regard class as an influence on behaviour they usually also want to say that people have some responsibility for their behaviour and fortunes, so that class disadvantages do not excuse anti-social behaviour. They may sometimes try to distinguish their disapproval of such behaviour from their feelings about the class identity of the actor, so that they condemn them for their behaviour and not their class identity. These explanations, distinctions and evaluations are inherently difficult, yet people sometimes reflect on them in trying to make sense of social inequalities, and they may make a difference to their own behaviour and self-evaluation.

This project therefore requires us to take lay normativity seriously, particularly regarding the ethics of everyday life, and attend to its content and internal rationales. Given the dominance in recent sociology of accounts that marginalise these matters and emphasise habitual action, interest-driven behaviour and the internalisation of prevailing discursive scripts, this emphasis perhaps requires some justification. I am not the first to call for more attention to be paid to the moral dimension of social life. Authors such as Alvin Gouldner (1971), Janet Finch (1989), Zygmunt Bauman (2001), Carol Smart and Bren Neale (1999), Ralph Fevre (2000) and Jane Ribbens McCarthy et al. (2003) and many others have done so too. However, these tend not to have been followed up. There is also scepticism in some quarters about the continuing usefulness of concepts of class. Let me address these in turn.

Lay normativity

[W]ithout a categorical opening to the normative standpoint from which subjects themselves evaluate the social order, theory remains completely cut off from a dimension of social discontent that it should always be able to call upon. (Axel Honneth, 2003, p. 134)

In everyday life, the most important questions tend to be normative ones. Of course we need to have a positive practical knowledge of what there is and of how at least some things work, but unless we are particularly curious, or are involved in education, these things matter less to us than questions of what is good or bad, how we or others should behave and what we or others should do. This is not to suppose that we always need to think directly about such things, for we tend to have 'a feel for the game', as Bourdieu would say, although we are likely to be pulled up and made to reflect upon things that happen to us that seem wrong or out of order.

Social scientists are taught to adopt and prioritise the positive point of view and, unless they also read philosophy, to suppress normative reasoning. The gradual separation of positive and normative thought that has occurred over the last 200 years in social science has involved not only an attempted (though incomplete) expulsion of values from science, but an expulsion of science or reason from values, so that values appear to be mere primitive, subjective beliefs, beyond the scope of reason.[1] This de-rationalisation of values is at odds with the fact that when necessary, as in the case of perceived injustices, we do reason about values, and not by appeal to personal preferences or mere convention.

This divorce of normative and positive thought has rendered much of critical social science unable to identify not only its own normative standpoints but the normative concerns, distinctions and valuations that figure so prominently in the lives of the people it studies. Consequently, social scientists are prone to theory/practice contradictions, that is, to producing accounts of action which do not fit their own mundane behaviour, and which they could not themselves live. Thus, while the behaviour of others is explained in terms of social positioning and discourses – in effect, implying 'they would say/do that, wouldn't they' – sociologists generally explain their own behaviour, like everyone else, by justifying it.[2] They do not, for example, say that the arguments that they put forward in sociological debate are no more than products of their position or self-interest. In the face of such theory/practice contradictions '. . . we ought to examine what has been said by applying it to what we do and how we live; and if it harmonizes with what we do, we should accept it, but if it conflicts we should count it [mere] words' (Aristotle, cited in Griswold, 1999, p. 49).[3]

Of course there are indeed important respects in which our justifications are indeed influenced by our social position and by wider discourses, but reflexivity is needed not only to examine such influences, but also in the opposite direction, to examine what they do *not* explain, that is, how everyday situations often require us to justify what we do.

Lay normativity should be taken seriously precisely because it matters to people, and it matters to them because it is about things that seriously affect their well-being. The struggles of the social field, between different groups, classes, genders and ethnicities, certainly involve habitual action and the pursuit of power, but they also have a range of normative rationales, which matter greatly to actors, as they are implicated in their commitments, identities and ways of life. Those rationales concern what is of value, how to live, what is worth striving for and what is not. It might seem that these are just different 'values', only important in

[1] The early founders of the social sciences combined positive and normative discourses seamlessly (see O'Neill, 1998; Barbalet, 2001).
[2] See Manent, for a profound historical analysis of the development of this spectator view of action in social science (Manent, 1998).
[3] Similarly, Marx comments: 'The idea of *one* basis for life and another for *science* is from the very outset a lie' (Marx, 1975, p. 355).

terms of how they correlate with social position. There is certainly some interesting sociological research on this, for example, in the writings of Pierre Bourdieu and Michèle Lamont (Bourdieu, 1984; Lamont, 1992, 2000), but what matters to people is whether these different values are defensible, and whether what they imply for well-being is true. There may be specific worries such as how they should bring up their children (Lareau, 2003; Reay, 1998b; Walkerdine and Lucey, 1989), concerns about whether others are treating them fairly and respectfully (Skeggs, 1997), or reflections on the way their lives are going in terms of balancing goods such as friendship and achievement (Archer, 2003).

Thus, if we are to understand lay normativity we need to go beyond a sociological reductionism which deflates and demeans lay justifications or rationales for beliefs and actions. Actors' rationales may indeed sometimes be little more than rationalisations of their position: the economically successful would value achievement, wouldn't they?; and the poor would say that other things than money are more important, wouldn't they? But while we all are capable of rationalisation, we are also sometimes capable of taking different views from the ones that fit our position most comfortably. Sociologists often do this themselves but are occupationally inclined to assume that those they study do not. I shall argue that it is as important to acknowledge how far moral evaluations of self and others are independent of class as it is to acknowledge how far they relate and respond to class. Indeed, it is only in virtue of this dual nature of lay moral judgements that we can understand why class is also a matter of embarrassment, resentment and shame. This is not to say that people necessarily have particularly coherent normative ideas. They tend to be disparate and sometimes inconsistent; middle class people may both resent snobbery from those more highly placed and be snobbish towards those below them. But however incoherent, the rationales are important in themselves, and as actors ourselves, we can hardly avoid engaging with them at least sometimes.

To be sure the rationales are to be found within available discourses, but they are more than mere internalised and memorised bits of social scripts. Discourses derive from and relate to a wider range of situations than those directly experienced by the individuals who use them, thereby allowing them vicarious access to the world beyond them. While they constrain thought in certain ways, they are also open to different interpretations and uses, and endless innovation and deformation, and they tend to contain inconsistencies and contradictions, making them open to challenge from within. Although they structure perception they do not necessarily prevent identification of false claims; for example, just because someone believes that the social world is organised on a meritocratic basis, it does not mean that no experience could ever lead them to have doubts about this. Many of the discourses relating to inequalities are also clearly normative, and normative discourse presupposes a discernible *difference* between what ought to be and what is – otherwise they would be redundant. Thus, feminism has developed an enormously rich critique of gender orders, showing, in effect, how patriarchal assumptions that legitimised and valued gender differences were ideological. In so doing it has not merely provided an alternative set of values which we can take or leave like individual preferences for colours, but has demonstrated that assumptions about what was good about traditional roles of women and men were *mistaken*, i.e., untrue, in that they had no natural basis and caused suffering and limitation of capacities rather than flourishing or well-being. As such it provides a compelling alternative moral discourse with which actors can engage.

The main kind of normativity that I shall focus on, and the most important one for our well-being, is concerned with morality. By morality I mean simply the matter of what kinds of behaviour are good, and thus how we should treat others and be treated by them. Moral feelings, ideas and norms about such things also imply and merge into what philosophers term 'conceptions of the good' – broader ideas or senses of how one should live – though in everyday life these are generally less coherent and explicit than philosophers assume. I shall follow older senses of 'morality' and include these implicit conceptions as part of what moral concerns are about. Some may prefer the term 'ethics' to 'morality'. Sometimes the two terms are assumed to correspond to a distinction between informal, embodied dispositions deriving from social life, perhaps from particular communities, and formal norms and rules, though confusingly the referents of the two terms are sometimes reversed. I shall be referring mainly to the informal embodied dispositions, but I shall use the adjectives 'moral' and 'ethical' interchangeably.[4]

To treat morality simply as a set of norms and rules, backed up by sanctions, which tend to produce social order, is to produce an alienated

---

[4] Following Hegel, it is also common to distinguish *moralität*, which identifies a universal conception of human needs or rationality against which existing social and political arrangements can be assessed, and *sittlichkeit*, in which 'the good of individuals – indeed, their very identity and capacity for moral agency – is bound up with the communities they belong to, and the particular social and political roles they occupy' (Kymlicka, 2002, p. 209). Hegel argued that *moralität* was too abstract to offer guidance and too individualistic, ignoring our embeddedness in communities. Of course, particular communal ethics may make claims to universality, and, conversely, universal claims may become part of a community's ethos, as at least partially seems to be the case with liberal societies. Another form of the distinction often made by political philosophers, particularly liberals, associates ethics with the good and morality with the right. This version of the distinction is very fuzzy and not useful for my purposes.

conception of the moral dimension of social life, for it omits what matters to us and why morality should have any internal force. We don't treat others in a certain way simply because there are norms dictating that we should and because we fear sanctions if we don't. We also usually behave in a certain way because we sense that it is right, regardless of whether there are any penalties for not doing so, and because to do otherwise would cause some sort of harm.

In view of the prevalence of alienated conceptions of morality in sociology, in which it is viewed as of minor importance and as an external system of regulation of behaviour, and an inherently conservative and reactionary one at that, it is perhaps necessary to remember how important it is to our very identities and well-being. I would ask any readers who are accustomed to thinking of morality in this alienated way to pause and think awhile about the following questions:

• What matters to you in life – what do you care about?
• How do you feel you should be treated by others, and how do you feel you should treat them? Why do you get upset if someone mistreats you? And if you try to remonstrate and reason with them, how do you do this and through what kinds of argument? Why shouldn't they treat you like that?
• What kinds of behaviour would you feel ashamed of or guilty about and why?

It would be strange to claim that these are unimportant matters or ones that we could avoid, and there is nothing inherently conservative about them.[5] Considering them should bring home the gravity of morality and how it is tied up with our conceptions of ourselves and our happiness and well-being. Of course it is not usually simply other individuals that cause suffering and unhappiness but the very organisation of society, and its prevailing discourses with their taken-for-granted assumptions and ways of understanding, which pre-exist any particular individual and influence their identity. But these *matter* to us. The nature of these causes is important precisely because of the harm or good they do. Social science tends to be better at thinking about such causes than why they and their effects matter to us.

The moral dimension is unavoidable. Hardly any social relationship 'is intelligible without a recognition of the ethical responsibilities and obligations which it carries with it, and . . . much of our moral life is

---

[5] Nor need they have anything to do with religion. For those curious about the possible bases of a plea for taking morality seriously, I should perhaps point out that I am an atheist. I would argue that secularisation creates the possibility of our becoming responsible, reflective moral subjects instead of relying upon established religious authority and dogma for guidance, though of course we may fail to respond to this opportunity.

made up of these kind of loyalties and commitments' (Norman, 1998, p. 216). Moreover,

> *Moral judgment is what we 'always already' exercise in virtue of being immersed in a* *network of human relationships that constitute our life together.* Whereas there can be reasonable debate about whether or not to exercise juridical, military, therapeutic, aesthetic or even political judgment, in the case of moral judgment this option is not there. The domain of the moral is so deeply enmeshed with those interactions that constitute our lifeworld that to withdraw from moral judgment is tantamount to ceasing to interact, to talk and act in the human community. (Benhabib, 1992, pp. 125–6, emphasis in original; see also Habermas, 1990)

Contemporary social scientists rarely talk about the moral dimension of social life. They are generally happier talking about the bad than the good, particularly about broad categories of exploitation, oppression and domination such as sexism and racism, and they tend to describe certain behaviours in these terms rather than in terms of virtues and vices such as kindness, sensitivity, callousness and selfishness. The emphasis on the bad rather than the good is not surprising, as it is what most needs attention.[6] Also, many of these bad things arise not out of ill will but on the basis of customs and practices, some of which are widely assumed to be justified, indeed as 'moral' or having some basis in nature. On the one hand, it therefore seems reasonable to by-pass their moral significance and provide a more political focus on the structures and discourses which reproduce them. On the other hand, if they did not produce some kind of mistreatment or limitation of people's capacities they would not be considered as problems. And without morality, any politics is directionless – as capable of increasing oppression as reducing it.[7]

Moral norms and sentiments or emotions are of course culturally variable, but this requires careful consideration. The specific practices about which actors feel proud or ashamed, the specific properties of which they approve or disapprove, the specific conventional forms of showing respect and disrespect, are all of course culturally variable, but emotions like pride and shame, respect and disrespect, along with more primitive ones like fear and security, appear to be transcultural. The variation seems to be less in the emotions themselves than in their referents or stimuli, but

---

[6] By contrast, moral philosophers – particularly Anglo-American ones – say remarkably little about evil, generally assuming that all that needs to be said about it is that it is the absence of good. Thus, with a few exceptions (e.g., Glover, 1999), one reads little in moral philosophy about the worst evils of modern society. These complementary deficiencies of moral philosophy and sociology cry out for a dialogue.

[7] As Carol Steedman (1985) notes, to enter the arena of subjectivity is not to abandon the political – on the contrary, subjectivity is a precondition of politics.

just how far such sentiments and norms are variable is emphatically an empirical question, not an *a priori* matter.

There is an idealist version of social constructionism which assumes that anything can be socially constructed, as if by an exercise of collective wishful thinking, and hence that flourishing or suffering are no more than what prevailing ways of thinking define them as, regardless of how they relate to our capabilities and susceptibilities – indeed, the latter are themselves deemed to be voluntaristically constructed. On this view, concepts of oppression, or violation, or abuse are incomprehensible, for there is nothing independent of the practices to which they refer that can be damaged by them: the damage can only exist in the mind of the beholder (Soper, 1995). Certainly morality is socially constructed and hence culturally variable, but if we are to understand this and avoid voluntarism we need to take the metaphor of construction more seriously, not less. All construction uses materials, and a necessary condition for the success of attempts at construction is that they use the materials according to their properties – properties that exist largely independently of the constructors and are not merely a product of wishful thinking, though they may be products of earlier incidents of social construction, which in their turn were constrained and enabled by the properties of the materials used (Sayer, 2000a). The materials may be ideational as well as physical, but ideational materials also have a degree of independence from the intended uses to which actors attempt to put them. Some discursive constructions fail because they fall on deaf ears, fail to resonate, or attempt materially impossible projects. The object of morality is human well-being, and we are beings who are capable of both suffering and flourishing, sometimes regardless of how suffering and flourishing are *construed*.

Our judgements of such matters are fallible ('subjective') assessments of objective possibilities. When we use terms like 'domination', 'oppression' or 'exploitation' we imply that some harm, injustice or suffering is objectively done, not merely, as subjectivism implies, that observers don't like what they refer to and are upset by them. They allude to damage and suffering that we have good reason to believe exist objectively, indeed exist even if we fail to recognise them (for example, presumably sexism actually inhibited women's flourishing before it was identified as doing so). Such terms have a descriptive as well as an evaluative content, indeed the two are inseparable in such cases. Contrary to idealism, such harms or suffering do not just exist in the mind of the beholder but refer to damage done regardless of whether anyone observes it. To be sure, there are many kinds of well-being and ideas about them are themselves culturally variable. But they are also fallible (which is to say there is something independent of them about which they can be mistaken). Solitary confinement and female genital mutilation, for example, are objectively damaging. Wishful thinking does not always work, and some kinds of cultural definitions of well-being have a blatantly apologetic function, for example, patriarchal ideologies that women are naturally suited to tedious work, and that bearing the burden of unpaid care-work should be seen as a virtue. No matter how wary contemporary radical social science may be of defending or criticising value positions, no matter how fearful of being ethnocentric it may be, it depends completely on the assumption that not just any way of life is as good as another. The negative valuations of sexism, racism and homophobia are based on fallible but probably practically-adequate assessments of the nature and consequences of those things.[8] While my interest is primarily in the positive analysis of lay normativity in economic life, it is impossible and arguably undesirable to assume a sharp distinction between positive and normative in matters such as the nature of human needs, well-being or suffering. A 'critical theory' that takes no interest in normative implications is a contradiction in terms.

To summarise: how people treat one another is of extraordinary importance to them; it can make the difference between misery and happiness. There is a danger of a form of bland, sociological reductionism according to which moral sentiments and norms are nothing more than arbitrary social conventions, which people internalise and become habituated to, just as they become habituated to holding a knife and fork or chop-sticks in a conventional way. This completely fails to understand the *seriousness* of moral issues, the way in which they concern matters that affect our well-being and often present difficult problems and dilemmas (Midgley, 1972). Even sociological reductionists, at least when off duty, do not respond to mistreatment by merely complaining that the local norms have been contravened, or that they just don't like that treatment, but by arguing why the behaviour in question was unreasonable and hurtful, and by pointing out the kind of damage that has been done. Hurt and suffering are not just constructs. People's lives may be blighted by shame and low self-esteem, and at the extreme they may value their commitments to others or to particular causes more than their own lives. The normative force of such feelings – the most important aspect of them to actors – is completely effaced by reducing them to mere norms backed by sanctions.

Rehabilitating class

For some, 'class' may seem, if not an obsolete category, one of declining relevance today, despite the widening of economic inequalities in many

---

[8] I will expand on this defence of a realist theory of value more fully in chapter 9.

countries over the last twenty-five years. There are several possible reasons for this. The decline of deference and the blurring of distinctions
between popular and elite culture might imply that class inequalities matter less in the way people value themselves and others. And yet, popular
culture is still not only differentiated by class but, especially in literature
and television, very much *about* class – or class stereotypes – even though
it is rarely named as such.[9] In mainstream British politics, New Labour's
aversion to Old Labour appears to have made it risky to acknowledge
class, except in heavily coded terms, though the 'underclass' is occasionally mentioned. In life-politics as well as mainstream politics, other
axes of inequality and difference – particularly gender, 'race', and sexuality – have come to the fore, and rightly so, given their previous neglect.
With the rise of feminism and anti-racism, important advances have been
made in popular and mainstream politics in establishing the injustice and
immorality of discrimination in terms of gender, 'race', and indeed other
differences such as sexuality and disability. But in many quarters their
recognition has come at the expense of interest in class. Thus egalitarianism has progressed on some new fronts while retreating on the class front,
producing an apparent shift from a traditional politics of distribution to
a new politics of recognition.[10]

There is a logic to this uneven development. bell hooks notes how class
has become an 'uncool' subject in a US becoming ever more unequal
(hooks, 2000, p. 1). As a black woman living in Greenwich Village, she
is often assumed by local people to be a nanny or shop assistant. Her
mostly white neighbours

> are social liberals and fiscal conservatives. They may believe in recognizing mul-
> ticulturalism and celebrating diversity (our neighborhood is full of white gay men
> and straight white people who have at least one black, Asian, or Hispanic friend),
> but when it comes to money and class they want to protect what they have, to
> perpetuate and reproduce it – they want more. The fact that they have so much
> while others have so little does not cause moral anguish, for they see their good
> fortune as a sign they are chosen, special, deserving. (hooks, 2000, p. 3)

The liberal, affluent, educated whites regard treating others unequally
on the basis of their gender, 'race' or sexuality as immoral, and they
presumably realise that if they were to be sexist, racist or homophobic,
they would themselves be responsible for reproducing injustice and undeserved inequality. They do not, however, see class inequality as unjust and

---

[9] See Skeggs, 2004.

[10] As Honneth argues, this description is inaccurate to the extent that traditional distributional struggles were generally motivated by demands for recognition of equal worth too
(Honneth, 2003).

they probably do not regard it as their responsibility either. The important point is that in a sense they are right in the latter respect. Some kinds of economic inequalities – for example, among white women or among black men – can[11] be produced without deliberate class discrimination, simply through the workings of the identity-neutral 'lottery of the market'. By contrast, inequalities of gender and 'race' (including economic inequalities of gender and 'race') are primarily products of identity-sensitive processes.

One of the signs of moral progress in the sphere of employment in recent decades has been the rise of equal opportunities policies, which attempt to prevent discrimination in relation to gender, 'race', age, ethnicity, sexuality, disability, religion, etc. Some such policies mention class too, but it is striking that class is generally forgotten in their implementation.[12] It is hardly a defence of this omission to argue that class is so strongly correlated with employment qualifications and so deeply embodied that it creates real differences in fitness to undertake different kinds of jobs and therefore can't be discounted, for similar arguments might be made about some of the other sources of social division. More convincing is the argument that while capitalism could cope with equality in relation to gender, 'race', age, sexuality, etc., it could not withstand the removal of class. And of course, the very act of creating jobs with widely differing pay actively reproduces class, so it would be strange, to say the least, to try to ensure that class origin of job applicants made no difference to their ability to get a different place in the class structure.[13] Even if those selected were chosen in a way that discounted their class, their children will still inherit their new class advantages or disadvantages, with lasting objective effects that would strongly influence their fitness for particular jobs. It is bizarre to argue for equality of opportunities in relation to class when the job opportunities are themselves unequal and fundamental to the reproduction of class.[14]

---

[11] The word 'can' is carefully chosen, precisely to acknowledge that economic inequalities can *also* derive from ascriptive, discriminatory processes. See below, chapter 4.

[12] E.g., Article 13 of the European Union's Treaty of Amsterdam (Walby, 2004).

[13] For a review of the literature on social mobility and meritocracy, see Savage, 2000, and for an interesting sustained analysis, see Marshall et al., 1997. It might be hoped that an equal opportunities policy for class would change the reproduction of class from a competition in which the winners of each race started the succeeding race with an advantage, to a meritocratic one in which all started at the same point regardless of their past position, but this would be wholly to underestimate the strength of path-dependence of class reproduction in early life in terms of the mutual reinforcement of struggles for economic, social, cultural and educational capital.

[14] A more radical line of argument would be to argue that the only way to get equal opportunities in employment would be to equalise the economic rewards of the opportunities.

In social science itself, concern with class has, until recently, also been on the retreat, though research on social stratification has continued (Goldthorpe and Marshall, 1992); as Michèle Barrett famously remarked in 1992, class has become 'non grata' – or, as Beverley Skeggs commented, 'ignored by those with the privilege to ignore it' (Barrett and Phillips, 1992; Skeggs, 1997). This may be because interest in class was previously tainted by its association with socialist discourses which ignored or marginalised gender, race and sexuality.[15] It may also be that class cannot easily be interpreted from within the theoretical frameworks that are necessary for understanding phenomena such as gender and sexuality; although class, like gender and 'race', is confirmed and contested at the level of recognition and identity, it is also produced to a significant degree by processes operating independently of ascriptive processes.

Whether class itself is considered to be of declining importance depends on which of the variety of sociological concepts of class one uses.[16] If one takes class to presuppose class-consciousness and collective action on the basis of strong subjective class identities, then these phenomena of course have indeed declined. However, in addition to continuing, indeed widening, economic inequalities, there is still, as Mike Savage argues following Bourdieu, a keen sense of class difference in terms of multiple differentiations rather than simple, clear-cut boundaries along which many differences fall (Savage, 2000). Actors have remarkably sensitive class antennae, even if they cannot always articulate the distinctions that they make. And whatever the sociological disputes over the meaning of 'class', it continues to be 'a loaded moral signifier' in everyday life (Savage et al., 2001a, p. 875).

After many years of neglect, there have recently been signs of a revival of interest in class, especially regarding how it is subjectively experienced. It may help the reader to know how this book relates to this and other literature.

Theoretical and empirical influences

This is not the first attempt to explore the moral significance of class. There have been landmark studies by Tawney (1931) on equality, by

---

[15] Strange complicities have resulted from the – in my view justified – critical reactions to the practice of assessing class in terms of male head of household, and to patriarchal socialist assumptions that class is about men, which, bizarrely, rejected class instead of this restriction of class to men.

[16] For reviews of the debates, see Crompton, 1998; Goldthorpe and Marshall, 1992; Savage, 2000.

Runciman (1966) on relative deprivation[17] and by Sennett and Cobb (1973) on 'the hidden injuries of class'. The major initial theoretical influence on my attempts to revive this topic came from the work of Pierre Bourdieu, particularly his *Distinction* (Bourdieu, 1984). This is impressive both for its theoretical apparatus and its remarkably – indeed, wickedly – perceptive analyses of the 'soft forms of domination' associated with class. If there was ever an example of the power of naming in social science, *Distinction* provides it through concepts such as 'cultural capital' and 'habitus', articulating hidden structures and experiences of domination. However, in this and in much of his other work, Bourdieu's analyses of the struggles of the social field pay little attention to their moral aspects, tending instead to emphasise their habitual and instrumental character, as if a combination of habit and the pursuit of status and power animated everything. Insofar as he considered the evaluative character of lay understandings, he did so primarily in terms of embodied dispositions and aesthetics rather than ethical judgements. Nevertheless, an ethical dimension is implicit in such struggles, and of course it is the ethical, more than the aesthetic, aspects of inequalities which matter to individuals, since they have more bearing on whether they can live with self-respect, feeling valued by others and engaged in a worthwhile life. This is evident in the accounts of interviewees presented in *The Weight of the World*, the major study of social suffering in France carried out in the 1990s by Bourdieu and associates (Bourdieu et al., 1999); these do not merely tell of material hardship and insecurity but emphasise lack of respect and self-esteem.

Although I am critical of some of the most basic features of his approach, especially the crypto-normative stance of much of his writing, the underestimation of actors' rationality and reflexivity, and the heavy reliance on economistic metaphors (Sayer, 1999), I regard these as problems which can be corrected in a way which enhances the analysis of the 'soft forms of domination'. In the detailed application of his ideas in empirical research, he used a much richer and less reductive set of interpretive tools than those implied by his best-known concepts such as 'habitus', 'field' and 'capitals'; indeed, these are best regarded as incomplete summarising concepts.

Other convergent influences come from empirical studies of the subjective experience of class, mostly ethnographic, by sociologists such as Beverley Skeggs, Diane Reay, Valerie Walkerdine and Helen Lucey,

[17] Runciman summarises his aim as understanding the 'relation between objective social inequalities and people's attitudes towards them' (2nd edn, 1972, p. 382). While this is a major part of my agenda too, I am also concerned with how inequalities can also be a product of people's attitudes to others.

Annette Lareau, Maria Kefalas, Jay Macleod, Michèle Lamont, Simon Charlesworth, and Mike Savage, Gaynor Bagnall and Brian Longhurst. These have greatly illuminated matters such as the relation of class and gender, how class affects people's sense of self-worth, how normative conceptions of important matters like childrearing practices vary across classes, how groups define themselves against others partly through drawing moral boundaries, and how people regard the phenomenon of class itself.

Contributions by feminist researchers of working class origin (e.g., Lawler, 2000; Reay, 1997b, 1998a and b; Skeggs, 1997, 2004; Walkerdine and Lucey, 1989) have been prominent here.[18] Their work has focused on the way in which gender is classed and class is gendered, coupled with arguments that they are not separate phenomena and can only be adequately understood jointly, rather than through separated abstractions which are then recombined. I shall argue that while they are indeed lived and experienced jointly, classed and gendered experience and behaviour are nevertheless responses to different sources of inequality and domination. Moreover, it is vital to understand in what respects class differs from inequalities of gender, race or ethnicity, for they are increasingly confused in everyday understanding, so that some actors imagine class differences to be primarily a product of prejudice. In developing social theory it is normal and legitimate to abstract the key object of interest from the mass of other phenomena in which, in concrete cases, it is contingently embedded, provided one remembers that to understand such cases we need to recombine our object of interest with the other processes from which it has temporarily been abstracted (Sayer, 1992). As this is primarily a theoretical work, for much of this book I will abstract class from other relations of inequality, though at various points I will comment on their similarities, differences and common interactions.

Most of my illustrations of the moral significance of class come from these recent studies, but the sources of my analysis of the normative structures which they report are quite different. Through serendipity, I have found that Adam Smith's analysis of moral sentiments, and the work of more recent moral philosophers such as Alasdair MacIntyre and Martha Nussbaum, provide the resources for a critique of Bourdieu's tendency towards sociological reductionism in his treatment of lay normativity, for developing an alternative account of the struggles of the social field, and

---

[18] The analysis of the moral dimension of social life has progressed much more with respect to gender than class. Although feminism tends to be wary of the concept of morality, perhaps because of its conservative associations, its critique of patriarchy is very much a moral one, in the sense I have defined (Finch, 1989; Smart and Neale, 1999; Sevenhuijsen, 1998; Tronto, 1993).

for deepening understanding of feelings such as pity, envy, shame and guilt in relation to class. I have also drawn upon the work of philosophers regarding the relationship between the politics of distribution and recognition (e.g., Fraser and Honneth, 2003; Taylor, 1994). This helps us understand the similarities, differences and interactions between class and other kinds of inequality. It also illuminates the nature of goods and their valuation (Anderson, 1993; MacIntyre, 1981), and how these are objects of the competitive struggles of the social field.

Finally, insofar as this book is a critique of class some readers may want to know where the critique 'hails' from. In some parts of social science this is now a common challenge to anyone who puts forward explicit normative arguments. It is a good question and I will try to answer it, but first we should note that the question does not tend to be asked of those whose 'critiques' leave their normative criteria implicit – those who use terms like 'oppression', 'racism', 'domination' without explaining what is wrong with them (all are undeniably evaluative terms). My objection is not to the question but to the fact that it's not asked widely enough. My answer is that this book hails from a position which might be termed a 'qualified ethical naturalism'. I shall explain this more fully in the conclusion to the book but for now it is sufficient to note that it argues that the basis for judgements of good and bad is what allows humans (and other sentient beings) to flourish or suffer. Again, to be sure, different cultures provide different perspectives on what human flourishing and suffering are, but not just anything can successfully be passed off as flourishing or suffering, and much dissent and resistance within cultures is directed at questionable assumptions about them. Wherever possible, I shall also attempt to make my arguments hail from opponents' own premises, in the standard manner of philosophical argumentation. I invite sceptical readers to explain the bases of their own normative views.

Chapter outline

Before we can address the moral dimension of class there are certain preliminary issues that need to be clarified, about the nature of lay morality, and recognition, and about the meanings of 'class' itself. These matters are addressed in chapters 2 to 4.

In chapter 2, I take some first steps towards an analysis of the moral dimension of social action through a critique and revision of Bourdieu's concept of habitus, in order to take account of the evaluative, including moral, character of people's dispositions. This requires moderating Bourdieu's 'Pascalian' view of behaviour to allow for lay reflexivity as an influence upon their behaviour. By examining the preconditions for the development of the habitus, it is argued that dispositions towards resistance as well as compliance with circumstances can arise, even in the absence of shifts to different parts of the social field where the habitus has not adjusted to its context. Drawing upon the work of Adam Smith and Martha Nussbaum I argue against certain sociologically reductionist treatments of morality as a system of external, regulative norms. Instead, the moral character of behaviour is held to be based primarily on actors' moral sentiments, which in turn are developed through social interaction. Emotions are argued to have a cognitive aspect that provides evaluations of actors' circumstances in terms of their implications for their well-being. Exploring the nature of 'commitments' further illuminates lay normativity in a way that acknowledges not only its habitual, embodied or strategic aspects but its non-instrumental and moral character.

As many observers have noted, there has been a shift in political concern from matters of economic distribution, traditionally associated with class politics, to a concern with issues of recognition, associated with the politics of gender, 'race' and sexuality. But of course the experience of class also involves unequal recognition or misrecognition, or what Bourdieu termed symbolic domination, or 'soft forms of domination'. In chapter 3, I outline how recognition has a moral element, how it is important for individuals and groups, how it takes two forms – conditional and unconditional – and how it is related to matters of distribution of wealth and resources.

Class is itself a contested concept, both in academe and everyday life, and how academics and lay actors understand class makes a difference to the moral significance they attach to it. In chapter 4, I attempt to clarify some of the different versions of the concept, arguing that, properly understood, some of them are not mutually exclusive but compatible, indeed indispensable. We need both abstract concepts of class to deal with economic power and more concrete concepts to deal with the combination of economic power and status in influencing lives and experience, or, in Bourdieu's terms, different combinations of economic, social, cultural, educational and other forms of capital. I also develop here the distinction between identity-neutral and identity-sensitive mechanisms that produce inequalities, and provide an alternative to Bourdieu's approach to the relations between class and gender.

The remaining chapters deal with the anatomy of 'the struggles of the social field', the competitive strivings for goods – in a broad sense – among individuals and groups with different assets and advantages, or amounts and kinds of capital. In chapter 5, we deal first with the nature of the struggle, and what it is for or over, and whether different groups are striving for similar or different goods. Then we apply some distinctions (elided by Bourdieu) between different kinds of valuation and goods that are crucial for understanding the struggles of the social field, namely use-value and exchange-value, and internal and external goods, and ask how those goods are distributed across the social field. We then analyse the implications of the way in which evaluations of goods are influenced by their class associations, producing elisions of the distinctions between the posh and the good, and the common and the bad. Finally, we draw together and illustrate the points made in the chapter by reference to the example of parents' commitments to their children's upbringing, in relation to class, and analyse the complex normative issues involved.

In chapter 6, we turn from the kinds of goods that are sought to the moral (and immoral) evaluations that people make of others, themselves and behaviour in relation to class position. Building on the work of Adam Smith, Martha Nussbaum and others, we analyse some key sentiments in this context, such as benevolence, compassion, sense of justice, envy, class contempt and, most importantly, shame.

In chapter 7, we then apply this to interactions between people of different classes, looking at 'othering' and moral boundary drawing, and egalitarian currents. I argue for an approach which is able to register both inter-class enmity and respect and benevolence. We examine the implications of the pursuit of respect or respectability, showing how these are particularly important in 'social tests' involving encounters with class others.

In chapter 8 we consider how actors evaluate others' behaviour and how they respond to class itself, in effect developing 'folk' sociologies and philosophies. In not only judging but trying to explain others' behaviour, they run into difficult philosophical problems of attributing responsibility, sometimes attempting to take into account their class position. Finally, I suggest an explanation for the common lay embarrassment and evasiveness about class, arguing that resentment and various forms of shame are responses to the injuries caused by class inequalities.

In the conclusion to the book (chapter 9), I draw out two kinds of implications. The first are mainly to do with social theory and its neglect or misunderstanding of the moral dimension of social life, and the need for a more post-disciplinary approach, one that is more attuned to normative issues. The second concern the substantive issues posed by class, how class should be understood in social science and politics, what makes it different from other forms of social division, and how the lived experience of class partly obscures and partly highlights and registers its immoral character. Finally, I make some suggestions regarding what might be done about it.

It is my belief that in social science, as in everyday life, we will understand people better if we take their normative dispositions, concerns and rationales seriously, rather than treating these as mere facts about them which can be given a social location in relation to class, gender and 'race', and then left at that, as if they were no different from facts about their age or height. This does not require us to agree with their beliefs or approve of their behaviour. Nor need it involve overestimating the extent to which they deliberate on their actions and views, and underestimating how much they do 'on automatic', though much of what we do in this way is learned and intelligent. Nor need it imply an individualistic, voluntarist, explanation of social forms, as if the latter were simply the product of the exercise of the will, which in this context would lead to a moralistic explanation of social problems. What it does allow us to address is the subjective experience of inequalities, how relations and differences are negotiated, and above all what it is about them that *matters* to people.

2 From the habitus to ethical dispositions

Introduction

Class is something beneath your clothes, under your skin, in your reflexes, in your psyche, at the very core of your being. (Annette Kuhn, 1995)

As Annette Kuhn's much-cited comment indicates, class is not merely a sociological concept or a location in the social field; it is deeply embodied, permeating our experience and sense of self. Even though we may not be able to articulate our feelings regarding class very well we can 'see it a mile off' in other people's appearance and behaviour, as they can in ours. It also affects what we value, including how we value others and ourselves – for example, whether we feel pride or shame, envy or contentment. To understand the subjective experience of class we need to consider the emotional and evaluative aspects of the relations of self to self and self to other. While much of this experience is deeply embodied at the level of unarticulated feelings and emotions, evaluations can also be more considered, frequently featuring in people's 'internal conversations' (Archer, 2003).

If we are to understand how class matters to people we therefore need to address how it is embodied and how it colours so much of our behaviour. An obvious starting point for understanding this is the work of Pierre Bourdieu, not only because of his emphasis on the embodied, practical character of action but because of his lifelong interest in class. Bourdieu interprets action via the concept of habitus – which refers to the set of dispositions that individuals acquire through socialisation, particularly in early life, and which orient them towards the social and physical world around them. For our purposes I want to emphasise the intelligent nature of these dispositions, and their relation to emotions, which in turn have a cognitive, evaluative and rational character.

While Bourdieu examined actors' embodied dispositions towards others, and towards practices and objects, he did so mainly in terms of aesthetic and practical rather than *ethical* matters, with the latter being only occasionally acknowledged,[1] and then in somewhat reductionist ways as functions of actors' social position and interests. This is perhaps surprising given his suppressed but obvious moral-political rage at the injustice of class, though as we shall see his approach makes it difficult to address the ethical dimension of social life. More generally, as many commentators have observed, his emphasis on the adaptation of the habitus to actors' circumstances exaggerates actors' compliance with their position and makes resistance appear to be an anomalous form of behaviour occasioned only by special circumstances. I wish to argue that if we are to understand resistance and actors' normative concerns and orientations regarding class we need to develop and modify some of Bourdieu's key concepts, starting with that of habitus. In particular, we need to develop an understanding of the normative orientation of the habitus, especially its ethical dispositions, which are scarcely acknowledged by Bourdieu. In addition, I shall suggest that these modifications to the concept of habitus allow us to see that resistance can be intrinsic to the formation of the habitus rather than extrinsic.

I shall begin by summarising the key elements of the concept as Bourdieu defines it, and then develop a constructive critique of it by focusing on several related problems: the relationship between habitus and habitat and the explanation of resistance; the relationship between embodied dispositions and reasoning, including reflexivity; the normative and evaluative character of the habitus; and finally the nature of emotions, commitments and ethical dispositions.

I should make it clear that the point of this argument is not to develop a critique of Bourdieu's approach for its own sake but to modify his concepts so that they can do new work.[2] Bourdieu's writings contain many different elaborations of the concept of habitus, some of them – particularly from his later writings – closer to what I want to propose than others. While I do not want to misrepresent Bourdieu, I am not concerned with how close or distant my modified concept of habitus is from his, only with whether it is defensible.

The habitus qualified

Habitus refers to those deeply engrained dispositions which are the products of socialisation, particularly in early life, and which orient individuals

---

[1] For example, Bourdieu makes a passing reference to ethical dispositions in *Practical Reason* (Bourdieu, 1998, p. 70).

[2] For critiques, see Alexander, 1995; Fowler, 1997; Sayer, 1999; Shusterman, 1999; and especially Crossley's (2001) constructive critique, which deepens and strengthens the concept of habitus by drawing upon the work of Merleau-Ponty.

at a subconscious level towards the world around them. The dispositions have a structure which reflects that of the corresponding habitat in which they were formed. This habitat is not merely a milieu but a position within a wider *field* of social relations, including relations to both similar and different others, for example to members of both the same and different gender or class. Habituation to this location within structures of social relations and material conditions produces a corresponding structure of dispositions which is attuned to them. When activated, these dispositions produce actions which tend to reproduce the external structures. Most of the dispositions composing the habitus are relational; they are oriented to other people and objects, such as a disposition towards serving others or being served. According to their location in the social field and their socialisation, one person becomes used to being respected, deferred to and listened to, while another, who is more often ignored, whose welfare is secondary to that of others, develops a habitus which is attuned to this treatment.

This internalised structure operates partly as a classifying mechanism, classifying any and every experience: discursive and material objects – people, places, practices, sounds, sights, smells and feelings. Thus, with respect to gender, the habitus classifies people, practices and objects as masculine and feminine, correlating these with the public and the private, the hard and the soft, reason and emotion, and so on. With respect to class, the upper class habitus classifies things as refined or vulgar, high or low, implicitly valuing the first term over the second.[3] The tacit classifications are formed by oppositions related by homologies among disparate phenomena. The habitus is therefore both productive and economical, using a small number of distinctions to classify not only a vast range of familiar objects but novel phenomena too. Thus, for working class men, their classed and gendered habitus, embodying distinctions between toughness, physicality and mobility on the one hand and gentleness, contemplation and confinement on the other, provides them with an aversion not only to caring or education but to novel phenomena like the use of computer keyboards (Cockburn, 1985). The habitus is thus more generative, flexible and multi-dimensional than mere habit (Bourdieu, 1993, p. 87). Yet it is not deterministic. The powers and susceptibilities of the habitus may or may not be activated. Whether they are

---

[3] 'Our perceptions and our practice, especially our perceptions of the social world, are guided by practical taxonomies, oppositions between high and low, masculine (or manly) and feminine, etc. The classifications which these practical taxonomies produce owe their value to the fact that they are "practical", that they make it possible to bring in just enough logic for the needs of practice, neither too much – fuzziness is often indispensable, particularly in negotiations – nor too little, because life would become impossible' (Bourdieu, quoted in McCall, 1992, p. 840).

depends on the context. When they are activated, they produce results which are always mediated in some way (facilitated, blocked, overridden or refracted and modified) by the context, and indeed actors may be able consciously to override them.[4]

The concept is used to explain the fact that the governance of most of our actions lies in the middle of a continuum ranging from unconscious reflexes to rational deliberation and choice. Our responses to the world are mostly at the level of dispositions, feelings and embodied skills. When we are in a familiar context, these dispositions give us a 'feel for the game', an ability to cope and go on effectively without conscious deliberation and planning. In such conditions, the workings of the habitus tend not to be noticed; its influence is clearer when we experience the discomfort of finding ourselves out of place, in an unfamiliar social setting, in which we *lack* a feel for the game.

The early years are particularly formative.

Early experiences have particular weight because the habitus tends to ensure its own constancy and its defence against change through the selection it makes within new information by rejecting information capable of calling into question its accumulated information, if exposed to it accidentally or by force, and by avoiding exposure to such information . . . (Bourdieu, 1990c, pp. 60–1)

However, later experiences can modify the habitus and produce new dispositions, and skills, enabling people to react in new ways. To the extent that their habitus does become modified, they may feel comfortable in contexts where they might not have done earlier. Thus new parents gradually develop a changed habitus and feel for the game of parenting, as they get used to caring. As Bourdieu acknowledges, 'a habitus can undergo modification in the face of different fields or even due to an awakening of consciousness and social analysis' (Bourdieu, cited in Aboulafia, 1999, p. 167).[5]

Although Bourdieu is usually at pains to stress actors' attunement to their circumstances and their acceptance of their lot in life it should not be assumed that social habitats or positions present actors with harmonious, complementary influences. On the contrary, people may find themselves pulled in quite different, incompatible directions. The habitus is formed through involvement in a variety of relations that intersect in the habitat and extend to other parts of the social field, and there is no reason

---

[4] This is a critical realist way of elaborating the generative powers of the habitus (Sayer, 1992, 2000a). Failure to appreciate this double contingency leads to a deterministic version of the concept of habitus.

[5] In *Sociology in Question* he had referred to the 'permanent' dispositions of the habitus (Bourdieu, 1993, p. 86).

why these different relations should be compatible, in fact they may be in contradiction: 'Such experiences tend to produce a habitus divided against itself, in constant negotiation with itself and with its ambivalence, and therefore doomed to a kind of duplication, to a double perception of self, to successive allegiances and multiple identities' (Bourdieu et al., 1999, p. 511). Here the contradictory influences are internalised so that different dispositions resist one another. This is plausible, and indeed likely to be common, given the complexity of the social world. There may be not just one but several lines of division within the habitus, leading to fractured identities.[6]

The model of development is one of subconscious bodily learning through repetition or practice. Just as the competent tennis player anticipates where the ball is coming without thinking about it and moves to the right place at the right time in order to return it ('protention'), so social action is a product of individuals' feel for the game, rather than a product of 'rational' deliberation and planning. This Pascalian view of human action is a vital antidote to the tendency of academics to project the special nature of their contemplative relation to the world and their consequent scholastic disposition (which has become a feature of their own habitus) onto those they study. Bourdieu pushes the Pascalian approach as far as he can and strenuously resists making concessions to critics. Although he occasionally admits that he is 'bending the stick' in response to overly rationalist approaches rather than refusing a role for conscious choice altogether (Bourdieu, 1990a, p. 106), he frequently follows up any concessions by immediate qualifications which neutralise them and allow the reassertion of an extreme Pascalian line (e.g., Bourdieu, 1998). However, I now wish to argue, in a series of seven stages, that concessions can be made to these and other criticisms of the concept without abandoning it altogether.

1.   *The feel for different kinds of game*

Even in the case of Bourdieu's favourite example of the tennis player, the habitus and the feel for the game are not acquired without some conscious monitoring of actions on the part of the actor. As those who have tried to acquire a feel for a complex, technical game know, be it tennis, dancing, or indeed learning how to go on in a new social situation, these skills are not acquired purely through unmonitored osmosis but require some

---

[6] While there is therefore no reason why the concept of habitus should tie us to a unitary conception of the self, we don't need to go to the opposite extreme of denying any degree of autonomy, reflexivity or coherence in subjects, for susceptibility to social influences presupposes them (Archer, 2000, 2003).

conscious effort. The tennis novice will never become skilled unless she is motivated to learn and concentrates on what she is doing. ('Wake up! Start your backswing earlier! Move!' shouts the coach.) Dancers talk about getting a new move or style 'into the body', and this requires concentration and practice in the sense of drilling. It is tempting to call this a shift from intention to achievement or from plan to practice, but usually the intentions are ill formed and ignorant. As readers of instruction manuals on learning complex skills know, descriptions can be more trouble than they are worth; rather, there is a creative process of adaptation or trial and error, and attempts to imitate others (Crossley, 2001; see also Collier, 2003).[7]

2.   The habitus and conscious deliberation

In most of Bourdieu's accounts of the habitus, the structure of disposi-tions seems to arise through a process of osmosis and shaping, through accommodation to material circumstances and social relations, like liv-ing in crowded housing or being accustomed to hard manual labour or serving others. However, he does note that the habitus generates 'mean-ingful practices and meaning-giving perceptions' (1984, p. 170). Ways of thinking can become habitual. Once learned they change from some-thing we struggle to grasp to something we can think *with*, without thinking *about* them. In other words, for much of the time our con-ceptual apparatus is not itself the subject of reflection. One can there-fore acknowledge the conceptual and concept-dependent dimensions of social practices without assuming that this necessarily takes the form of an ongoing rational discussion, as in the scholastic fallacy invited by many interpretivist or hermeneutic approaches to social science. Orienta-tions and behaviours such as condescension and deference involve habit, feeling and comportment but they also imply tacit understandings and evaluations: they involve 'intelligent dispositions' (Wood, 1990, p. 214). As Raymond Williams noted, thoughts can be felt, and feelings can be thought (Williams, 1977, p. 132). Further, these dispositions relate to a

---

[7] Processes of embodiment range from those which need no conscious apprehension or monitoring to acquire, through to highly technical skills which require considerable con-centration and continual practice, such as those of playing a violin concerto. There is no trade-off in such practices between the physical work and the thinking. By analogy, facil-ity in more complex forms of social action may require regularly repeated performance. It should thus be clear that insofar as the concept of habitus is conflated with that of 'feel for the game', it is expected to cover an extraordinarily wide range of phenomena, from primitive embodied modes of classification (e.g., hard/soft) through to wondrously complex embodied skills.

social field that is not 'inert materiality', but 'a complex imbrication of material and symbolic relations of power' (McNay, 2001, p. 146).

It is therefore important not to reduce the formation of the habitus to mere conditioning, although some conditioning is likely to be involved. Some dispositions are based on understanding: the difference between merely learning by rote or emulation and understanding is that in the latter case one grasps reasons or rationales – not merely memorising them but seeing their point (Winch, 1958). We become habituated to stopping at the traffic lights when they turn red, but we also see the point of doing so.[8]

Although Bourdieu's Pascalian view of action acknowledges the capacity of the habitus to generate meaningful practices it leaves the status of discourses unclear. His antipathy towards rationalist accounts of action implies a possible underestimation of the implications of the fact that subjects continually interpret and understand various discourses, including ones which present ways of thinking which are at variance with their dispositions. For example, while Bourdieu discusses many examples of responses to discourses in *Distinction*, he sees these only in relation to the habitus and the social field, not as discursive structures, conceptual schema in their own right. As Michèle Lamont notes, he underestimates the influence of remote, national discourses, which have deep historical roots and an inertia which make the experience of class differ between countries (Lamont, 1992, p. 135). Thus, for example, his explanations of racism largely ignore the role of racist discourses and how they reflect countries' particular histories (McRobbie, 2002).

While it is possible to absorb contradictory ideas deriving from this discursively mediated involvement in social life without noticing their contradiction if they apply to different spheres of action, the fact that we sometimes do notice them, for example, the hypocrisy of a top executive calling for pay restraint on the part of workers, indicates the co-presence of a more rational monitoring. This capacity need not be seen as radically distinct from that of the habitus, for we often sense an inconsistency ('smell a rat') before we manage to articulate it. Embodiment and rationality are not as opposed as generally assumed.

Bourdieu himself notes that the distinction between conscious and unconscious knowledge is overdrawn: with reference to 'the paradoxes of the scientific habitus', he argues:

---

[8] Understanding the point of complex matters such as the meaning of an unfamiliar technical concept may be gradual, because it takes time to learn how to use it in all the practical contexts which give it sense. We can gain a feel for a certain kind of reasoning, such as that used by economists or sociologists, but it still involves understanding and not merely conditioning.

The opposition between conscious and unconscious 'knowledge' . . . is actually totally artificial and fallacious: in fact, the principles of scientific practice can be both present to consciousness – to varying degrees at different times and different 'levels' of practice – and function in the practical state in the form of incorporated dispositions. (Bourdieu et al., 1999, p. 621n)[9]

Nevertheless, despite his outstanding skill in the interpretation of discourses, discourse lacks a clear place in Bourdieu's framework.

3.   Mundane reflexivity: internal conversations

In bending the stick to correct for overly rationalised approaches which ignore embodiment, Bourdieu (like many social theorists) ignores a mundane but crucial aspect of our lives: our 'internal conversations'. Our streams of consciousness – ranging from day-dreaming, through more or less distracted ruminating, to concentrated reflection on particular problems – are central to our lives, going beyond thinking about what we are doing to other, often more serious, matters (Archer, 2003). It is evident from the interview transcripts presented in Bourdieu et al.'s *The Weight of the World* that some actors churn through their moral narratives in their internal conversations almost obsessively (Bourdieu et al., 1999). To be sure, Bourdieu is right to emphasise the dangers of projecting features of the special conditions of academic life onto others, particularly the contemplative relation to the world, but there are also dangers of doing the opposite – denying or marginalising the life of the mind in others. Significantly, some commentators have criticised the denial of the life of the mind in the working class in much sociological writing, a tendency also present in lay middle class thinking (hooks, 2000; Reay, 2002). As Margaret Archer's research shows, reflexivity is certainly not the preserve of academics but is common to people regardless of their social position.

   As with any causal power, the effects of this exercise of reflexivity may be overridden by other obstacles or forces. That many of the intentions

---

[9] In these ways we can begin to get beyond the kind of mind/body dualism that is implicit in philosophies of social science and social ontologies which produce a split between understanding and material causation. Instead we can think of mind as a kind of form or organisation exhibited by the body in its structure and behaviour which has emergent powers (Wood, 1990, p. 19). Reasons and other discursive objects can be causes and become embodied (Fairclough et al., 2001). As Archer elaborates, practice is 'the wordless source of reason', for logic obtains its force indirectly from the practice of coping with the differentiations, affordances and constraints of the world, including ourselves, from representing necessity in the world through logical necessity in the relation between statements (see Archer, 2000, pp. 145–52; also Harré and Madden, 1975). The contrast between the 'fuzzy and creative logic of practical understanding . . . [and] . . . the abstract process of self-decipherment characteristic of scholastic interpretation' (McNay, 2001, p. 140) can therefore be overdrawn.

and plans developed through our internal conversations are frustrated by external constraints does not mean that they can be ignored by social scientists, for they also influence what we do within the constraints, and the failures certainly matter to the subjects, and affect what they do subsequently, whether they increase their resolve or moderate their ambitions. Sometimes we manage to change or escape the constraints. That we should even want to try indicates a tension between our situation and our wishes. (Inner worries like: 'What can I do about this relationship that has gone bad?', 'How can I pay off my debts?' presuppose the possibility that we know we are not in control of the game and that we need more than just a 'feel' for it.) Bourdieu cannot of course fail to acknowledge these tensions, and his normative critique of society presupposes a tension in his own relationship to it, and therefore his Pascalian approach to social action has to be moderated and supplemented.

Putting this point together with the role of practice and drilling in the development of embodied dispositions and skills, it is possible for actors not only to deliberate on their situation and on what they have become, but to strive to change their own habitus. This is illustrated by Farida, a French woman of Algerian parentage interviewed by Abdelmalek Sayad in *The Weight of the World*; she had struggled not only to escape her father's domination and oppression but to change and heal herself through considerable 'work on the self', which ranged from insomniac introspection to forcing herself to learn to do and enjoy what other young women had learned to do throughout their youth (Bourdieu et al., 1999, pp. 583–9).

. . . when I left, I realized the damage and destruction, as you say. I had to relearn everything . . . No, I had to learn everything. To speak normally, to listen without trembling; to listen and think at the same time, something that I had never learned to do, I didn't know how to listen, to reflect on what someone's telling me since I wasn't listening. I learned to walk, to associate with people and not to run away; in a word, to live. Something still remains: I can't stand public spaces, I took a long time before going to the movies . . . (p. 586)

Accounts like this are both a testimony to the power and inertia of habitus and the way in which it can be changed deliberately, at least in part, by repeated practice aimed at the embodiment of new dispositions.

4.   *The alleged complicity of habitus and habitat:*
      the necessity *of resistance*

Our fourth qualification concerns the relationship between habitus and habitat and wider field, or between dispositions and positions. Bourdieu *asserts* that there is an 'ontological complicity' between habitus and field, which implies a high degree of adaptability on the part of the subject, such that no matter what the habitat, s/he will gradually acquire a habitus that corresponds to it. We could try to test this empirically or we might even try to treat the empirical findings of studies such as *Distinction* and *The State Nobility* as tests of such a hypothesis, though they would hardly be conclusive (Bourdieu, 1984, 1996a). One of the noticeable features of the diagrams in the former text depicting the relationship between particular dispositions and social positions is the wide dispersion of responses within any particular group; indeed, in some cases the differences between responses of individuals in different social positions are only limited. Bourdieu would presumably have argued that this could be explained by variations in the paths by which actors had arrived at their current position, and in chance external influences, but it could also indicate that the adjustment of their original habitus to their original position had only been partial in the first place.[10]

Because of his prior assumption of complicity, Bourdieu is only able to note non-correspondence or tension between the habitus and the habitat either where people have been politicised (apparently 'from outside') or in cases where they have moved to a different part of the social field, so that it is an alien habitat that they now confront. But why should human beings be such that whatever the nature of their habitat in their early years, be it comfortable or wretched, a corresponding habitus that completely accommodates to and internalises their relations to the rest of the social field from the standpoint of their location should automatically form? This is a model of a perfectly malleable human, a model which makes it impossible to understand how anyone could react against and resist at least some parts of their habitat. I shall argue that the body already has aversions to and inclinations towards particular conditions, already has a sense of lack, before it gets habituated to a position within the social field, *indeed these are a necessary condition of the efficacy of socialisation.* That socialisation also generates new preferences or inclinations and aversions and modifies the innate ones is not in contradiction with this.

This 'default assumption' of complicity and compliance makes resistance hard to understand, and it is therefore not surprising that *Distinction* gives such an unrelentingly pessimistic view of the struggles of the social field, in which the dominated accept and rationalise their domination rather than challenging it. Ironically, it renders *The Weight of the World*, a book documenting people complaining and resisting, unintelligible. Where Bourdieu does occasionally acknowledge resistance it is usually

[10] John Frow suggests that some of these diagrams are misleadingly presented (Frow, 1995, pp. 40–4).

only to describe how it is doomed to failure, unless it is politically informed. Moreover, the assumption of perfect complicity renders mysterious those situations where there is no subordination and no resistance, and indeed in which we *relish* freedom, or *enjoy* and *feel empowered* by respect, for within the Bourdieuian nihilist framework such responses can only be construed as dull compliance.

To understand resistance, we must first recognise that it need not involve the pursuit of change or take progressive forms. Change is not necessarily progressive and conservatism not necessarily bad.[11] We need to avoid restricting acknowledgement of resistance to cases where it challenges the status quo or seems politically progressive. It is also sometimes difficult to distinguish resistance from compliance, especially when faced with contradictory influences: is refusing what you are enjoined to seek but actually refused resistance or compliance?; equally, is longing for what you are enjoined to want but not allowed resistance or compliance?

We can now question the assumed ontological complicity between habitus and habitat. This requires us, first, to note that the habitus must have some degree of independence from its corresponding habitat precisely because it is a different kind of thing, and, secondly, to examine more closely the process of the *shaping* of the individual that the formation of habitus presupposes. For it to be possible for anything to be shaped, it must have a particular structure, which, through its powers and susceptibilities, its constraints and affordances, *allows* such shaping to take place. Humans can only be shaped if they have structures and powers which resist some influences and yield to others.[12] Without capacities for resistance, then, like air, we could not be shaped. Firm, compacted snow is easier to shape into a ball than soft, powdery snow because it offers more resistance, owing to its different structure. Moreover, particular kinds of bodily structure are needed to enable us to become habituated to particular practices; we cannot develop a feel for the game of unassisted flight because we lack the necessary structure. The dialectic of resistances and susceptibilities is presupposed in any process of formation; resistance is

---

[11] Conservative resistance to change may be good, as many academics resisting audit culture would argue.

[12] As Mary Midgley comments: '. . . some sociologists and existentialists, like to claim officially that there is no such thing as human nature, so that nothing is naturally more important than anything else. This means that (for instance) total immobility or total solitude would be as good ways of life as any other, provided you were brought up to them or decided to choose them. Man is supposed to be infinitely plastic . . . I find this contention so obscure (even a piece of plasticine is not *infinitely* plastic: everything has *some* internal structure) that I propose simply to wait till I find someone living by it . . . Meanwhile, I propose to take it that we are so constituted as to mind more about some things than about others' (Midgley, 1972, p. 222).

presupposed by shaping but it also limits shaping. Thus, *provided we do not arbitrarily limit acknowledgement of resistance to cases where it seems progressive, we can see that resistance is intrinsic to the formation of the habitus rather than extrinsic and exceptional.*

Not just any kind of attempted social influence or construction works, because of the otherness of human nature. This suggests that just what the relationship between habitus and habitat or social field is in particular cases should be an empirical question. People are not 'discursively constituted' – which would presuppose the universal efficacy of wishful thinking – but discursively *influenced, selectively and fallibly,* and a precondition of this influence is that they – unlike logs or fish – are beings which are susceptible to such influence, and it is the specificity of their particular mix of causal powers and susceptibilities which makes the causal efficacy of social influences selective. Social being presupposes and is emergent from physical being (Archer, 2000). Critical realist philosophy reminds us always to ask what so many social constructionist accounts of socialisation forget, namely, *what is it about humans which makes them susceptible to a certain kind of change or 'construction'?* (Archer, 2000; Soper, 1995). Not just any object can become culturally modified and imprinted; a plank of wood remains the same whatever kind of cultural meaning we care to give it. The success of any kind of shaping or social construction depends on the relation between the shaping process and the pre-existing (including social) properties of the materials being used and worked upon (Sayer, 2000a).

One of the features of humans – though one shared by many other species – is a capacity to suffer and inflict pain:[13]

No durable social arrangements can be indifferent to the amount of pain they entail or allow to be inflicted. Even behaviourists like Skinner depend upon a judicious mixture of pleasure and pain in the process of social conditioning. Our inescapably incarnational nature presents society with non-negotiable intolerances which are no less salient for the societal enterprise because they are not species-specific. (Archer, 2000, p. 41)

As Archer adds, we should not allow a sociological imperialism that fills the body with 'social foam' (p. 317) and denies the relative autonomy of the biological and psychological, and hence renders pain, distress,

---

[13] The fact that this is not unique to humans does not of course prevent it being part of our nature. Rorty falls into this simple non-sequitur in presuming that its non-uniqueness means that it cannot be part of human nature (Archer, 2000, p. 41). Unique or distinctive properties don't always tell us much about objects' natures; e.g., a tiger's stripes are certainly distinctive but they don't tell us much about what it can and can't do, while less distinctive features such as its anatomy, musculature and reproductive system tell us a great deal.

pleasure and well-being incomprehensible, or at least as forms of self-delusion. When a child resists something it is not necessarily because it is subject to contradictory external influences, for there could be mutually consistent external influences to which they cannot adjust; some of the younger interviewees in *The Weight of the World* seem to have resisted their first habitat from the start (Bourdieu et al., 1999). Ironically, despite his emphasis on practice and embodiment, Bourdieu does not deal adequately with their nature and preconditions in terms of corporeality. What kinds of beings are people, such that they can acquire a habitus?

We can still acknowledge that most of our powers and susceptibilities are socially acquired (though this very process presupposes enabling pre-discursive and biological powers (Archer, 2000)). To see this we need to avoid collapsing time, and note that our susceptibility to social shaping at time t is constrained and enabled by the products of social shaping at time $t-1$, and hitherto. Thus, it is usually easier for a university tutor to induce an upper middle class student to talk in seminars than a working class student because of the way they have been shaped in the past, which has given them different dispositions and skills or powers and susceptibilities. Similarly, a person's susceptibility to guilt and shame presupposes already-acquired ethical and other values.

We should therefore not assume a perfect harmony or complicity between habitus and habitat, or try to reduce one to the other, as in either voluntarism or various kinds of determinism. Unless we recognise the differences between habitus and habitat then we will prevent analysis of their interplay (Archer, 2000, p. 6). The phenomenon of the feel for the game lends credibility to the idea of some kind of ontological complicity between habitus and habitat, but the extent of the complicity may vary; there might even be some familiar situations in which it may be difficult for actors to acquire a feel for the game. Moreover, they can know or sense (fallibly, but with some degree of success) a rough difference between circumstances which enable them to flourish and circumstances which do not, indeed this is a condition of their survival. People are not merely shaped, but flourish or suffer. That some kinds of beneficial or damaging effects may not be noticed, or may be misconstrued by actors, does not invalidate the obvious point that people do not merely 'classify' – as if they subconsciously constructed disinterested typologies – but actively discriminate between the good and the bad, the safe and the threatening, and so on. In their mostly subconscious and fallible, but mostly practically-adequate ways, they *value* the world. That so much social theory could miss such an obvious point is a sad testament to its estrangement from practice and the normative character of life.

Certainly we can come to care about some of the things and relationships to which we are habituated, but there are also many for which we do not care and indeed from which we would rather escape, despite having an appropriate feel for the game. We can get used to living in crowded conditions but still want space of our own; we can get used to doing without holidays but still want one; we can get used to a relationship and yet still want to end it.

Bourdieu often comments on the way in which goods that are prescribed as socially valid and desirable for all are often only available to a minority. He writes of activities, particularly those of education, in which the subordinate class are expected to compete, noting that this is a competition which they have effectively lost before they have begun to play. Yet this tension between expectations and possibilities need not always result in resignation, compliance and the refusal of what is refused. It can also result in *longing for what is denied* to the actor. As Carolyn Steedman's account of her working class mother's life shows, refusal of what one is given and encouraged to identify with (mothering) and intense longing for what one is denied can become central to one's inner life, dominating how everything is seen (Steedman, 1986). It is hardly surprising given the relentless seduction of commodities, the glorification of educational advancement and economic success, the pressure to conform to gender norms, and to be popular and attractive, accompanied by economic insecurity, anomie, and loneliness, that unfulfilled longing can be so powerful.

Longing and desire have a more primitive basis than mere internalisation of social influences. Humans are characterised not only by animal lack, as in hunger for food, but desire for recognition and self-respect, which they can only obtain through certain kinds of interactions with others. The habitus not only classifies phenomena but *values* them, as the expressions 'ill-disposed' and 'well-disposed' suggest. An object or machine can have tendencies to behave in a certain way but it cannot be well-disposed to some and ill-disposed to anything or *care* about them. This is also central to the explanation of resistance, and why it can occur during the formation of the habitus, and indeed can be constitutive of the habitus. Acknowledging internal conversations and longing helps to make sense of the obvious point that our relationship to the world is not simply one of accommodation or becoming skilled in its games, but, at least in some ways, one of wanting to be different and wanting the world and its games to be different.

5.   Emotions

Bourdieu's emphasis on the habitus draws attention to our partly subconscious orientation to the world and our feel for the game. As such, it (curiously) ignores a much more conscious aspect of subjectivity, and one central to the experience of class, namely emotion. I shall argue later in the book that emotions such as pride, shame, envy and resentment tell us a great deal about class and the difference it makes to our lives.

Although emotions are clearly embodied, sometimes visibly so, they are not to be understood, as commonly supposed, as the antithesis of reason, but as responses to and commentaries on our situations (Archer, 2000; Barbalet, 2001; Bartky, 1990; Helm, 2001). They are cognitive and evaluative, indeed, essential elements of intelligence (Nussbaum, 2001, p. 3).[14] They are strongly related to our nature as dependent and vulnerable yet intelligent beings. Like reason, emotions are *about* something, particularly things which are important to our well-being and which we value, and yet which are not fully within our control. Thus, the loss of a friend occasions a stronger emotional response than the loss of a pencil. Emotions are not a redundant accompaniment to the business of life, like muzak in a supermarket, but commentaries which relate to our concerns and evaluations of the import of things (Helm, 2001). They are highly discriminating evaluative commentaries on our well-being or ill-being in the physical world (for example, pleasure in warmth), in our practical dealings with the world (for example, the frustration of failing to execute some task successfully), and in the social-psychological world (for example, self-esteem or shame) (Archer, 2000; Nussbaum, 2001).[15] They are relational – not merely 'subjective' in the sense of dispositions and emanations of subjects having no relation to objects/referents. Rather, they are about the relation between the objective[16] qualities of the subject, and objects such as the actions of others. Their physical side, though often prominent, is different from other kinds of physical experience; the physical pain from, say, backache, is different from the physical emotional pain of bereavement or shame in that one knows that the latter have a cognitive aspect.[17]

---

[14] Mind/body dualism must be rejected if we are to understand emotions. We need to take seriously the proposition that bodies are intelligent and that reason is one emergent power that arises from them.

[15] This anti-subjectivist, anti-idealist claim that emotions have referents is borne out by social psychological research on aggression reported by Scott (1990, p. 186), which shows that victims' anger towards agents of injustice is not reduced where they displace it onto others or give vent to it in 'safe', legitimate activities such as sports (the 'safety-valve theory'). Experiences of injustice may also make people more disposed to aggression against innocent others, but such displacements have been found not to resolve the problem and the anger remains. Such emotions are clearly not undirected, non-specific urges having no referents and capable of remedy through just any means.

[16] Here by 'objective' I mean neither 'true' nor 'value-free' but 'pertaining to objects themselves' – in this case the subject as object (Sayer, 2000a, pp. 58ff.).

[17] Thanks to John O'Neill for discussions of this and the point made in the next footnote.

Emotions tend to have a more complicated relation to circumstances than unemotional commentaries not only because they involve valuation, but because they are often influenced by previous experiences. In a manner reminiscent of the formation of the habitus, early experiences, especially from childhood, when we were most needy and vulnerable, may have a lasting effect on our emotional dispositions or susceptibilities. At first sight, when we note how emotional reactions sometimes seem to be disproportionate to the events that prompt them and linger long after the events are over, we may be tempted to conclude that this is evidence of their irrationality.[18] For example, emotional dispositions towards confidence or diffidence, which often correlate with class and gender, tend to form early in life and subsequently prove durable. Or a childhood instance of humiliation, perhaps by someone of higher class, may influence emotional responses to other situations many years later. In other words, emotions evident on particular occasions in adult life may have a narrative character, though this is inevitably difficult to interpret, not least because subjects can remember little of their early experience (Nussbaum, 2001).

The commentaries which emotions provide are *fallible* – but then the commentaries of reason are fallible too – yet they are usually sufficiently practically-adequate to warrant being taken seriously. We should also take them seriously precisely because they may be wrong or misplaced, as in the case of racist anger towards asylum seekers. The idea of 'listening to our emotions' is not mere psycho-babble but acknowledges the fact that emotions are about something, and that by taking them seriously we might be able to appreciate hitherto unnoticed things and assess what they tell us about what is happening to us and others. The relation of particular emotions to specific referents or causes may often be unclear, and of course such causes may themselves be complex and diffuse; we have all had the experience of not being sure just what has put us in a bad mood – but again that is a good reason for reflecting on precisely what they are about. Emotional responses to the inequalities and struggles of the social field and how people negotiate them are to be taken seriously both because they matter to people, and because they generally reveal something about their situation and welfare; indeed, if the latter were not true the former would not be either.

Emotions like anger, happiness, pride and shame appear to be common to all cultures, but what they tend to be aroused by or about varies among

---

[18] Emotional reason differs from unemotional reason in being hard to control. For example, while one can choose to stop thinking about something of no emotional import, when under stress, feeling ashamed, angry, anxious or bereaved it may be difficult or impossible to stop the continual emotional churning through the same thoughts and feelings.

cultures, and within them, according to social position. 'If emotions are evaluative appraisals, then cultural views about what is valuable can be expected to affect them directly . . .' (Nussbaum, 2001, p. 157). Thus in a liberal culture, limitations of individual liberty are more likely to cause anger than in a communitarian society which values individual liberty less. Emotions do not escape discursive influence and may be deepened and enlivened by discourses. But they are not deepened by just any discursive phenomena; they are not deepened by reading the telephone directory or a language one doesn't understand, but by discourses that refer to the kind of things whose implications for one's well-being and that of others make them matters of emotional concern. Again, there is no contradiction between acknowledging both the fact that many of these matters depend on 'cultural constructions' like religious beliefs or lifestyles rather than on matters relating to physical well-being, and the fact that humans must have the causal powers and susceptibilities (many of them socially acquired), such that they can be enculturated. In particular, vulnerability and dependence, lack, and desire, including the psychological need for recognition,[19] provide the 'hooks' with which social constructions or discourses can engage. To understand how inequalities are lived we have to come to terms with actors' ambivalent responses of compliance, resignation, rationalisation, resistance and longing. Unless we take emotion seriously, and our capacity for suffering and happiness, and for discrimination and evaluation, we cannot understand why any circumstances should prompt resistance or critical reflection. For any kind of social condition to 'affect' us, we must be the kinds of beings capable of suffering, happiness, love, humiliation, shame, etc. As Mauss argued, this implies some kind of integration of the physiological, the psychological and the social (Probyn, 2002). To be sure, some emotions (secondary emotions) depend on understandings and dispositions acquired in culturally mediated ways, but it would be a mistake to treat emotions as purely or voluntaristically constructed: again, not just any construction or construal succeeds in producing conformity.[20] Cultural mediation is not the same as cultural determination.

Finally, emotions are not trivial. At the extreme, emotions such as shame and hatred may concern matters which people value more highly than their lives. So much social science ignores the force of emotions in everyday life, alienating itself from what lay people might recognise as their experience. Renato Rosaldo comments on the inability of much anthropology to grasp emotions, particularly rage, presenting instead sophisticated accounts which wholly miss this force, treating behaviour as

---

[19] See chapter 3.   [20] See also Barbalet, 2001, p. 25.

defined by mere discursive and practical convention – a kind of insensitivity which would be considered appalling if exhibited in an emotionally charged social situation such as bereavement (Rosaldo, 1993). As words are often insufficient to describe them, the strongest emotions may be concealed by the thinness of actors' accounts of them. Though not as strong as the emotions of grief and rage that Rosaldo had in mind, the emotions associated with class are central to its experience. The very word 'affect', with its academic, cold, clipped, distant, unemotional ring, seems symptomatic of intellectual disdain and belittles the force and enormity of what it refers to.[21] Significantly, as a verb, to 'affect' means to merely simulate a response, such as surprise (i.e. to *dis*simulate or deceive), and 'affect*ations*' are *artificial* manners.[22] While the rationalistic tendencies common in social science incline many to ignore emotions, to do so is extraordinarily irrational: 'simply, emotions matter because if we did not have them nothing else would matter. Creatures without emotion would have no reason for living, nor, for that matter, for committing suicide. Emotions are the stuff of life' (Elster, quoted in Archer, 2000, p. 194).

6.   Commitments and investments

The causes, practices, or other people that matter most to actors are not merely things which they happen to like or prefer but things in terms of which their identities are formed and to which they are committed, sometimes to the extent that they will pursue them against their self-interest. The ability to develop commitments is central to people's well-being, and one of the main reasons why inequalities of class are so important is that they influence this process.

It might seem that Bourdieu acknowledges this since he comments frequently on the way in which actors *invest* in particular practices, and in many cases he frames this in terms of games, stakes and prizes (e.g., Bourdieu, 1998, pp. 76ff.; 1993, p. 18). The investment of the middle classes in education is an example. However, the metaphors of investment and games are in tension with Bourdieu's Pascalian view of behaviour, and inadequate for understanding the nature and strength of the attachments involved in commitments. Such metaphors, like those of capital, profit and calculation, invite us to interpret investment as egotistical, instrumental, involving competitive, reward-seeking behaviour. The tension created by the combination of economic metaphors associated with

---

[21] 'Affect' is also associated with non-cognitive views of emotions that I wish to oppose (Nussbaum, 2001, p. 61n).

[22] Ironically, 'affection', a common-enough emotional feeling and one that is hugely important for our well-being, is rarely acknowledged in sociology.

rational calculation, and exorbitant claims for the power of habitus relative to reasoning and reflexivity, runs throughout his work and structures
responses to it. Yet Bourdieu also vehemently rejects the rationalist, utili-
tarian reading (1998, p. 79, see also 1993), though the grounds on which
he defends himself are significant. They are primarily that actors are not
rational, self-interested decision-makers making investments, but, rather,
their habitus attunes them to the game. However, we don't have to flip
from a rationalist interpretation to an anti-rationalist one; as we have
pointed out, there is often a cognitive element in the learning/habituation
process, and actors clearly do sometimes think about what they have
invested themselves in – as is implied by 'taking an interest'. But the
important point is a rather different one. Actors also tend to invest emotionally in certain things not merely for the rewards but because they
come to see them as valuable in themselves, sometimes regardless of any
benefit to themselves.

The concept of commitments is superior to that of investment in games,
because it implies a stronger and more serious attachment, one that has
an emotional dimension and involves objects, practices, others and relationships which we *care* about. If we omit from the relationship between
habitus and habitat our ability to discriminate among phenomena according to their perceived implications for the well-being of others or ourselves, if we ignore emotions, then commitment seems little more than a
strong correspondence or deeply entrenched habit. Commitments imply
emotional, reasoned attachment. They can be in our self-interest – for
example, allowing us to indulge ourselves – but they can also be based on
altruism or be related to causes such as social justice or nationalism (Sen,
1999, p. 270).[23] Did Pierre Bourdieu have a commitment to uncovering
the mechanisms of domination in society or did he merely have a feel for
the game of sociology? To be sure, his habitus presumably evolved in a
way which disposed him to do this, and he clearly had an outstanding feel
for the academic game, but it was surely also a commitment supported
by a rationale which was not mere rationalisation of the unavoidable but
had some normative justification.

Few people can list their commitments, and they may only notice
them when they are threatened. They usually emerge gradually and unintentionally through continued immersion in relationships and activities,
and through embodiment. Although the distinction between commitments and preferences is a fuzzy one, it is not merely one of strength of

---

[23] Not every activity in which we invest our energies leads to a commitment. There may
be relatively short projects we get involved with that are complex, challenging and interesting, but to which we are not committed in the same way as we might be to, say, our
child. As always these distinctions are fuzzy.

attachment; there are important qualitative differences too. Where preferences are concerned we are generally willing to substitute something else for what we prefer. I would prefer to do x (stay with my current bank), but if y (another bank) is a good substitute I will give x up for y. If I am committed to, say, my child or my political beliefs, then they can't be sold or swapped for something else. I am committed to certain people, ideas and causes and I can't be bought off, for they are ends in themselves, not merely means to other ends. Moreover, in pursuing commitments we tend to choose means that already prefigure and are consistent with those ends, which is not necessarily the case for preferences (Archer, 2000, p. 84).

Though they are rarely things that we plan to have in advance, our commitments make up our character and without them we are likely to feel rootless and lost. Losing or being prevented from pursuing commitments we have already formed leads to something akin to bereavement, since through our commitment to x, x has captured something of us. Changing my bank may cause me some trouble, but it need not affect the kind of person I am or my well-being, as the loss of a commitment might. It is nevertheless possible for commitments to weaken or 'go sour' over a period of time, producing a sense of disillusionment and loss, and re-evaluation of priorities. Commitments also tend to be gendered, with commitments to people being primarily associated with women, and commitments to technical projects primarily associated with men. Class and other social hierarchies further influence the kinds of commitment we are able to develop, both in terms of differentiating them and in unequally distributing the resources needed for pursuing them.

Not surprisingly given their importance for our well-being, commitments figure prominently in the struggles of everyday life. Consider a familiar example: if we listen to people talking about their jobs, particularly in professional work, we are often reminded that workplaces are fields of struggle in which self-interests clash, in which commitments may differ from self-interest – or be too closely related – or in which non-work-related commitments may be in conflict with work duties and commitments. People may work for organisations for decades and become thoroughly habituated to them, yet while they certainly have a feel for the game they can still experience conflict between how they feel they ought to act and are allowed to act, and between how they feel they ought to be treated and are treated. They may feel that they are struggling to maintain their integrity in the face of pressures from others, be they fellow workers, clients, or managers relaying budget pressures or government directives. Neither an economic instrumentalist account nor a purely Pascalian view does justice to what can be for some workers an overwhelming experience.

From the outside many of the conflicts may seem petty, but the mixtures of ambition, struggle for self-esteem and emotional commitment (all of which can be tangled up together) can have a huge impact on workers' lives – at the extreme, prompting them to leave secure jobs and uproot their lives. The identities and commitments which are being challenged are invested in consciously and normatively, and not just through habituation. They are not simply about power and resources, but over what is considered to be good. This reminds us that not all struggle is for power or for resources; while these may sometimes be seen as ends in themselves, their importance lies in the fact that they are necessary conditions for allowing people to live fulfilling lives, in which commitments are an essential part.

7.   Ethical dispositions

Having developed the concept of the habitus and proposed that emotions are evaluative judgements of matters perceived to be important to people's well-being, and acknowledged the way in which people come to value certain things in themselves rather than merely instrumentally, we can now address what often matters to them most – namely their sense of, or feel for, how people should treat one another. Again we can start from Bourdieu.

At one level, Bourdieu recognized the deeply evaluative character of social behaviour in terms of how people judge themselves and members of other groups, and the practices and objects associated with them. However, his interests in this regard lay primarily in the valuation of these things in strategic, functional and aesthetic terms. This is partly a consequence of his Hobbesian, interest- and power-based, model of social life. But actors also value others and their conduct in terms of their goodness or propriety. I wish to argue that the habitus includes ethical dispositions, which, when activated, produce moral emotions or what Adam Smith termed 'moral sentiments' (Smith, 1759).[24] It is in virtue of these that people often produce moral responses spontaneously, without reflection; indeed, it is interesting that we would have doubts about the moral character of someone who couldn't respond morally to events without first deliberating on them. Thus, on seeing a pensioner being mugged we might respond instantly with horror, anger and sympathy, before we had chance to reflect on what had happened. Like other dispositions,

---

[24] In a rare reference to the ethical dimension of the habitus, Bourdieu argues that the word 'ethos' better refers to these dispositions than does 'ethics', which suggests coherent explicit principles (Bourdieu, 1993). For a slightly different analysis to mine of the relationship between sentiments, dispositions and emotions, see Rawls, 1971, pp. 479–85.

ethical dispositions, virtues and vices are acquired and become embodied through practice involving relations with others, so people become habitually honest, trusting, or deceitful and suspicious. The activation of these dispositions has an emotional aspect, evident in sentiments such as gratitude, benevolence, compassion, anger, bitterness, guilt and shame.

There can also be *un*ethical dispositions and *im*moral sentiments.[25] As Norman Geras notes, we all know the 'motivational range' here:

> comprising, with all the admirable qualities and excellences, also elements which are less than admirable, and indeed some which are downright repugnant. This range is simply the stuff of ordinary existence. It is a form of practical experience taken from every area of life: every family, every circle of friends and acquaintances, every neighbourhood, every milieu, social stratum, vocation, organization. It is an experience – again, together with what is generous, loving, courageous and so on – of jealousies and vanities, petty unkindness and hatreds, wilful deceits, self-importance and self-promotion. (Geras, 1998, p. 99)[26]

In addition there may be xenophobic, racist, sexist and homophobic dispositions, involving the projection of bad or feared characteristics onto the other; like dispositions which we would be happier to term 'moral', they have an evaluative character.

It is common to draw a distinction between ethics and morality in which the former refers to actors' sensuous dispositions which they absorb largely subconsciously through socialisation, while the latter refers to relatively formal, universal, public norms, though sometimes the terms are reversed (Smith's 'moral sentiments' are closer to ethical dispositions than norms; philosophy students generally study 'ethics' rather than 'morality'). There is indeed a difference between the two, but there are also strong relations between them, as acknowledged in Hegel's concept of ethical life (Wood, 1990; Yar, 1999). While it is mainly the informal practices that concern us in this book, it is possible for formal moral norms to be internalised and embodied. Thus, although the Kantian theory of morality has rightly been criticised for being alienated from actors' dispositions and feelings, it is possible for actors to accept, invest in and identify with such principles and others so that they become habitual. We may acquire an embodied sense of duty and self-restraint that overrides certain dispositions which we formerly held; indeed, this process

---

[25] Normative moral and political philosophy understandably focuses on the nature of the good and the right, and if bad and wrong are acknowledged at all they are treated as aberrations rather than all-too-common tendencies whose origins need to be explained (Alexander, 2003). For a rare exception see Glover, 1999.

[26] Geras continues: 'It yields to us a knowledge complementary to the one we have from the Holocaust itself: a knowledge of the ordinary raw materials of great evil, those common vices and human failings which can become, in another setting or combination, suddenly exorbitant.'

is a large part of what moral education is about. Again, the rationale of such internalised norms may sometimes be brought to consciousness, and sometimes changed through reflection. In the opposite direction, it is possible for moral principles to be little more than formal expressions of ethical dispositions.[27] The two sides come together in the realm of inner or public conversation about moral issues, jointly influencing moral decisions. Actors come to grasp the complex evaluations of their culture, which relate to the range of their daily experience and beyond, partly at the level of having a feel for the relevant games (activities and situations), and the various kinds of feelings that they occasion, and partly through a more discursive consciousness; indeed, the latter mediates and provides a vocabulary, and sometimes a range of sensibilities, for such activities and situations. The distinction between moral norms and ethical dispositions should therefore be assumed to be very fuzzy.[28] The approach developed here regarding morality and emotions concurs with that of Martha Nussbaum: 'Instead of viewing morality as a system of principles to be grasped by the detached intellect, and emotions as motivations that either support or subvert our choice to act according to principle, we will have to consider emotions as part and parcel of the system of ethical reasoning' (Nussbaum, 2001, p. 1).

Since the concepts of ethical dispositions, moral sentiments or emotions and ethical life can be related to that of habitus, the same kinds of qualification that we made regarding the latter apply to the relationship between dispositions and norms.

- Just as the habitus need not be in harmony with the habitat or with wider discourses, even during individuals' formative years, so individuals' ethical dispositions need not be entirely consistent with the particular nexus of relations in which they are situated or with wider discursive norms. On the one side there can be a tension between the body and the practices and conditions in which people find themselves; on the other side, discourses, being both fallible and relating to a wider range of experience than that available to individuals at first hand, can engender dissonance too. Such differences can generate anomalous behaviour and resistance, whether deliberate or inadvertent.
- Ethical dispositions, once acquired, have some inertia, but their strength depends on their seriousness and the frequency with which they are activated. The mode and context of their activation can recursively change dispositions, making actors more, less, or differently

---

[27] Norms are as much outcomes of practices as guides for action.

[28] Hence '[V]irtues are [or can be A.S.] *intelligent* dispositions, dispositions to act for certain reasons, to be pleased or pained at certain things, to feel certain emotions' (Wood, 1990, p. 214).

ethical. Some experiences, like blood-doning, may be 'consciousness-raising', while others, like a night out with the lads, may be 'consciousness-lowering'. In either case the process of change is likely to take place through small steps. For example, in the negative direction, people may find that minor immoral acts pave the way for the sanctioning of major ones, though they may realise, usually too late, that they have crossed a moral boundary (Glover, 2001, p. 35).[29]

Social action is influenced by an ongoing mutual and self-monitoring of conduct, as expounded by Adam Smith in the *Theory of Moral Sentiments*, not only in confronting serious moral dilemmas but in the most ordinary situations, such as conversation, where we have to evaluate how we are being treated and how we are treating the other (Smith, 1759:1984). We imagine how others' well-being will be affected by our actions, and how a spectator would evaluate our own actions, so as to consider what to do. This process of self- and mutual evaluation is crucial both for our well-being and for social order, and of course the two are linked. The self-monitoring need not involve invoking a 'generalized other', as Mead called it, nor need we suppose that the imagined spectator succeeds in being impartial or achieves an Archimedean position (Griswold, 1999). In familiar situations, the monitoring and evaluation can be done 'on automatic' as part of our feel for the game, but in more difficult and less familiar situations it may require conscious deliberation. Evaluative behaviour is not reducible to mere primitive responses like those to heat and cold, for we also develop an evaluative feel for the game, indeed a feel for the evaluative game, and become practised in forms of judgement which have particular logics or structures, albeit unnoticed ones. It is these structures that moral philosophers often try to identify, for example in distinguishing envy from resentment, shame from guilt, or compassion from pity.[30] These are not merely conceptual structures but embodied psychological dispositions which may be activated by certain events.

Ethics or morality have a conventional character because they are social products and we do not have to conform to them – indeed if this were not the case, there would be no need for normative ideas about what we should do. The conventional aspect is also implied by the etymological link between ethics and ethos, and morality and mores. This, coupled with an acknowledgement of the considerable degree of variety in such dispositions and norms among societies, is sometimes associated with

[29] This is a tendency taken advantage of in military training: for example, novice soldiers are made to alter their ethical disposition towards violence through bayonet practice.

[30] E.g., Nussbaum (1996, 2001), Williams (1993).

a reduction of morality to mere communal convention, or 'what we do round here'. However, we cannot endlessly bracket out the ought, the normative force and rationales for actions, though this is often what sociologists do.[31] While sociologists are often content to reduce the moral to the conventional in their professional explanations of others' actions, they are unlikely to explain their own actions in this way, nor would they accept an appeal to 'what we do round here' as a justification of actions of others who behaved unethically towards them. This reduction is both inconsistent and demeaning. Actors' own judgements and justifications, be they good or bad, have to be taken into account insofar as they influence what they do.

As Mary Midgley has argued, morality differs from mere convention in being *serious*, that is, about matters that affect people and their well-being deeply, whereas mere convention need not necessarily be serious (for example, ways of setting a table). Its seriousness derives from its significance for human well-being and is reflected in the expectation of some kind of justification for its norms, though of course these may be questionable (Midgley, 1972). Actors have varying degrees of awareness of these kinds of justification and use them to call into question unethical behaviour. Such justifications in turn imply some notion or recognition of human suffering and vulnerability.

Purely conventionalist understandings of morality tend to rest on untenable models of the communities to which the conventions or moral norms belong. As critics of communitarianism have pointed out, communities are usually internally differentiated and hierarchical and include inconsistent as well as consistent forces and beliefs. 'What we do round here' might be seen as oppressive and immoral by some of the community's own members. There may therefore be resistance to norms from within as well as without. Fallibly, but usually with some degree of success, actors can often distinguish the harmful and the oppressive from the beneficial and the supportive, though of course both may be entangled and embedded in particular practices and interests and difficult to resolve. In making or sensing such distinctions actors draw upon both their

---

[31] For example, even Durkheim, in *The Division of Labour in Society*, views moral rules as obligatory, desirable and having an aura of sacredness and tending to be functional for the survival of society, hence ignoring their normative content and force and reducing them to special conventions backed up by sanctions (what is moral about such rules?) (Durkheim, 1984). In *Suicide* (1951) he equates the moral with the social, but presents a more sophisticated analysis which acknowledges the psychological, insofar as the social engages with longing and desire (pp. 246ff.), both as a precondition for their fulfilment and as a regulative and moderating influence on them. While he examines moral motives for certain kinds of suicide, he does not go deeply into their meanings, being more interested in their distribution and sociological correlates.

non-discursive dispositions and their discursive awareness and knowledge. Actors make sense of themselves and their well-being in terms of their cultures, just as scientists can only observe the world in theory-laden ways. But just as in science, theory-laden observation is not necessarily theory-determined but can still register certain mistakes and failed expectations, so actors may find some of their own cultural interpretations unsatisfactory without going beyond the interpretive resources offered by their own culture. Like any discourse, cultural discourses are heterogeneous and fallible and they often provide resources for their own critique.

To be sure, to some extent, actors' ethical dispositions and beliefs relate to their social location and interests, for example, in relation to gender and class (e.g., Bartky, 1990; Lamont, 1992; Tronto, 1994), but they can also be based on reflection and engagement with different ideas and hence come to differ from what might be expected. We do not treat Bourdieu's work merely as an expression of his social position and trajectory; rather we *evaluate* his claims and assume the reasons he offers for them to be causally responsible[32] for his making them, though of course they could be rationalisations, disguises or evasions of the real reasons for making them. The interviewees in the *Weight of the World* do not merely explain to Bourdieu and his fellow researchers their local conventions; rather, they voice deeply felt disapproval of many of them. In some cases their despair and rage appears to be all-consuming. A bland, anti-naturalist conventionalism simply cannot begin to understand the extent or profundity of the normative contestation of social life. Ethical dispositions, beliefs and norms are indeed likely to vary across social space, reflecting social divisions and how people have been treated and how they have been allowed to treat others, but they also strikingly *cross-cut* social divisions. Smith himself noticed this, arguing that moral sentiments were less affected by 'custom and fashion' than are aesthetic sentiments (Smith, 1759:1984, V.2.1, p. 200). There are several, related, reasons for this.

First, ethics, concerning primarily how people (ought to) treat one another, is more socially regulated and momentous than matters of aesthetic taste.[33] For example, it matters little to me what you or your possessions look like; what is more important is how you treat me, whether you respect my autonomy and needs, whether you take advantage of my vulnerability, and so on.

---

[32] For defences of the assumption that reasons can be causes see Bhaskar, 1979; Collier, 1994; Sayer, 1992, 2000a.

[33] I argue later in chapter 9 that although they are always culturally interpreted in various ways, at least some moral issues concern transhistorical features of humanity.

Second, while ethical dispositions are likely to be influenced by social-isation under specific, concrete circumstances, they are also applied to novel situations; indeed that is their practical point – they do not merely provide us with evaluations of what exists or has happened but orient our future actions. There is more at work here than a merely pragmatic logic – an 'economy of practice' like that associated with the deploy-ment of other dispositions – for the generalisation of ethical behaviour is *normatively* enforced. Moreover, as Jeffrey Alexander puts it: 'Values pos-sess relative independence vis-à-vis social structures because ideals are immanently universalistic. This is so . . . because they have an inherent tendency to become matters of principle that demand to be generalized' (1995, p. 137). Alexander cites research in developmental psychology, which with 'the signal and revealing exception of behaviourism' supports the acquisition of this process of generalisation. The recognition of a form of morality involving concrete rather than abstract others is not incom-patible with this for this too involves a process of going beyond one's own position (see also Benhabib, 1992, chapters 5 and 6). Preferential treat-ment of certain others (for example, one's children) is therefore typically expected and seen as proper rather than as unethical, though how far responsibilities are expected to extend to others varies and is a subject of debate (see, for example, Goodin, 1985; Tronto, 1994; Unger, 1996). This generalising tendency of morality is not at all in contradiction with its localised origins in particular relations:

It is because we have specific commitments to specific individuals and groups that we can then go on to recognize the claim of all human beings . . . It is because we first form ties with parents, siblings and friends that we are subsequently able to extend our sympathies to other human beings with whom we are less closely connected. (Norman, quoted in Goodin, 1985, p. 4)

Third, the reciprocal character of relations with others produces not only a generalising tendency but a concern with consistency and fair-ness, other things being equal, though to differing degrees. Integrity – coherence and consistency in action – is also valued and sought after: it is not simply an imposition. This is often overridden by sectional interests and inequalities of power and situations of near-Hobbesian (dis)order. However, the strength of the ideal of fairness is even evident in spurious appeals to it by the dominant, which show a realisation of the need at least to appear to be fair in their dealings with the subordinate if they are not to lose legitimacy. The legitimation of relations of domination depends on a combination of naturalisation of inequalities, as in the case of gender, and the appearance of fairness, at least in matters which do not threaten dominance.[34]

To some extent then, moral behaviour and evaluation may vary *independently* of divisions such as those of class, 'race', gender, or age. Sociology's understandable concern with the bad should not be allowed to obscure the simple fact that people also often behave not merely civilly and respectfully but generously and warmly towards others, and not purely those of their own group. Sociologists may be reluctant to accept that any actions could cross-cut gender, class and ethnic divisions in a way that is neutral towards them, though presumably their pessimism doesn't prevent them wishing that this were indeed the case and at least trying to make their own behaviour more consistent across such divisions. It would be bizarre for progressively minded social scientists to argue that ethics was unavoidably purely relative to gender, or class and ethnicity, for this would essentialise it and render sexism, class discrimination or racism as beyond criticism. The very question of whether ethical behaviour should be influenced by these divisions is itself implicit in the micro-politics of everyday life as well as in academic discourse. The fact that actors sometimes accuse one another of selfishness, hypocrisy, racism, sexism, and other kinds of unfair or discriminatory treatment, shows the presence of norms of fairness.[35] Feminism, socialism, anti-racism, and liberal notions of tolerance have had some influence on social relations and ethical sentiments and norms and all of them rely on more basic ethical ideas; for example, while sexism and racism are not unusual in education, many teachers try not to be sexist or racist in their treatment of pupils and parents. At least some actors try to behave in a way that is indifferent to these divisions.

Sociology's investment in ideas of social divisions, boundary drawing and 'othering' is such that it is easily overlooked that we can be well or badly treated by people regardless of their social position; members of our own social group can behave well or badly, as can those of others.[36] Radically different kinds of behaviour can coexist within the same groups or contexts: for example, as John Stuart Mill noted, families can be schools of both love and despotism (Mill, 1869). Moreover, the moral education we gain within our own groups influences our relations with others. Through all these relations, we develop expectations and

---

[34] Even the success of acts of deceit depends on others' assumptions of honesty and trustworthiness.

[35] It's also interesting that racists and sexists sometimes preface expressions of prejudice with protestations that they 'believe in equality, but . . .'.

[36] I shall elaborate this discussion of moral boundary drawing in chapter 7.

norms which to some extent are treated as universal rather than group-specific. Insofar as they concern actual behaviours, not mere stereotypes, it is possible to identify behaviour which *contradicts* rather than confirms such stereotypes; we may sometimes notice that the stigmatised other behaves ethically while the respected peer sometimes behaves unethically. To be sure, we may relate to others in ways that imply double standards, but we do not operate with *totally* different standards in different contexts. Treating the same action in the same way whoever does it, acting 'without regard for persons', is itself a common moral principle, indeed it is intrinsic to concepts of fairness and the virtue of integrity.[37] Hence, although it may be incompletely carried through, moral thought involves a generalising moment which can cross the boundaries between social groups; indeed, it is to this that we owe our ability to criticise inequalities such as those of class. Criticism – whether by lay people or academics – of domination, unfairness, hypocrisy and inconsistency therefore implies the existence of moral norms in the sense that I have defined them. Later in the book, I shall argue that we cannot make much sense of lay understanding of class, in all its ambivalence, unless we appreciate this duality.

Conclusion

The concept of habitus is expected by Bourdieu to carry a heavy explanatory burden. It functions as a summarising concept for complex processes which have not just a sociological dimension but aspects studied by psychology and neurophysiology. In effect, the concept is a product of sociological disciplinary imperialism, reflecting the discipline's competition with and aversion to psychology and biology.[38] However, suitably qualified, the concept can serve as a provisional filler for a space in which a great deal of further post-disciplinary work needs to be done. To abandon the concept of habitus because Bourdieu exaggerates its influence would be to throw the baby out with the bathwater. No other sociological concept can help us understand the embodied character of dispositions, their generative power and their relation to the wider social field. The difficult question is how far to invoke it. I want to retain and modify rather than drop the concept and the associated Pascalian view of action. This requires us to moderate the claims made by Bourdieu for the explanatory power of the concept, and to supplement it with a recognition of the close relationships between dispositions and conscious deliberation,

---

[37] This does not exclude the possibility of also recognising that to treat unequals as equal is unfair.

[38] Bourdieu's disciplinary imperialism (e.g., 1993) is surprising given his perceptive analysis of the struggles of the academic field in works such as *Homo Academicus* (1988).

the powers of agency and mundane reflexivity, and by addressing actors' normative orientations, emotions and commitments.

Despite the centrality of what we care about to our lives, much of social science abstracts from this ordinary phenomenon, presenting us with bloodless figures who seemingly drift through life, behaving in ways which bear the marks of their social position and relations and of wider discourses, disciplining themselves only because it is required of them, but as if nothing mattered to them. This picture is a product not only of sociological imperialism, but of a kind of intellectual elitism, in which theorists elevate themselves above the drone-like masses they study, and congratulate themselves on being able to see what the latter cannot, when in fact in some respects they can see less. We might add that nothing in our argument leads to any kind of Cartesianism; people are social beings, embodied and psychologically and materially dependent on others, discursively and socially embedded, with many-sided, often fractured, habituses. As we have noted, evaluative capacities such as susceptibility to shame or guilt or embarrassment depend on socialisation and culturalisation; they are not innate, even though they presuppose capacities – presumably born of an integration of the physiological, psychological and social – not possessed by objects which cannot be socialised. And of course, our deeply social character in no way negates the force with which we care about things, indeed it is a precondition of emotions such as shame, pride and affection.

The habitus has a moral dimension; ethical dispositions develop through socialisation and are not reducible to expressions of mere interests, nor are the norms with which they are associated reducible to mere conventions. Rather, they have a normative force deriving from their implications for well-being. Like commitments, ethical dispositions and beliefs need not merely promote actors' self-interest, but to varying degrees can include the welfare of others, thus being eudaimonistic rather than egotistic – that is, oriented to social well-being and happiness. While actors' ethical dispositions and beliefs vary to some extent according to social position, they also cross-cut them. To understand how these phenomena vary with social divisions we need to understand how far they do not. Emotional values, cares, concerns and commitments are of course gendered and classed and culturally embedded, and it is important to analyse in what ways they are so, but those are not the only important things about them. It is also important to understand what circumstances (subjective and objective) these cares are about and how they affect people's well-being; otherwise, why should class or gender matter?

3   Recognition and distribution

Introduction

As many commentators have noted (e.g., Fraser, 1995; Honneth, 2001; Phillips, 1999), until the 1980s, equality in terms of distribution was seen as central to political philosophy and radical politics, whether under the banner of Rawls and other social democratic positions or various kinds of Marxism, whereas since then, the avoidance of exclusion and disrespect has in many cases overtaken inequality as a priority. Repeated refusal of recognition to an individual can produce serious psychological damage and refusal of recognition to a group also damages its well-being and ability to function in wider society (Taylor, 1994). As Nancy Fraser puts it, it prevents people 'participating on a par with others in social interaction' (Fraser, 1999, p. 34). Many oppressive social relations such as those of racism and homophobia involve systematic misrecognition – part refusal of recognition and part stigmatised recognition. While this shift from distribution to recognition has been progressive in highlighting hitherto ignored forms of oppression, some observers have regretted the fact that it seems to have been coupled with an abandonment of concern for class politics, which have been associated with the politics of distribution (Phillips, 1999). The retreat from class was not merely illogical but decidedly untimely, for it coincided with the rise of attempts by neoliberals to legitimise class inequalities.

The most prominent kinds of recognition claims in contemporary politics have been ones relating to cultural difference, including differences in sexuality, religion and lifestyle. In such cases the groups in question claim recognition for their legitimacy and value. However, the micro- and macro-politics of class are different. The poor are not clamouring for poverty to be legitimised and valued. They want to escape or abolish their class position rather than affirm it (Coole, 1996). At the same time, they do not merely want more material wealth, but recognition and respect

This chapter is particularly indebted to John O'Neill's essay on 'Economy, equality and recognition' (O'Neill, 1999). Thanks too to Majid Yar for discussions.

as well, in terms of their moral worth, and perhaps for certain aspects of their culture.[1] Class antagonisms are therefore about more than distribution of income and material goods, but they involve a different kind of recognition from that highlighted in identity politics, one that is as old as inequality itself. As historians such as E. P. Thompson and James Scott have argued, political antagonisms, including those of class, are typically driven by moral concerns and a sense of injustice, and not merely by the pursuit of wealth and advantage (Honneth, 2003; O'Neill, 1999; Scott, 1990; Thompson, 1963).

> Even in the case of the contemporary working class, it appears that slights to one's dignity and close surveillance and control of one's work loom at least as large in accounts of oppression as do narrower concerns of work and compensation. (Scott, 1990, p. 23)

It is this kind of politics of recognition which relates most clearly to the subjective experience of class inequalities and therefore forms the main subject of this chapter. Recognition has an important ethical dimension and implications for the normative significance of inequality, which we need to explore in order to understand matters such as lay feelings towards inequalities and the struggles of the social field. This older kind of recognition has more to do with the struggle for equality than the recognition and legitimation of difference, though arguably it is not necessarily incompatible with the latter. There has not only been a decline in interest in class and a neglect of the politics of distribution, but a failure to notice how central recognition is to the micro- and macro-politics of class.

As Fraser and a number of other authors have argued, the struggles of the social field have to be understood as involving *both* recognition and distribution (Fraser, 1995, 1999; Honneth, 1995; Taylor, 1994; see also Anderson, 1999; Butler, 1997; Phillips, 1997). I very much agree with this, but I shall argue that the relations between recognition and distribution are closer than many have realised. Later, I shall contend that although class inequalities are not a product of relations of (mis)recognition, except contingently and secondarily, the everyday micro-politics of class are very much about recognition and misrecognition. The latter, in the form of what Bourdieu terms 'symbolic domination', deeply shapes the quality of individual lives, and adds its own influences to the arbitrary inequalities produced by market forces. Chapters 5–8 of this book amount to an examination of the nature of this misrecognition and its close association with inequalities in distribution.

---

[1] Gender politics are more mixed in that they involve complex mixtures of legitimation and refusal of gendered characteristics, for example attempting both to value skills associated with women without idealising them and to de-gender them.

The kind of recognition we shall be concerned with has a necessary psychological dimension that is sometimes overlooked in discussions of the politics of recognition in relation to identity. Recognition matters to people, not just for their status in adulthood, but as a condition of their early psychological development as subjects and for their subsequent well-being. They need recognition of both their autonomy and ability to reason and their neediness and dependence on others – indeed recognition of their need for recognition. The vulnerability of individuals consists in their dependence on others not only for material support but for ongoing recognition, respect, approval and trust. While this may be adequately provided by small numbers of others, its absence can cause severe distress, shame and self-contempt – indeed, sometimes individuals may value respect more than their own lives (Gilligan, 2000; Sedgewick and Frank, 1995). As Axel Honneth notes, 'forms of reciprocal recognition are always already institutionalized in every social reality, whose internal deficits or asymmetries are indeed what can first touch off a kind of "struggle for recognition"' (Honneth, 2003, p. 136). We shall address these sentiments and needs later, but for now it is important to note that recognition is not a luxury that ranks lower than the satisfaction of material needs, but is essential for well-being.

The concept of recognition is a more complex issue than that of distribution, and therefore requires some analysis before we can apply it. I shall begin with a discussion of the reciprocal nature of recognition, which owes much to Hegel's view of recognition in relation to ethical life and the nature of human social being. It involves a social, bilateral or multilateral view of recognition whose implications for inequality are made clear in his celebrated account of the master/slave dialectic. In principle, it seems to imply that our need for recognition requires equality among persons, but in practice, localised conditions for recognition can also be partly met in highly unequal societies, and indeed can degenerate into forms of recognition or misrecognition involving 'othering'. This practice of defining one's identity through a contrast with a stigmatised other is a central target of the politics of recognition. Next, I shall differentiate recognition into unconditional and conditional forms, drawing particularly on the work of Charles Taylor and Axel Honneth. This will provide tools for exploring the relations between distribution and recognition in ways that, though indebted to Fraser's analysis, also differ from it. Finally, I shall suggest that, important though recognition undoubtedly is, there is a danger of focusing too much on recognition itself and not enough on what it is for; in particular the kinds of goods, practices and ways of life that are regarded as worthy of recognition – matters which figure prominently in struggles over distribution.

Recognition, equality and 'othering'

The need for recognition is at once familiar and mysterious, for it is largely only implicit in social interaction, and noticed more in its absence than its presence. We are dependent on others not only for material support and not purely in instrumental ways. Though we may sometimes fail to realise it, we need others non-instrumentally too, as ends in themselves, and as sources of non-instrumental valuation of our own being and standing in terms of respect and esteem. Recognition is implicit in the way people address and deal with one another, whether they are kin, friends, associates or strangers, and in the merest looks of 'civil inattention', as Goffman termed it. It is also institutionalised in the rules governing matters such as immigration, citizenship, and equal opportunities policies. Through both subtle and unsubtle differences in recognition of others, people are in varying degrees included or excluded, and allowed access to different opportunities.[2] In this section I draw selectively on Allen Wood's *Hegel's Ethical Thought* (Wood, 1990, especially pp. 90–1) and on Majid Yar's defence of Hegel in response to post-structuralist theories of recognition (Yar, 2001a). Note, however, that it is not my intention to stick faithfully to Hegel's view, but merely to draw certain ideas from it that can serve as a starting point for thinking about recognition and equality.

To begin with, it is necessary to acknowledge that we have not only susceptibilities to social and physical influences, and not only dispositions or powers that can be activated, but *lack* and *desire*, which are continually in need of satisfaction. They both influence and are influenced by our social contexts.[3] Lack and desire are preconditions for autonomy since it is contingent whether and how they are satisfied, thus leaving a space for autonomy. But in virtue of our social nature they also create dependency on others. The relations between autonomy and dependence are fundamental to our psychological development and to ethical systems and normative ethical theories. Autonomy requires us to have certain capacities, such as confidence, which can only be acquired through the support of others and via their recognition of us as subjects. To be trusted is to be granted independence on the understanding that we will not abuse it by taking advantage of the others' dependence on us. Without others

---

[2] In Sen's terms, to be discussed later, recognition influences people's 'capabilities', their freedom of access to various functionings or ways of life they have reason to value (Sen, 1992).

[3] Lack and desire involve special kinds of causal powers, ones which are internally activated as well as socially influenced. Their omission from many social theories and ontologies is extraordinary.

on whom we can depend, our freedom is drastically limited. Whereas lack concerns things such as food and warmth, desire is more related to subjectivity, and our need for recognition by others in order to become subjects.

Recognition can be given only by another subject, and it cannot be achieved simply through unilateral demands. Although it may be implied and inferred in mere looks and mannerisms, it is more fully affirmed dialogically and hermeneutically. To develop a sense of self we need others. Even though we may objectify ourselves through labour by producing objects, objects are not capable of reflecting back to us our conception of ourselves as subjects, having some degree of freedom and responsibility. Only other persons, also subjects and having some degree of freedom and responsibility, can do this. While producing things (including providing services) and hence changing the social world around us can indeed help to create a sense of self-worth, this too depends on others who (a) recognise us as subjects capable of self-determination, and (b) are capable of judging and confirming the worth of our labour. One-sided recognition cannot succeed. If, for example, the dominated are denied anything more than the most limited education, they are unlikely to be able to make a worthwhile judgement, so recognition by them would have little value. For similar reasons, an adult cannot expect the same recognition from a three-year-old that she can expect from a fellow adult. In addition, if the dominated lack the freedom to make an independent judgement, their recognition is worthless to the dominant for they cannot be expected to say what they really think. Moreover, as we shall see, recognition through deeds can speak louder than verbal recognition. I may *say* things that indicate recognition of you but if everything I *do* indicates insensitivity to your needs and disrespect of your intelligence and worth my words will be worthless. Adequate recognition therefore demands freely given acts as well as freely given words. Putting these points together, we can see that nothing that a subordinate says or does towards the dominant can match the recognition in words and deeds that an equal can give. To be adequately recognised by the slave, the master would have to abolish the relation of domination and cease to be a master. The development of a sense of self-worth therefore requires mutual recognition among subjects who are in a strong sense equal and free to exercise autonomy, not merely formally in terms of their rights but in terms of their capabilities for living in ways they have reason to value.

Mutual recognition of this sort is much more straightforward where the subjects are members of the same culture than where they are radically different. In such cases, recognition may be blocked, distorted or rendered spurious by mutual ignorance, and by the projection of familiar characteristics, often stigmatised ones, onto the other. Yet while this is common it is not inevitable. Though difficult, dialogue that is sensitive to possible ignorance and difference, working from whatever common premises can be found, may in the long run be able to establish a non-spurious basis for recognition through a hermeneutic engagement of their respective frames of meaning (Yar, 2001a).[4]

This account of recognition involves a strongly social conception of self-hood, and yet one which does not wholly reduce it to the product of external forces, as if each individual were a passive object lacking any powers of its own. It also implies that individuals depend on external social relations for the development of some of these powers. Recognition is central to the slow process of development of the emergent properties of the self from infancy, through the co-development of biological powers and social influences (Nussbaum, 2001). Human beings have a psychological need for recognition, and its denial, especially in childhood, can produce long-lasting damage;[5] we should not allow sociology's imperialistic rivalry with psychology to obscure this. There are indeed dangers of exaggerating the extent to which individuals can be autonomous subjects and underestimating the extent of social influences upon them, but there are also dangers in reducing them to such influences, for this renders recognition and its significance completely unintelligible.[6] If people were in no sense subjects, they would neither need nor be able to give recognition. To recognise a person is different from recognising a tree; both are constituted by internal and external powers but the latter lacks emergent powers to desire and reason, and it does not need recognition to flourish.[7]

---

[4] It is easy to be sceptical about this in the abstract but what else would sceptics propose we ought to do? I therefore follow Yar in rejecting the 'pathological' renditions of recognition inferred by Levinas and others (Yar, 2001a). To recognise the other properly is precisely not to colonise them or deny their difference. In the absence of this possibility, progressives are ironically thrown back onto the bleak alternative of a quasi-liberal contract of mutual indifference (Geras, 1998), in which strangers merely avoid their others (e.g., Young, 1990).

[5] As James Gilligan's work on violent criminals shows, their behaviour derives consistently from severe deprivation of recognition and violent treatment in earlier life (Gilligan, 2000).

[6] To achieve an adequate account of this process, it is essential to avoid collapsing development into an instant, so that it appears that subjects are either pre-social or purely the product of externally induced subjectification. The development of subjects at time t is predicated on earlier rounds of development involving the interaction of both biological and social influences and preconditions.

[7] 'Reason' in this context should not be equated with the elevated, highly reflective forms it takes in philosophy, including the philosophy that reflects on it, but should be understood as everyday thought processes. Note, also, that I would want to relate recognition of others not only to their freedom but to their vulnerability and capability of suffering. This could also be taken to involve a natural capacity for sympathy, which although highly developed in humans appears to be present in some non-human species too. These emergent powers presuppose but are irreducible to those of our physical being.

In principle, this mutuality of recognition is hugely significant for arguments about equality and human well-being for it seems to imply that only in a relatively equal and free society can all achieve recognition; indeed, the recognition and freedom of each would seem to be a condition of the recognition and freedom of all. However, in practice, it is possible that the conditions for recognition can be met selectively and locally within particular groups, and therefore the need to be recognised by others does not provide a powerful impetus for equality unless it is institutionally reinforced. The dominant can find recognition within their own group, be it one of class, gender or some other kind, while simultaneously exploiting others:

[I]n modern societies people prefer to conceal from themselves their dominion over others, by sequestering the others in different parts of town or in distant lands, or by representing the others as formally free and equal to themselves. In these ways, people enjoy simultaneously the (real) advantages of oppressing others and the (at least pretended) self-certainty that only a society of free and equal persons can offer. . . . Consistently with Hegel's argument, I might find self-certainty in the parochial society constituted by a privileged race, caste or class, whose members mutually recognize one another as persons but treat outsiders as non-persons. (Wood, 1990, p. 93)

Equivalent possibilities exist for localised mutual recognition among the subordinate.

There is a complex social geography of moral communities here in which actors consider certain other groups as less worthy of moral consideration than the members of their own group.[8] An implication of the need for recognition is that forms of domination involving denial of recognition are unlikely to operate simply on the basis of dyadic relationships between individuals, since the dominant need to belong to a group which can provide them with recognition and solidarity, including support for their domination of others. This is acknowledged, for example, in definitions of patriarchy that refer not only to men's domination of women but to the solidarity and peer pressure among men in support of that domination. Similarly, solidarity among the dominated helps them to endure domination, as well as to resist it.

The situation is made worse by the common tendency for identities to be sought through 'othering', that is, by a process in which groups define themselves in opposition to and exclusion of their others, by attributing negative properties to them, in contrast to which their own identity is defined as normal and good. At the same time, this self-definition via

---

[8] In the extreme, others may be treated as if they were completely outside actors' moral community, but I suggest that it is more normal for there to be gradations in moral considerability.

contrasts with the other means that their own identities become negatively rather than positively constituted, so that either granting recognition to the other or removing them would mean a loss of their own identity. Any demands for recognition from those who are stigmatised in this way cannot be met because it would come from those not considered fit to give it. In addition, the resulting identities have nothing positive to offer other groups or communities from which they could benefit, and which would bring further recognition.[9] Othering is likely to support and be supported by relations of economic inequality, domination and social exclusion, and indeed to be stimulated as a rationale for these (Tilly, 1998), but it can also derive from xenophobia. Once formed, it is difficult to remove, and at worst it can prompt self-fuelling mutual contempt and revenge. I shall comment further on these issues in chapter 7.

Gloomy though these conclusions undoubtedly are, especially after the hopes raised by the arguments concerning mutual recognition, they do not at all mean that the demands of the subordinate for recognition are necessarily ineffectual, for they can also appeal to the need for recognition on which the dominant depend, and this in effect is what struggles for recognition do, such as those of civil rights, anti-racist and feminist movements. Nor does it mean that the dominant can afford completely to disregard the recognition of the dominated, although such recognition will necessarily take flawed forms. Even if they do not need it to stay in power, that is, even if its pursuit is not strictly necessary for maintaining their material advantages and the recognition that these bring *within* their own group, they typically strive to establish their legitimacy beyond it, as Weber noted.

The framework I have outlined here enables us to understand the incomplete, restricted forms of recognition that exist in modern societies, while indicating the tendencies that could generalise them through egalitarian movements. In one sense the latter points might be seen merely as normative arguments, but what is important is that they are grounded in existing tendencies or potentials which derive from our character as social beings, albeit tendencies that can all too easily be overridden. Without this, the demand for recognition would be empty and arbitrary, with no rationale or connection to existing tendencies, and lacking any connection to equality.[10]

---

[9] Although Hegel is sometimes unfairly associated with a conventionalist, communitarian view of ethics (Wood, 1990), he regarded it as important that communities have positive things to offer other communities.

[10] The only reasons for granting it to the subordinate would be tokenistic and instrumental, for example as a means by which politicians can win the votes and acquiescence of a subaltern group.

Conditional and unconditional recognition

'Recognition' takes a number of forms. Charles Taylor draws a distinction between unconditional and conditional respect.[11] The former is or should be granted simply in recognition of others' humanity, even in the absence of knowledge of their particular characteristics and behaviour.[12] By contrast, the latter is conditional upon the particular behaviour of others, whether in terms of its moral or other qualities: it has to be earned (Glover, 2001, p. 23; Taylor, 1994; see also Collier, 1999, chapter 7). Granting recognition to others is therefore a two-stage process. To claim recognition or respect of the second (conditional) kind without having behaved in a way that warrants it is absurd, and equally to grant it in such circumstances is meaningless. It would be meaningless, for example, for a person to claim respect because she had inherited a large sum of money, but it would not be meaningless for such a person to claim respect as a human being. There are some similarities here to Honneth's distinction between self-respect and self-esteem (Honneth, 1995). Thus, recognition of others' humanity, particularly their autonomy, is necessary for them to acquire self-respect,[13] while recognition which is conditional upon their specific behaviour and achievements is the source of self-esteem. Many situations involve both; for example, the ethics of teaching require both forms of recognition of students.

Of course, what exactly is worthy of conditional recognition may be contested. To devalue the particular achievements or forms of life of a particular group may damage its self-esteem (Honneth, 2001), but, as the conditionality of this kind of recognition implies, we should not assume that recognition is always warranted, for individuals or groups may behave in ways that do not warrant recognition. As Taylor notes, not all forms of life are worthy of esteem, for example, those of racists or paedophiles.[14] There is a danger of assuming that in all cases of 'misrecognition' or refusal of recognition, the problem lies with those called upon to grant recognition, rather than those making the recognition claims.[15]

---

[11] In common with many other authors I do not find it useful to distinguish respect from recognition, but see respect, along with esteem, as part of recognition.

[12] This need not preclude recognition of unavoidable or benign differences.

[13] Honneth also identifies recognition of others as equal citizens as the basis of self-respect, but this can be a product of an instrumental, contractual approach to recognition, having little to do with respect.

[14] Significantly these are groups which, by their very nature, deny even the unconditional kind of recognition to their victims.

[15] Such an assumption would be (a) idealist (problems only exist in the mind of the beholder or are constructed performatively); (b) relativist (there are no grounds for choosing among competing claims), and (c) crypto-normative (the concern with problems of recognition indicates a normative concern for well-being, but one which is not carried through into judgements of what is good or bad and why), and hence useless.

In other cases, where the others concerned are from a different culture from our own, judgements about whether to grant conditional recognition can only reasonably be made after some success has been achieved in coming to understand the other in non-ethnocentric terms – a process which, as we have noted, may be long and difficult. Not surprisingly, in practice, premature (mis)judgements about conditional recognition are common.

Although theorists like Mead and Honneth have argued that conditional recognition depends on individuals achieving things which others have not (Honneth, 1995, p. 125), I would argue that while this is sometimes the case, conditional recognition is also given for 'good enough' performance in valued but ordinary activities such as parenting, teaching, cooking, nursing, or professional work, etc., and indeed for mundane virtues such as fortitude, civility and sociability. In such cases there can be not only self-esteem from recognised proficiency but a sense of pride and solidarity in having abilities, skills and virtues shared with others.[16] There is also sometimes an awareness of the downside of individual achievement, in terms of unbalanced lives, aloofness, ruthlessness, selfishness and exploitation of others whose contributions do not get to be objectified and celebrated. The achiever in one area of life may be compensating for deficiencies in another, such as sociability. The everyday pursuit of well-being can involve consideration of such trade-offs (Lamont, 2000).[17] Judgements like these about conditional recognition are part of ordinary life; as we shall see in chapter 7, they are part of the complex mix of lay feelings about class.

However, it is vital to appreciate that in some cases, lack of achievements or of behaviour deserving recognition may result from distributional inequalities. If you have only the bare minimum of resources, you cannot achieve much. Literature on the struggle for recognition has tended to overlook that it implies not simply unspoken or occasionally more explicit demands and counter-demands for recognition by others, but a striving to be able to live and act in ways *deserving* of recognition. It is thereby connected to distributional demands through the need for access to conditions that support such ways of living. The suffering of the unemployed derives from denial of income and lack of recognition,

---

[16] One can also take pleasure from being involved in activities in which there are others whose performance is superior to one's own but which serve as a source of inspiration and pleasure rather than low self-esteem (O'Neill, 1999). (See chapter 5.)

[17] A white American worker interviewed by Lamont said of ambition: 'You miss all of life . . . A person that is totally ambitious and driven never sees anything except the spot they are aiming at' (ibid., p. 110). This could be a rationalisation of the worker's own lack of success, but it is patronising to assume that such critical judgements are never any more than this.

and lack of access to the means to remedy it. Disregard of these mitigating circumstances by the dominant and continual disrespect or refusal of recognition to the less fortunate and the excluded often produces anti-social behaviour in the latter, which then in turn strengthens that refusal. Those who scorn the demands of socially excluded groups for respect or esteem, on the grounds that they have not clearly earned it, callously overlook the need of such groups for both resources to be able to achieve much and unconditional recognition of their needs and powers as human beings. These dynamics of recognition and misrecognition are typical of the micro-politics of the social field.

Conditional recognition, like unconditional recognition, is distorted by relations of domination. In relations among equals, where recognition is freely given, conditional recognition of someone's exceptional virtues may give rise to (conditional) deference, but this is of a different kind altogether from deference within a relation of domination. I may defer to someone who has qualities I admire, where those qualities have in no way been achieved at my expense or anyone else's. But deferential behaviour of the subordinated towards the dominant is of a different kind, implying resentment of advantages and contempt. Even though the dominant may have certain admirable qualities, their reliance on the subordination and unreciprocated service of others is liable to taint admiration and deference from the subordinate, in both its production and reception. At times this may be made more explicit through expressions of excessive deference involving thinly disguised sarcasm. This is a soft weapon that the subordinate can use against the soft forms of domination, for it can make the dominant feel uncomfortable and disrespected. If the dominant then castigate the subordinate for their sarcasm, this is likely to backfire, for it makes it all the more clear that the hoped-for recognition is devalued by being mandatory rather than freely given, and hence doomed to be unsatisfactory. Alternatively, if the admiration and deference are sincere, but disproportionate to the virtues which are the object of their admiration – a common situation where the subordinate have been denied access to the means both to achieve such things and to make well-founded judgements about the qualities in question – it may also make the subject of their deference uncomfortably aware that they do not deserve this recognition. Those who, like the middle classes, find themselves, by the accident of birth, in advantageous positions such that they can easily achieve valued things, may be embarrassed and disturbed by the compliments of those who lacked those advantages; as a middle class academic, I am sometimes embarrassed by the apparently sincere deference of those less fortunate than me regarding the fact that I have written books, because I am aware of the unjustified inequality in our positions. But if I receive compliments from those who are similarly positioned, such that they can make an informed judgement of their quality and significance, then the recognition is free from such taint because it is embedded in a relation of equality.

Conditional recognition is itself differentiated according to the kinds of qualities being evaluated. Most clearly, recognition of achievements is different from recognition of moral virtues such as those of friendliness or generosity, and often neither of them are reflected in individuals' economic position and rewards (which might be seen in terms of 'economic recognition'). Actors are commonly well aware of these differences ('Don't think this makes you any better than us'), though some may treat one kind of quality as a surrogate for another, for example, income as an index of worth (Lamont, 1992, 2000). Moreover, as we have seen, under conditions of inequality, feelings about self and other become further complicated by awareness of the uneven and arbitrary distribution of conditions favourable to the development of the valued achievements and qualities.

Criteria of recognition are also culturally variable, insofar as different goods may be differently valued, as Michèle Lamont's comparisons of US and French working class and upper middle class men demonstrate (Lamont, 1992, 2000). Further, difference itself implies differential understanding of others and hence problems of recognition. These may vary from the minor – simply feeling out of place or not fitting in when in the company of certain others – to damaging forms of misrecognition which blight one's life-chances. To some extent culture may also vary with economic circumstances and vice versa. Especially in the light of Lamont's work, which shows class differences in the valuation of achievement relative to moral qualities of integrity, solidarity and reliability, it is interesting to speculate on whether the former are more valued in highly unequal societies and the latter in more equal societies.

Links between recognition and distribution

This account already implies the existence of strong relationships between distribution and recognition, but we can now make them more explicit. Rather than counterposing recognition to distribution, with recognition referring to the ideational realm and distribution to the material realm, we need to appreciate that 'recognition' cannot be limited to the realms of 'idealised' communication and signification, but is thoroughly materialised in the distribution of material goods (Fraser, 1999; Yar, 1999, p. 202; see also Yar, 2001b). If a rich university department were to give all of its students computers, except for a minority to whom it gave nothing, while claiming that it recognised them all as of equal worth, it would be accused of unfairness and hypocrisy: the inequality of the distribution would itself falsify any claims about equality of recognition. In the very act of distributing the material goods the university would be conferring or denying recognition. By the same token, it is difficult to accept claims that all members of a society are recognised as of equal worth if they face major inequalities in access to health care.[18] Recognition is not just something we say or think, it is also evident in material actions, in the things that institutions or we do to others, in particular in what is given to others. In the micro-politics of everyday life, this includes the time that we give to others: as Bourdieu points out, one of the clearest indicators of the relative social position of individuals is how much of their time they are expected to give to one another (Bourdieu, 2000).[19] But not only can words and deeds differ, thoughts and actions can differ too; within relationships of domination, spoken words and deeds of apparent recognition are likely to differ from unspoken feelings or 'hidden transcripts', which may be ones of resentment and contempt (Scott, 1990). Those in such relationships may be well aware of this in their others, but usually they have to collude in the fiction that this is not the case, acting as if words and deeds were transparent and sincere.

Recognition at the level of discourse and attitudes is of course important, but it is not enough, and at worst may be tokenistic. It is easy for the dominant to grant discursive recognition and civility to the dominated or socially excluded; giving up some of their money and other advantages to them is another matter.[20] An egalitarian politics of recognition at the level of professed attitudes is easier for the well-off to swallow than an egalitarian politics of recognition-through-distribution, and it suits them to regard the former as progressive and the latter as passé, indeed the former can be a source of kudos. In fact, it seems that in British political culture over the last three decades, the more everyone is discursively acknowledged as being of equal worth, the *less* the pressure to change

[18] '. . . a society that condones excesses of poverty in the midst of wealth or arbitrarily rewards one skill with one hundred times the wages of another is not recognizing its citizens as of equal human worth. On the contrary it is making it harder than ever for members of that society to keep up the pretence that they consider their fellow citizens their equal' (Phillips, 1999, p. 131).

[19] Those who are familiar with organisational life will know that when we request a meeting with our superior he or she may only give us a few minutes, and even then end up doing most of the talking so that we struggle to get across the very point for which we requested the meeting. See also Scott, 1990, p. 29.

[20] My thanks to John O'Neill for this point. Tokenistic recognition can involve not only unwillingness to redistribute money but reluctance to counter symbolic domination, for example, in education, in the use of cultural and social capital (string pulling), to win advantages. See also the quotation from bell hooks in chapter 1.

the distribution of material goods, because the inequality of the latter is increasingly seen as a separate matter. As culture has become more egalitarian, it has been supposed that economic equality matters less.

Further, the grounds for an egalitarian politics of distribution lie in an egalitarian politics of recognition: any argument for distributional equality must ultimately appeal to criteria of recognition – that all are of equal moral worth.[21] Similarly, more sectional distributional claims such as the pay demands of particular groups of workers are often supported by claims of inadequate recognition of the moral as well as the economic worth of the work.[22] Honneth acknowledges this when he notes that there are cases where 'social esteem for a person or group is so obviously correlated to the level of control over certain goods that only the acquisition of those goods can lead to the corresponding recognition' (1995, p. 166; see also Honneth, 2003).

It might also be argued that there are grounds for unequal recognition, and hence unequal distribution, such as differences in needs, or more contentiously, differences in merit. This would imply that roughly speaking, while the distributional implications of unconditional recognition of citizenship and humanity imply equality (except where needs differ), those of conditional recognition might imply inequality, depending on whether we judge the particular inequalities in achievement to be earned rather than unearned and to warrant unequal rewards. Whatever we as observers might think about such normative views, they are common in lay attitudes towards inequality (for example, see Bowles and Gintis, 1998; Lamont, 2000; Miller, 1992).

While these arguments might seem sound where economic distribution is consciously planned in relation to recipients and their characteristics, distribution under capitalism is in large part unplanned and arbitrary, being the product of the anarchy of market forces, strategies of closure, political manipulation and symbolic domination.[23] In the neoliberal guru

---

[21] By the same token, defenders of inequality have to appeal to criteria for unequal recognition. As Fraser argues, redistributive policies may backfire in terms of recognition – thus the receipt of means-tested welfare benefits may be seen as demeaning and stigmatising (Fraser, 1999).

[22] 'Because we're worth it' – a slogan now used in pay bargaining – is, interestingly, an adaptation of the slogan 'Because you're worth it', first used by advertisers to persuade us to buy their products. In the latter case it fits with the contemporary amoral emphasis of neoliberal culture on individuals 'feeling good about themselves', in which self-esteem is not necessarily tied to doing anything worthy of esteem. Of course the workers have publicly to justify their claim whereas consumers do not.

[23] Defenders of capitalism often offer a rationale in defence of this arbitrariness, to the effect that the amoral mechanisms and the inequalities they produce are necessary for the efficient functioning of capital, from which the poor arguably benefit in the long run, by being better off than they would in the absence of markets.

Hayek's case, he is quite explicit that fortunes in markets may have more to do with luck than merit (Hayek, 1960).[24] Justifications of superior wealth on the basis of achievements worthy of conditional recognition are always open to contestation. Up to a point, conspicuous wealth may (intentionally or unintentionally) produce envy and even admiration, but others may discover or suspect that the owner has not done anything to deserve the wealth. As regards the pre-requisites of capitalism (as opposed to its contingent forms and accompaniments), the relationship of recognition to economic distribution is therefore not reversible: economic distribution depends on luck and scarcity and hence does not necessarily reflect qualities worthy of recognition. Moreover, modern economies do not operate simply according to the pre-requisites of capitalism but are responsive to other, contingently related, sources of inequality such as divisions of gender and 'race', which influence distribution via unequal recognition. As a matter of fact, then, distribution under capitalism does not have much to do with recognition; but from a normative point of view, one could argue that it ought to.

The mistaken idea that distribution through markets does in practice reflect and provide due recognition of merit ('you're paid what you are worth and worth what you are paid') is likely to appeal to the rich, and it is also not unusual to encounter deferential versions of the idea in popular discourse. (There are equivalents of this with respect to gender where women 'generously' accept men's advantages as deserved.) This kind of deference may sometimes be seen positively as an unselfish acceptance of others' merits, though it might also result from wishful thinking, that is, from a slide from normative feelings that distribution should reflect recognition to positive assumptions that it actually does. Such are the twists and turns of moral sentiments regarding inequality.

Conclusions

A broadly Hegelian analysis of recognition illuminates its role in the development of subjects, and hence the social psychology of interpersonal relations. The master/slave dialectic identifies the limits and tendencies of recognition within relations of domination, as compared to recognition among equals. Although the analysis points towards the need for more equal relations, the very durability of actual relations of domination shows that these normative pressures can easily be overridden by interests in

---

[24] This is not an anomalous element of his philosophy, for it enables him to argue that the poor are just unfortunate rather than unjustly treated, and therefore in no need of transfers from the rich.

continued domination, while the negative consequences in terms of failures of adequate recognition between dominant and subaltern can be compensated by recognition among equals within their respective communities. Nevertheless, the analysis is still useful for understanding the micro- and macro-politics of recognition in relation to class, and the associated feelings of frustration, deference and resentment that are likely to be generated.

Recognition and misrecognition are undoubtedly important aspects of social life and sources of conflict, ones that are not reducible to matters of distribution, though as we have seen recognition and distribution are closely related. Recent interest in recognition harks back – often unknowingly – to early concerns of the Enlightenment (O'Neill, 1999), but goes beyond it in addressing the misrecognition and othering that are central to sources of oppression such as those to do with 'race', gender, sexuality and disability. The focus on recognition developed by authors such as Honneth also helps to take us beyond interest-based views of conflict such as Bourdieu's. However, it does not take us far into 'the moral grammar of social conflicts' (the subtitle of Honneth's book, *The Struggle for Recognition*), precisely because it only deals in the broadest and most abstract of ways with the question of *what* is valued in acts of recognition. 'Recognition' is too thin and unspecific a concept to get us very far in this respect and there is more to the moral grammar and semantics of social life and conflict than recognition. To understand the significance of both distribution and recognition we have to consider what they enable and what they are *for*.[25]

We need to consider the goods or valued ways of life for which people strive and for which they may also seek recognition. The struggles of the social field are partly about what is worthy of pursuit and respect: they are about what is needed to flourish and what deserves recognition. Recognition is always of something, in virtue of something, and what it's for is what is most important. Moreover, there is a crucial *asymmetry* between goods and recognition. While recognition is itself a good (since it acknowledges individuals' and groups' rights and allows them to pursue their conceptions of the good and gain self-respect), it is partly conditional upon other goods: people *also* pursue activities, commitments and relationships regardless of whether they bring them recognition. In addition, lack of necessary resources is itself a source of suffering, independently of its association with lack of recognition: the homeless need a home as

---

[25] For example, while recognition encourages confidence, confidence is not in itself a moral quality; it may, for example, be falsely based, and confident people are not necessarily morally good, or diffident people bad (Alexander and Lara, 1996).

shelter and not only for the recognition that it signals.[26] An occupational hazard of studying recognition itself, in abstraction from goods, is that it is easy to forget or reverse this asymmetric relation, so that it seems that what is good is simply whatever happens to bring recognition (O'Neill, 1999). As I shall argue in later chapters, people do not just strive for resources and recognition, they strive to flourish by living in ways they have reason to value and this depends on more than either resources or recognition.

Consequently, *both* interest-based struggle and the pursuit of recognition are related to the struggle for goods in the broad sense of ways of living that people value. The pursuit of interests, if it is not misguided, also involves the pursuit of goods, albeit often in a selfish way rather than one that leaves enough and as good for others. Recognition of the particular goods that people achieve gives them self-esteem. In both cases there is a basis in goods – in things, practices and goals – that are valued. Without this basis, recognition would be tokenistic and worthless and interests would be delusory. This is not at all to foreclose the thorny question of what *are* goods in this sense. On the contrary, the point of this critique is to elevate the position of that very question in social science and in public debate. It is important both from an external normative view and for understanding actors' own normative concerns. In chapter 5, as part of an analysis of the nature and structures of the struggles of the social field, we will introduce some ways of conceptualising some of the goods that people pursue and in virtue of which recognition is likely to be granted.

I have argued that a different form of recognition is involved in the politics of class than in identity politics and have attempted to analyse what the former involves. The differences between them can be summarised by reference to their *normative implications*, as Diane Coole has shown in an important article (Coole, 1996). She conceptualises class as a type of 'structured economic inequality which often correlates with cultural differences in values, perspectives, practices and self-identity but which is not primarily produced by cultural distinctions' (ibid., p. 17).[27] Classes are not primarily life-forms requesting recognition as legitimate[28]

---

[26] We do not need to go to the extreme of arguing that perceived disrespect is the 'motivational basis of *all* social conflicts' (Honneth, 2003, p. 157, emphasis added). Some are purely about getting more resources regardless of their implications for recognition.

[27] This, *pace* Lawler (1999, p. 4), does not entail that class is not also figured in cultural or symbolic terms.

[28] Or as Nancy Fraser notes, 'The last thing the proletariat needs is recognition of its difference.' Nevertheless, my colleague Maureen McNeil reports that some students think of class in these terms (personal communication).

(though demands for recognition of some aspects of particular class cultures might be made); they are not differences to be celebrated; they cannot be reduced to their performances; they cannot be subverted by parody; and, unlike gender, class 'does not need denaturalizing since everyone agrees it is conventional' (ibid., p. 23). These differences matter. However, some versions of the concept of class, including lay versions, do include more cultural distinctions as partly constitutive of class and not merely responsive to it. It is therefore necessary to confront the many different meanings of 'class' before we can proceed any further.

4 Concepts of class: clearing the ground

Introduction

The normative significance of class for actors depends partly on their understanding of what determines class. Thus the evaluations that they make of their class others and themselves are influenced by what they assume to be the causes of class positions; in particular they involve assessments of whether people 'deserve' their class position or are undeserving beneficiaries or victims of it. For example, as Michèle Lamont demonstrates, while US skilled working men tend to see class inequalities in individualistic terms, as products of differences in effort and merit, their French equivalents have a more politicised understanding of class as a structure or set of forces positioning people (Lamont, 2000). As with any kind of practical sense, lay understandings do not have to be consistent or correct: people often waver between treating class differences as unfair or fair, or deny that classes exist when their actions imply the opposite. We therefore cannot simply reduce class to whatever actors imagine it to be, for it may have effects on them that they do not register, including ones that influence the positions from which they think about class. In subsequent chapters, like Bourdieu and other social theorists, I shall mostly simply use the everyday descriptions 'working class' or 'middle class' for locating actors, qualifying them where necessary. However, it is important to appreciate what lies behind those everyday terms, and for this we need to turn to sociological theory, where we encounter more examined concepts of class. Popular ideas about the nature of class embrace a chaotic mix of phenomena including not only occupation and wealth but matters such as accent, language, taste and bearing that sociologists would generally treat as secondary. They also tend to include inequalities that many sociologists would see in terms of status rather than class. Since lay understandings face social researchers both as an object of explanation (explanandum) and rival explanation (explanans), we need both to understand lay concepts of class – whether consistent or inconsistent – and to use a consistent set of sociological concepts to analyse them. If we are to assess the moral significance of class we need to understand how class is produced, and this may not accord with lay understanding. Of course there are many sociological concepts of class, ranging from the abstract or narrow, such as the Marxist concept, to concrete and inclusive ones such as that of Bourdieu, which subsume differences of status. Some give primary emphasis to economic mechanisms of distribution and control, others include forms of (mis)recognition and cultural differentiation. The point of this chapter is to consider these different concepts and how they might be synthesised. In so doing, I shall attempt to clarify a number of points about the nature and distinctiveness of class which may help the reader interpret subsequent chapters.

The basic points I want to make are very simple, though the devil is in the details. They are:

(1) For analytical purposes we need *both* abstract and concrete concepts of class, and both academic (sociological) and lay concepts, while keeping in mind their differences. To understand the many aspects of the lay sense of class we need to recognise a diversity of mechanisms, each of which needs first to be isolated through abstraction.

(2) While, for reasons which I will explain, a Bourdieuian approach is invaluable for understanding the subjective experience of class, it needs modification, (a) as regards gender, and (b) as regards the sources of economic capital.

(3) In theorising the reproduction of class differentiation, we need to take account of both mechanisms that are sensitive to actors' identities and those that are neutral or indifferent with respect to them, and to understand the interactions between these.

(4) Despite the fact that class and gender are fused in behaviour, so that, for example, we cannot neatly distinguish which aspects of working class men's behaviour are attributable to their class and which to their gender, the determinants of class and gender are different and separable, giving rise to different normative implications.

I shall come to the details shortly. Those who already accept these points may wish to proceed directly to chapter 5.

To progress further in these matters requires a plunge into the murky depths of concepts of class. First, so as to avoid confusion, we need to acknowledge the multiplicity of concepts of class in lay and academic discourse, and how these vary in terms of how abstract or concrete they are, whether they subsume or exclude ideas of status, indeed whether they have different referents or objects and different explanatory goals. Some may be compatible despite their differences. I shall then summarise key features and merits of Bourdieu's conception of 'objective class'. I then argue that despite these strengths it invites an unsatisfactory treatment of gender and other bases of inequality by subsuming them within class rather than treating them as distinct from it. Next I attempt to develop Bourdieu's concept of economic capital in order to identify its various components, in particular distinguishing between identity-sensitive and identity-neutral processes. This allows us to understand how class and gender can have different determinants despite being experienced conjointly.

This chapter is therefore mainly concerned with the analysis of concepts. Any exercise in trying to clarify confused concepts involves attempting to preserve and strengthen usages and conceptual links that seem to be successful while cutting those that do not. We can only forge new concepts out of old ones, and some of the latter may be part of the problem we are trying to escape. To abandon too much may result in our struggling to do what used to be straightforward. However, we cannot expect to assess either lay or academic understandings of class without working out a position on what they purport to be about.

Clearing the ground

Talking at cross-purposes is almost inevitable in any discussion of the nature of class. This is, first, because there is a common failure to recognise that there are not only many different conceptions of what 'it' is (which would imply that the debate was between different concepts of the same, single object, as it is when someone asks what it is I have in my hand), but also different concepts referring to different objects or referents (so that there is more than one 'it'). Conceptual dizziness is thus an occupational hazard in the study of class, but noting the different referents and explanatory ambitions of different concepts of class can reduce it. This implies that not all concepts of class need be mutually exclusive. Thus a Marxist concept of class is certainly different from Bourdieu's concept of class, but they refer to different aspects of the social world and are used for different, but possibly compatible, explanatory purposes.

Secondly, it helps to avoid confusion if we appreciate that concepts of class may differ according to how abstract or concrete they are. Some concepts are highly abstract, by which I mean not 'vague' (on the contrary), but *one-sided* or selective, in that they focus on a particular aspect of the social world, abstracting from others which may coexist with it. Marx's concept of classes in capitalism, anchored in relations of production, is – if not overstretched – relatively abstract, because it leaves out of account and makes no judgement on forms of variation and differentiation which are held to be capable of operating independently of the aspect being abstracted (e.g., gender, skill-levels, status).[1] Other concepts of class are more concrete, or *many-sided*, in that they attempt, more ambitiously, to synthesise diverse forms of differentiation. The concepts of class used by social stratification theorists are much more 'concrete', in this sense, since they see class as the product of many influences which they attempt to synthesise.[2] Again, the abstract and concrete concepts are not necessarily mutually exclusive: a social stratification theorist could regard Marxist or Weberian abstract concepts of class as reasonable identifications of just some of the elements of concrete classes.

It is an elementary but common mistake to expect an abstract concept of class to do the same work as a concrete concept, and vice versa; for example, a Marxist or Weberian abstract concept of class should not be expected to function on its own as a predictor of life-chances and forms of life.[3] They will inevitably fail to acknowledge those things from which they abstract, such as gender, which also affect life-chances, but then it is unreasonable to expect a single abstract concept to enable us to say much about concrete phenomena. Rather, the strengths of abstractions lie in enabling us to focus on the workings of influences that may be separable from (i.e., only contingently related to) other phenomena of interest, so we can isolate what is due to any particular source. The explanandum may not even be inequalities in life-chances and lifestyles; it could, as in the case of the Marxist concept of class, be primarily designed to explain the necessary conditions for the existence and functioning of capitalist eco-nomic mechanisms. On the other hand, such matters are not the focus of more concrete concepts of class, such as those used in social stratification analysis or Bourdieu's concept of class as used in books such as *Distinction* (Bourdieu, 1984). A more concrete concept of class would be expected to say more about life-chances, lifestyle and experience, but to do so it would have to acknowledge interactions with other axes of inequality, including

---

[1] This does not mean that they cannot work jointly with these other influences, only that they are *capable* of working independently of them. The difference between contingent and necessary relations is crucial in abstraction (Sayer, 1992).

[2] Given these definitions of abstract and concrete, how 'realistic', truthful or practically-adequate concepts are does not depend on whether they are abstract or concrete. The real is fallibly construed both through abstract and concrete concepts. Hence, 'concrete' does not mean 'real'. To talk of 'concrete reality' on these definitions is to refer to many-sided reality, not to add rhetorical weight to implicit 'claims to truth'. Nor does 'abstract' correspond to 'academic' or 'theoretical', for everyday language and concepts are also abstract; indeed, the power of all language derives from its ability to abstract in ways that can inform practice successfully: abstraction is eminently practical (Sayer, 1992, 2000a).

[3] In this way, the Marxist concept of class is routinely thrown out because it fails to do what it wasn't intended to do. This is not to deny that Marx and Marxists have often also expected too much of the concept. While ownership and non-ownership of means of production are still crucial to the functioning of capitalism there are many other influences upon economic power and security.

gender and status. I shall argue that Bourdieu's concept of class comes close to doing this.

To explain the complexities of the concrete one has first to abstract its various elements, analyse them, and then move back towards the concrete by recombining them, examining how they interact, often producing emergent properties irreducible to their constituents. In effect, this is what Bourdieu attempts to do, by resolving the determinants of social position into different kinds and volumes of capitals – economic, social, cultural, etc. – and then explaining the specific combinations of these held by actors in different parts of the social field, and the effects of those combinations. However, where researchers lack time and are attracted by the goal of explaining much by little, they may misguidedly seek to by-pass this arduous analytical process and instead try to identify an abstract concept which single-handedly will 'explain' – often in a merely statistical sense – the complexities of the concrete. This positivist approach mistakes quantitative regularities for causal mechanisms and invites identification errors – misattributions of causal responsibility to just those variables that have been selected (Sayer, 1992). Conversely, as we have seen, abstract concepts of class that can only be expected to be selective in their scope are often criticised and rejected for failing to explain the complexities of the concrete.

A third requirement for clearing the ground is that we avoid the common tendency of overlooking the difference between academic, sociological concepts of class, and those implicit in lay, everyday understandings of the social world. Again, the latter are both object and rival for the former. Confusion may arise from the fact that in attempting to explain or interpret lay senses of class we may want to invoke different academic concepts of class to explain them or certain elements of them; for this purpose it is not necessary that the latter corresponds to the former (though confusingly we may use the same word for them). This is not only because the academic concepts tend to be more examined, more abstract and hence less ambiguous and diffuse, but because an explanans needs to be different from an explanandum. However, sometimes not only lay people but academics feel that they should judge academic concepts according to how they match everyday concepts. Lay concepts of class may themselves fail to distinguish between different sources of inequality, for example, between wealth and status. Lay thought also rarely acknowledges gender, either as an influence upon life-chances as a whole or more specifically as an influence upon economic capital, and gender is still fundamentally naturalised in much lay thinking. Lay concepts differ from academic concepts of class in that, like any commonsense concepts, they are typically unexamined and used in a wide variety of situations, so that their meaning tends to shift without this being noticed. As Bourdieu would say, they are governed by a practical logic rather than a logic of categories, statements and relations of entailment; their development is driven by a pragmatic feel for the game rather than the pursuit of conceptual consistency and empirical corroboration. For these reasons, whatever the shortcomings of academic concepts of class, it is misguided to object to them simply because they differ from lay senses, though this kind of objection is common, as if lay senses were authoritative. While the unexamined nature of lay concepts renders them problematic for use as an explanans, they are of course part of the explananda of social science; indeed, in this case, they are matters about which people care a great deal and are not merely descriptive but constitutive of social life, and hence cannot be ignored.[4] In this book I intend to take them seriously – more seriously than much social science has done – but I want neither to dismiss nor to privilege them *a priori* as explanations of social life.

Since sociological concepts of class can and should differ from lay concepts, and since the latter are part of the object of study, we shall need to use and refer to both kinds of concept. Hence, where the meaning is not clear from the context I shall denote the sociological or academic concept 'class^S' and the lay concept 'class^L'. Note, however, that this does not necessarily correspond to the abstract/concrete distinction, for some sociological concepts of class, such as Bourdieu's, may be concrete rather than abstract.

Fourthly, matters are further complicated by the fact that academic concepts of class may filter into lay discourse, and affect how actors think about it. This does not mean that actors will interpret them in exactly the same way as academics. Although, if asked about class by social scientists, they may try to answer in terms that they imagine will be acceptable to their interviewers, they are also likely to appropriate academic concepts in ways that fit with their understanding and interests, sometimes deliberately changing their meaning, as when bosses describe themselves as working class because they work.

This highlights a fifth point, that concepts of class are likely to be contested:

---

[4] The rich diversity of contexts in which lay concepts are used has certain virtues which academics tend to miss. Lay interpretations of behaviour and motives can be highly skilled and subtle, compared to the lumbering efforts of academics, whose abstraction from concrete contexts not only highlights particular things for analysis but carries the occupational hazard of plunging others into darkness. While radical academic wariness of commonsense is warranted, it often goes not only with an underestimation of its practical efficacy but with a scarcely veiled form of class distinction, through which academics assert their superiority over the vulgar masses. Radical academia is no less vulnerable to forms of pretension than other kinds.

The word 'class' will never be a neutral word as long as there are classes. The question of the existence or non-existence of classes is a stake in the struggle between the classes. (Bourdieu, 1993, p. 21)

Later I shall argue that this struggle is more than just a competition for power but one influenced by various kinds and levels of awareness of the ethically problematic nature of class.

Sixthly, to some extent discourses of class produce real effects. In recent years, following the cultural turn in social theory, there has been increased interest in cultural constructions of class, for example, in the history of discourses of class (e.g., Day, 2001; Finch, 1993; Skeggs, 2004). These contributions are important not only for understanding the subjective experience of class: the ascriptions of value or lack of value to self and other produce real effects on people in terms of how they are treated, and hence on their life-chances. As a result of such work, we now have a much richer understanding of cultural constructions of class. However, there is a danger that it may be assumed that class is little more than a product of such constructions. To be sure, discourses have real effects, but rarely ones that are identical to those to which they refer. Identifying discourses is not the same as identifying what they are about, or their reception and effects. Discourses are usually performative to some degree, but the extent to which they produce what they name is a matter for empirical research, not *a priori* assumption. Careless, hyperbolic uses in social theory of the metaphors of 'construction' and 'constitution', in ways that conceal their fallibility and limited effects, lead us to exaggerate the power of representations.[5]

Having cleared the ground a little as regards the general nature of concepts of class, I turn now to Bourdieu's approach to the subject, as one which is particularly appropriate for interpreting lay understandings of class.

Bourdieu's approach to class

I shall first draw attention to the strengths of this approach for understanding the subjective experience of class, and then identify some problems with it, albeit ones which can be rectified without abandoning it altogether.

Bourdieu defines an '*objective class*' as:

the set of agents who are placed in homogeneous conditions of existence imposing homogeneous conditionings and producing homogeneous systems of dispositions capable of generating similar practices . . . (1984, p. 101)

[5] As Skeggs notes, representations are not always taken up by the represented (2004, p. 117).

(1) This definition of class, with its reference to correspondences between conditionings and dispositions, obviously complements Bourdieu's concepts of habitus and field, reflecting the fact that it is not merely an *ad hoc* concept but part of a social meta-theory. Bourdieu's definition is relatively concrete compared to most sociological concepts of class, yet flexible enough to identify class differences in more than one dimension, hence enabling it to illuminate lay senses of class which tend not to differentiate it from status. It embraces differences not only in economic capital but in cultural, social, educational, linguistic and other forms of capital too, so that classes or class fractions are differentiated not only by their total amount of capital but by its composition.[6] Class differences are therefore understood as lying not on a single axis, but on several, each relating to different forms of capital. Thus, for example, the dominant classes include both commercial fractions (strong in economic rather than cultural capital) and professional fractions (strong in cultural and educational capital and moderately strong in economic capital). The inclusion of non-economic capitals allows Bourdieu to take a more searching analysis of differentiations normally treated simply as matters of 'status'. He is therefore able to provide unparalleled insights into symbolic domination, and hence into the subjective experience and sense of class, which is always far more than an awareness of differences in material wealth. It therefore differs from social stratification approaches to class, which are often little more than operational taxonomies for empirical research, weakly supported by a combination of *ad hoc* references to various theoretical abstract concepts of class and other 'variables' ('human capital', status, education, etc.), sometimes coupled with appeals to supposed lay senses of class. Bourdieu does not merely list and add up variables, and look for empirical regularities among them, but theorises the character and tendencies of the constituent elements and how they interact. Thus, insofar as it is an unusually concrete concept of class, embracing many different elements, it is closer than other sociological concepts to lay senses of class in all their complexity, though of course in abstracting and then recombining different elements it provides a deep analysis of what is unexamined in everyday life.

Bourdieu's approach allows us to analyse the interactions between sources of inequality relating to different types of capital. Usually, there is a positive covariation between holdings of most of these forms of capital. For example, although people with the same amount of economic capital

---

[6] I have omitted symbolic capital, that is, capital of any kind which is recognised as legitimate, and have assumed that such recognition applies in some degree to all types of capital.

may vary in the amount of cultural capital they have, cultural capital is nevertheless generally positively associated with economic capital. There are unlikely to be individuals or groups with very high cultural capital but very low economic capital, though the lottery of economic markets may in a few cases allow the reverse – i.e., for individuals who lack non-economic capital to enjoy monetary windfalls (the nouveau riche). While cultural and other non-economic forms of capital can to a limited extent compensate for lack of economic capital, they can also be converted into it, usually without loss.[7] Conversely, a certain amount of economic capital is necessary for acquiring many forms of cultural and other non-economic capital. The degree of convertibility and hence the extent to which they covary tends to be gendered. While the different kinds of capital tend to be closely related for men, they are less so for women, for whom patriarchal constraints can easily prevent them converting their cultural and educational capital into economic capital. Thus the new generation of women graduates has not had the same success in developing careers as male graduates. Those who have children and divorce are particularly likely to experience difficulty in converting their cultural and educational capital into economic capital.

Although, in a highly commodified society, not much can be done without money, cultural and other non-economic forms of capital cannot themselves be directly bought, for they require processes of social osmosis, embodiment, learning and self-change which can take considerable time – generations in some cases. This relative durability of capital holdings – particularly in the case of embodied capital – means that there is a great deal of path-dependence in the evolution of inequalities; yesterday's winners and losers tend to be tomorrow's. For example, outlay of money is only a necessary, not a sufficient, condition for gaining the know-how and feel for the game of high culture. This limitation betrays the nouveau riche. Here, in the difficulty and slow rates of acquisition, we see another significant difference between economic and non-economic capital. Whereas one can tell people's origins by their accents, demeanour, speech, etc., one cannot tell where money has been before; it bears no traces of its origins and does not have to be embodied, as do non-economic forms of capital. As Offe puts it, 'an essential feature of markets is that they neutralise meaning as a criterion of production and distribution' (Offe, 1985, p. 82). However, money and markets do not

---

[7] The fact that non-economic forms of capital (such as social or cultural capital) can be deployed without depleting the 'stocks' – indeed they may be augmented through use – indicates a disanalogy with the more familiar economic capital. It also gives those with more cultural and educational capital more security than those who lack these and have only economic capital.

easily neutralise meaning in relation to cultural, social and educational capital.[8]

Educational capital is of particular importance, because the mechanisms governing access to it appear to be purely meritocratic and hence legitimate (at least where education is free), when in fact its acquisition is strongly facilitated by cultural capital. Indeed, as Bourdieu brilliantly demonstrated, educational institutions tend to function as mechanisms for helping those with plentiful cultural capital convert it into the legitimate, indeed consecrated, form of educational capital, and for preventing those lacking in cultural capital from doing so (Bourdieu, 1996a). Educational capital in the form of certificates and degrees is also different from other forms of capital in that it has the effect of introducing sharp distinctions rather than mere gradients between groups.

(2) Bourdieu's approach provides not merely a description of differences in taste and lifestyle but an explanation of the hierarchical relations among them – for example, why certain kinds of art or literature have more cultural capital than others – showing that these correlations between specific kinds of goods and their standing are not arbitrary and merely conventional, but have a rationale in terms of a practical logic related to habitus. The most important axis is 'distance from necessity'. This divides the economically insecure from the secure – those for whom the need to make a living is an ever-present pressure, dominating all other decisions and influencing all other evaluations of objects, from those whose economic security and wealth are such that they can approach any object or subject without regard for its implications for their economic well-being. In *Distinction* Bourdieu shows how this difference colours the aesthetic evaluations of particular social groups, so that the economically insecure evaluate art in terms of its functionality for everyday life, while the bourgeois are willing to accept abstract art 'for its own sake', regardless of any functional associations, indeed their habitus disposes them toward it because it resonates with a life removed from the pressure of necessity.

(3) Aesthetic, and to a certain extent moral, judgements reflect the relation between the respective social positions of the judge and the judged. Symbolic domination, competition and struggle among groups take place within fields, structured by the hierarchical relations between different social positions and their occupants. Within the social field as a whole – i.e., that of the society as a whole – there are specific fields, each with its own variant of the latter's hierarchical relations, structuring the competitive strivings of individuals and groups; for example, the field of education

---

[8] This again implies a limitation of Bourdieu's economic metaphors.

has its own hierarchies of institutions and its own competing valuations of and struggles over different kinds of capital. The definition and pursuit of goods therefore take place according to contested criteria, which reflect the different positions of the competing groups within their field. This allows us to recognise that there is a social patterning to the valuations that actors make of themselves, others and goods, including the valuations they make of people according to class.

(4) The theoretical framework of habitus and field enables us to see that individuals sharing the same conditions may behave similarly even in the absence of any recognition of collective identity or interests: an objective class need not be a 'mobilised class'. As Bourdieu argues, the decline of class solidarity and the absence of mobilisation in no way imply that class is disappearing. It therefore enables us to understand how lay sensitivity to class difference persists despite the decline of class solidarity and class-based political organisation. As Mike Savage argues:

> What Bourdieu's arguments point towards is the need to consider the nature of contemporary identities in ways which are not premised on simplistic contrasts between either class collectivism on the one hand, or individualized identities on the other, but which are attentive to their intermeshing. (Savage, 2000, p. 108)[9]

(5) Bourdieu's definition of objective class cited above does not require the definition of sharp boundaries between classes. Differences in volumes of capital holdings generally form continua rather than steps, though processes of exclusion, and the bestowal of credentials by educational and professional institutions, can in many cases produce steep gradients of holdings between groups, thereby making some boundaries relatively clear. Since class boundaries are themselves contested in the very reproduction of class, their identification is a matter for empirical research rather than prior decision. In this way, Bourdieu is able to avoid sterile debates over where to draw class boundaries and where to locate particular groups on a single dimension.

(6) Unlike most social stratification approaches which posit classes in mainly non-relational terms and only contingently in antagonism or competition, Bourdieu conceptualises them in strongly relational terms, not so much in terms of exploitation, as in the Marxist concept of class, but in terms of a dialectic of competition, distinction and differentiation which is central to symbolic domination. Economically, members of different occupations such as accountants and teachers are only indirectly interdependent through the division of labour, but symbolically they not only

---

[9] The targets of Savage's criticism are the claims about 'individualisation' made by authors such as Beck and Beck-Gernsheim (2002) and Giddens (1991).

have different amounts of economic, cultural and educational capital but actively distinguish their own valuations of these and other goods from those of other groups. For Bourdieu, competition, struggle and domination are not incidental to class but constitutive of it. The competitive struggle is not normally politicised and organised but is the product of actors' dispositions and strivings for goods of various kinds. Some goods – be they commodities, relationships or practices – are elevated and invested in, others ignored or disparaged and hence devalued. Since the value of capital is inversely related to the number of people who hold it, as is particularly clear in the case of educational qualifications, success in increasing holdings of a particular form of capital may be self-defeating. Through these processes of competition, objective classes as Bourdieu defined them differentiate themselves from others.

Bourdieu summarises his position on points 5 and 6 thus:

[I]t is possible to deny the existence of classes as homogeneous sets of economically and socially differentiated individuals objectively constituted into groups, and to assert at the same time the existence of a space of differences based on a principle of economic and social differentiation. . . . From this point of view, the 'social reality' . . . consists of a set of invisible relationships, those precisely which constitute a space of positions external to one another and defined by their relative distance to one another . . . the real is the relational. (Bourdieu, 1987, p. 3)

Later I shall argue that Bourdieu's view of the processes of differentiation and competitive struggle is too Hobbesian and fails to do justice to its normative, including its ethical, aspects, but at this stage I want to focus on two different problems with his concept of 'objective class', one concerning gender and the other the origins of economic capital.

'Objective class' and gender

To repeat, for Bourdieu, an 'objective class' is 'the set of agents who are placed in homogeneous conditions of existence imposing homogeneous conditionings and producing homogeneous systems of dispositions capable of generating similar practices . . .' (Bourdieu, 1984, p. 101). At first sight, one might be tempted to protest that such a definition could be as much about gender as class, or indeed about ethnicity, for it fails to say how class differs from gender and other sources of inequality.[10]

---

[10] Elsewhere he writes: '[A] "class" [in a sense consciously used by actors], be it social, *sexual, ethnic* or otherwise . . .' (Bourdieu, 1987, p. 15, emphasis added). This usage reinforces the impression that for Bourdieu, class means just social position, and is not related to narrower senses of 'class' which tie it to economic capital, or distinguish it from gender.

By virtue of gender, men and women are placed in different conditions of existence, and therefore according to this definition could not ever be said to belong to the same class. However, when Bourdieu elaborates his definition of objective class, it turns out that gender and ethnicity are *subsumed* in it:

> [A] class or class fraction is defined not only by its position in the relations of production, as identified through indices such as occupation, income or even educational level, but also by a certain *sex-ratio*, a certain distribution in geographical space (which is never socially neutral) and by a whole set of subsidiary characteristics which may function, in the form of tacit requirements, as real principles of selection or exclusion without ever being formally stated (this is the case with *ethnic origin and sex*). (Bourdieu, 1984, p. 102, emphasis added)

Gender and ethnicity are therefore treated as elements which, with others, co-determine class. This would imply that, thanks to gender differences, men and women must always occupy different classes. While this would be a consistent use of the definition, the danger is that, while claiming to take gender into account, it invites us to overlook it or reduce it to a modifier of class in the more restricted, abstract sense which relates it to economic capital, so that its distinctive character is overlooked. The supposedly universal descriptor actually tends to marginalise what it claims to include. In Bourdieu's analyses, the logic of class and status is given the dominant, contextualising role, with gender as modifier. The dominant oppositions of symbolic domination are taken to be those of high/low, refined/coarse, rather than those of gender (male/female, public/private, hard/soft, etc.). Only in his *Masculine Domination* does gender escape a secondary role to be treated as an axis of inequality in its own right (Bourdieu, 2001). Gender, ethnicity and other kinds of social division have different bases from those of economic class^S in the narrow sense. To ignore these differences and treat each kind of division and group as reducible to particular combinations of various forms of capital is to obscure their most important and distinctive properties. Certainly, men and women do tend to have different volumes and mixes of capital, but this says nothing about the mechanisms – to do with gender – which make them different. Gender and class (in both a narrow and the broad sense) are not merely modifiers of each other but axes of social differentiation and inequality in their own right.

I therefore suggest we rename Bourdieu's concept of objective class simply 'objective social *position*', thereby retaining the strengths noted above while removing the awkward semantic tension with more restricted concepts of class^S, and making it clearer that we need to explicitly include gender as well among its prime determinants. Thus, adopting an abstract concept of class^S need not mean that gender is excluded from consideration among the determinants of objective social position; on the contrary, it leaves space for it instead of attempting to subsume it in a way that risks burying its distinctive features. This still allows us to take account of how these objective positions are associated with different amounts and combinations of various forms of capital, but without inviting the misapprehension that these are all to do with class in the abstract sense. Gender and class thus defined combine in various ways to influence objective social position and life-chances. The combinations are not merely additive. They may involve reinforcement, neutralisation or dissonance, or they may yield emergent properties. In analysing the concrete we therefore have to examine the manner and products of the interaction of elements previously analysed through abstraction. In this alternative approach, the struggles of the social field involve cross-cutting struggles of class, gender, and others such as age, ethnicity and sexuality.

Gender orders give rise to their own distinctive forms of capital. As Leslie McCall (1992) argues, gender can be not merely a secondary modifier of cultural, social and educational capital but a source of capital – masculine or feminine – in its own right.[11] As with other forms of capital, the value of masculine and feminine capital varies according to the particular field in which its holders find themselves. Middle class masculinity may be disparaged in a working class context, and vice versa, and equivalently with middle and working class forms of femininity. Masculine and feminine capital are strongly embodied and evident in appearance, demeanour, comportment and behaviour. Insofar as femininity and masculinity depend on socially valued inherited bodily characteristics such as size and shape which are difficult to alter or disguise, as opposed to more easily socially acquired ones, then as forms of capital they tend to cut across the others. Size and body shape vary to some extent with economic capital, but there is of course a great deal of variation around such averages, and the working class boy or girl who has the valued body shape and size has more opportunities for upward mobility than those who do not. Bodily features therefore function as a wild card in the struggles of the social field, offering possibilities for upward (and downward) mobility.[12] To the extent that bodies and appearances can indeed be shaped, they can be the subjects of investments in masculine or feminine capital.

[11] As McCall shows, Bourdieu's position on this seems to have varied between these two positions. Heterosexuality could also arguably be regarded as a source of capital, albeit one that is beginning to be contested.

[12] Thus, in part, gendered capital involves a valuation of nature; like any valuation, it is made according to social criteria, but it is *about* something that is partly beyond social construction. On the ambiguities of 'social construction', see Sayer, 2000a, chapter 4.

As forms of capital they are complex. No men or women conform exactly to masculine or feminine norms, which suggests that absolute conformity is either impossible or seen as undesirable. Moreover, valued masculinities and femininities vary not only according to particular subfields – for example, between artistic and professional middle class fields on the one hand and commercial fields on the other – but according to age and position. As Rosemary Pringle (1988) and Sylvia Gerhardi (1995) have shown, women in employment tend to fall into a number of gendered roles which resemble those of family members. Feminine and masculine forms of behaviour are valued through a system of gendered double standards, which are themselves inflected differently according to class and ethnicity: for example, assertiveness, submissiveness and hardness are valued differently in men and women. The particular hierarchical distinctions and criteria are neither stable nor consistent. They do not need to be. Their main function is to permit male dominance, and changes and inconsistencies may be necessary for maintaining it. Thus, as Cynthia Cockburn notes in her analysis of gender and technology:

[I]n engineering masculine ideology made use of a hard-soft dichotomy to appropriate tough, physical engineering work for masculinity and thus ran into a problem when it came to evaluating its 'opposite', cerebral, professional engineering . . . The ideology coped with this contradiction by calling into play an alternative dichotomy, associating masculinity with rationality, intellect, femininity with the irrational and with the body – incidentally turning an almost complete conceptual somersault in the process. (Cockburn, 1985, p. 235)

Masculinity and femininity are only conventionally associated with biological sex, and on appropriate occasions (whose determination again varies by class) feminine characteristics may be acceptable for men and masculine characteristics for women – usually on the proviso that outside these occasions they revert to expected type.[13] Gender norms are in varying degrees contested, particularly in groups with high cultural and economic capital. Conversely, as Beverley Skeggs shows, femininity may be the only source of capital to which working class women have access and hence they are likely to be sceptical of feminism to the extent to that it threatens the profits of femininity (Skeggs, 1997; see also Lovell, 2000).

---

[13] For example, a woman like Ellen MacArthur, who shows great bravery, toughness and technical skill in the conventionally masculine sport of sailing, is expected to be sufficiently feminine when off duty; indeed, it seems as if the latter is a condition for unqualified celebration of her exceptional qualities. The same applies to 'strong women' in politics.

Developing Bourdieu's concept of economic capital: identity-sensitive and identity-indifferent mechanisms

Bourdieu's contributions lie mainly in the analysis of symbolic domination rather than economic inequalities and exploitation, and he has relatively little to say about the latter: 'As regards economic capital, I leave that to others; it is not my area' (Bourdieu, 1993, p. 32). I shall argue that this needs more attention if we are to understand the origins of inequalities of economic capital, the moral significance of class^L and the struggles of the social field. I shall first introduce some of the determinants and components of economic capital, and then argue that we need to acknowledge both mechanisms determining economic capital which are neutral or indifferent to actors' identities and mechanisms which are sensitive to them.[14]

As we noted, Bourdieu's relatively concrete concept of class need not be taken to be incompatible with certain more abstract analyses of class, indeed it can be illuminated by them. In particular, his approach is compatible, first, with the argument that one of the determinants of economic capital lies, as claimed in Marxism, in the ownership and non-ownership of means of production. This makes some difference but not all the difference. Other things being equal, a cleaner who is a wage-labourer has less power than one who is a co-owner of the firm in which she works, and similarly with employee-managers compared to owner-managers. Another element in determining economic capital relates to the division of labour (often included in many sociological concrete concepts of class where it is operationalised in terms of groupings of occupations). Different positions in the division of the labour afford their occupants more or less power in relation to others; those involved in strategic activities on which others are dependent in the short term are likely to be able to use this to leverage more earnings and security than those in occupations whose services are less urgently needed. They further offer different opportunities for strategies of closure. Relative scarcity affects economic capital, and though it often correlates with the technical skill and training required for the job, or so-called 'human capital', it can also vary independently of this. Other economic possessions such as land and housing can also influence actors' economic capital; individuals may be beneficiaries or victims of house price inflation, for example. Access to

---

[14] I do not simply term the latter 'discriminatory' because some forms of discrimination are not in response to identities, but to other qualities, e.g., discrimination according to price.

economic capital is highly spatially differentiated, too – an aspect which is under-analysed in Bourdieu's work; labour markets are usually highly localised and economic opportunities vary considerably from one local labour market to another so that some regions offer greater prospects for upward social mobility than others (Fielding, 1995). Finally, a further important source of economic capital, one which is central to the reproduction of the wealthy, is inheritance.

Together these possibilities affect individuals' total economic capital in terms of income, wealth and security. They are the constituents of economic capital, though as we shall see other processes can also contingently influence them.

Whether on their own or in combination, these different elements of economic capital should not be expected single-handedly to explain differences in life-chances, for the latter – and access to economic capital itself – are also influenced by status, ethnicity and gender, matters dealt with by *other* abstract concepts (Crompton, 1996; Sayer, 1995). For example, as many researchers have pointed out, economic inequalities can also be influenced by differences of status and gender through the way jobs are designed, through the selection of employees, and through the economic valuation of practices. Sometimes distinctions made on the basis of gender or ethnicity may push individuals into a particular class; for example, gendered systems of inheritance may allow the eldest son to become a petty-capitalist through inheriting a family firm, while daughters are disinherited and propelled into the labour market as wage-labourers. However, the position of capitalist or wage-labourer can exist independently of these mechanisms and hence such practices are merely contingently related to capitalist economic classes^S, not necessary conditions of them.[15]

Sarah Irwin argues that this relationship in which the formal economy itself adjusts to gender and other non-class social differences can be generalised further:

[T]he marginality of certain groups is itself important in shaping the structure of employment . . . The structure of occupations and employment inequality is not 'given by' economic processes but is shaped also in relation to social divisions. (Irwin, 1995, p. 186)

---

[15] To elaborate: I did not include these in the elements of economic capital because none of them constitute necessary conditions for the existence of economic capital, though on occasion they may be sufficient but unnecessary conditions. Putting it the other way round, economic capital based on ownership and non-ownership, division of labour, inheritance, do not *require* status, gender or ethnic differences and the like as conditions of their existence. On this mode of abstraction, see Sayer, 2000a and b.

This is surely correct – economic inequalities are structured by non-economic, cultural mechanisms – but the 'also' is important too, if, that is, it is meant to imply that there are, *in addition*, some influences which are indeed determined by economic processes regardless of gender, ethnicity or status. To understand in what respects inequalities are necessary for capitalism to function we would need to distinguish whether the relations between these different mechanisms producing inequality are contingent or necessary.

More specifically we need to recognise the contingent co-presence of identity-neutral and identity-sensitive mechanisms in determining inequalities. One of the great disappointments of the last two decades of research on inequality has been a tendency to invert the former neglect of identity-sensitive, cultural influences by denying the co-presence of identity-neutral mechanisms (Sayer, 2000b; see also Holmwood, 2001 and Sayer, 2002a). In the process certain essential features of the operation of capitalist economies which can have major effects on people's life-chances and experience, regardless of their identity, are in danger of being lost to view. Just because economic relations are always socially embedded – which in our society inevitably means in ways that are gendered, 'raced', etc. – it does not follow that identity-neutral dimensions are not also present, any more than the fact that birds can fly means that gravity is suspended.

While the concrete forms of capitalism are contingently influenced by and responsive to misrecognition or discrimination according to identity, capitalism as an economic system is not dependent on these – there is no reason why it could not exist without them, and capitalism both produces and depends on inequalities in the distribution of economic capital regardless of these identity-sensitive processes. Whether people find, retain or lose their jobs as wage-labourers and members of particular occupations or succeed or fail as capitalists depends on (among other things) whether there is a market demand for whatever commodities – material or non-material – they produce. When consumers switch from buying typewriters to word processors the fortunes of the respective workers producing those goods are likely to diverge, as jobs are lost in the former sector and added in the latter. Further, some new people may be able to become capitalists in the expanding sector. The resulting changes in inequalities are not the product of discrimination by consumers according to the identities of the workers producing those goods, for consumers are likely to be ignorant of or indifferent to their identities. Similarly, de-industrialisation results primarily from the uneven rate of productivity growth in manufacturing and service sectors and produces change in the distribution of economic capital, indirectly affecting the class structure. This too does not depend on differences in identities or acts of ascription. Likewise, a weakening of the currency may make firms which are dependent on imported materials insolvent, resulting in job losses and a decline of economic capital, but the macro-economic causes of such events operate without regard for workers' identities.

These and many other identity-indifferent mechanisms are a normal part of capitalism. However, it does not follow that these identity-neutral mechanisms must have identity-neutral effects, since it is common for workers of different gender and ethnicity to be segregated in different kinds of work through identity-sensitive mechanisms, and, in particular, for those who are subject to racism and/or sexism to be confined to those jobs most vulnerable to redundancy. Yet even then, if they lose their jobs because consumer tastes have changed or because currency movements have undermined profitability, these are still cases of identity-indifferent mechanisms impacting on an identity-differentiated context, and it is the latter, not the former, that is responsible for the gendered or 'raced' outcome. Capitalism requires private property in the means of production to be concentrated into the hands of a minority and the majority to be wage-labourers (whether they be cleaners or managers), but any individuals can do these things. Nobody is born a capitalist or worker or doctor or cleaner. Other mechanisms not intrinsic to the basic structure of capitalism may contingently influence who becomes a capitalist or a worker or workers of particular kinds, but from the point of view of what is necessary for capitalism to exist, anyone can find a place in its structures. Of course, in practice, what exists is not only what has to exist for capitalism to function but what is contingently produced by other mechanisms. However, it only takes a little bit of sloppy thinking to mistake this contingent relation for a necessary one and thereby misunderstand the necessary conditions for the reproduction of inequalities. This slip has disastrous consequences because it invites the inference that capitalism doesn't just accommodate to sexism, racism and the like but depends on them for its very existence, which in turn implies that these latter forms of discrimination and domination can only be removed if capitalism is abolished.[16] This ironically produces the same conclusion as that of ultra-leftism – that nothing can be changed until everything is changed.[17] While the argument about the nature of the relation between identity-sensitive and identity-indifferent mechanisms might seem academic, its practical and

---

[16] Judith Butler's claims about the relationships between capitalism and sexuality, ably rebutted by Fraser, are an example of this kind of illogic (Butler, 1997; Fraser, 1998).
[17] The irony is that ultra-leftism was notable for its dismissive attitude to non-capitalist causes of inequality and oppression.

political implications are huge, namely, that progress in eliminating these cultural, identity-sensitive forms of domination and exclusion need not wait upon finding a successor for capitalism.[18]

Competitive market contexts can encourage either behaviour which is neutral with respect to identity, or behaviour which *appears* to be highly sensitive to it, though, as we shall see, in the latter case it is not the identity but the money or goods associated with it that count.[19] In the case of product markets, the need of sellers to get buyers' money makes it against their interest to discriminate against customers on any grounds other than ability to pay. Insofar as producers of consumer goods and services target particular identities of consumer, the reason for this is not any interest in the identities themselves, but their interest in earning more cash. In the case of labour markets, competitive pressures encourage firms to employ whoever will do the job best, regardless of matters of identity, such as gender or 'race', and they penalise those which forgo the best candidates on such grounds, though of course such incentives are often contingently overridden by racism and the like. At the same time, competitive pressures compel firms to take advantage of any differences in identity of groups which have economic implications, as when employers needing to cut labour costs employ workers from a culturally stigmatised group which can be paid low wages. However, note the logic of this kind of selectivity: competitive pressures encourage the exploitation of such groups literally *for all they are worth, and only for what they are worth in money terms, and – again – not necessarily for any particular interest – hostile or favourable – in their culture.*[20] In other words, market pressures encourage employers to take them on not because of their cultural identity but because of their economic exploitability. The latter may in turn be a consequence of the stigmatisation of their identity, but from the point of view of market incentives, it is the economic consequences that matter.

It might nevertheless be objected that there are cases where firms depend for their existence on employing a particular stigmatised group, such as marginal clothing firms in east London employing women of Bangladeshi origin. If these firms could not get labour that was cheap

---

[18] I recognise that a low class position can compound disadvantages of gender and 'race' or ethnicity, and add to stigmatisation of such identities, but the relation is contingent: low class positions could exist in their absence.

[19] '. . . the economic logic of markets interacts in complex ways with the cultural logic of recognition, sometimes instrumentalizing existing status distinctions, sometimes dissolving or circumventing them, and sometimes creating new ones. As a result, market mechanisms give rise to economic class relations that are not mere reflections of status hierarchies' (Fraser, 2003, p. 214).

[20] 'The market thrives on inequality of income and wealth, but it does not recognize ranks. It devalues all vehicles of inequality but the price tags' (Bauman, 2001, p. 21).

and exploitable, they could not survive. However, note, first, that what is essential for their survival as marginal capitalist firms is cheap, exploitable labour – not necessarily cheap labour of this particular gender or ethnicity: any group which happens to be available and is willing to do the work for equally low pay would do. Secondly, this cheap, exploitable labour-power may be a condition of the existence of these particular firms, but it is not a condition of the existence of capitalism. Capitals have to compete but there are many other ways of competing besides driving down the labour cost:output ratio – there are also automation, upskilling, product innovation, reducing material costs and overheads, to name a few. Capitalism, as such, therefore, does not depend on employing workers from particular gender or ethnic groups.

Capital also certainly needs its labour force to be reproduced if it is to survive, but it does not need its labour force to be predominantly male or domestic work to be done primarily by women. Anyone who can do these kinds of work will do, and men and women can do both. Moreover, as Sylvia Walby has argued (1986, 1990), although most capitalists are also men, patriarchal interests may often be at odds with capitalist interests. Capitalism and patriarchy or gender orders are two systems which, being both pervasive, have had to adjust to each other, though they could exist independently of each other; patriarchy has existed in non-capitalist systems, and no-one has ever demonstrated why capital accumulation, class, money, or competition among capitals could not exist without patriarchy. Hence, while they are everywhere in interaction, their interdependence is only contingent.[21]

Identity-sensitive, identity-constructing mechanisms are an important source of inequalities, both in their own right and in interaction with identity-indifferent ones. The economic capital, security or vulnerability of many workers has a great deal to do with their particular identity. Those who are excluded from the labour market through sexism or racism and the like suffer from economic disadvantages which are ultimately *cultural* in origin, involving symbolic domination, including discourses of sexism, racism and homophobia. With respect to their *gender* men and women experience what we might call 'first-order' moral judgements and taken-for-granted assumptions regarding them *as* men and women – e.g., as 'good' girls or boys, mothers or fathers – and different standards (i.e., double standards) are a prime force in the (re)production of gender differences and relations. They are cultural in the sense that they are constructed on the basis of cultural understandings of men and women

---

[21] Once again, refusal to use abstraction or distinguish between contingent and necessary relations – between can and must – is a recipe for misunderstanding.

and what should be expected of them. But they are also economic insofar as those constructions of gender assume particular economic roles for men and women, such as breadwinner or caregiver, whether work is to be paid or unpaid, and how work is valued in terms of recognition of skills and rewards.

Thus, the practice of actual organisations typically (but contingently) involves both identity-sensitive or -constructing mechanisms and identity-indifferent mechanisms. (Note that we are moving up to a more concrete level of analysis here, from particular mechanisms, to the manner of their combination in particular circumstances.) Giving certain jobs to people on the basis of gender identity and appearance, for example the customer relations job to an attractive woman, certainly indicates sensitivity to identity, but in the context of an organisation involved in economic systems, such as a bank, this is a process of selection oriented towards these cultural differentiations, albeit, in many cases, for reasons to do with identity-neutral mechanisms, particularly maximising profit. The decline of manufacturing employment in most industrialised countries was not a response to gender but it certainly impacted on the gendering of labour markets, for the over-representation of men in manufacturing jobs meant that many working class men's economic capital declined significantly, with major implications for working class culture. The expansion in the employment of women in Britain in the last two decades is a product of a combination of identity-neutral mechanisms, such as changes in the relative profitability of sectors in which women were already under- or over-represented, and identity-sensitive mechanisms, such as the beginnings of a feminisation of education and political culture.

The partial autonomy of market systems from the identity of those involved in them also provides an important reason for retaining an abstract 'structural' concept of economic class as product of those systems, in addition to more concrete concepts of class such as those of Bourdieu, or indeed lay actors. This still allows us to acknowledge that, at the level of the concrete, the way in which class[L] behaviour and identities develop is always in and through gender, ethnicity, age and sexuality. There are therefore significant differences between working class cultures of men and of women, of black and of white, and so on (Skeggs, 1997, 2004), and the same goes for higher classes. However, as we have seen, our economic capital can change for reasons that have nothing to do with our identity or behaviour, as well as for reasons that do.[22] Note also

---

[22] This identity-neutrality of formal economic systems gives a certain *justification* to the 'insulation' of *abstract* political economic theory of such systems from the study of culture, though of course it does not justify any such bracketing out of the latter in concrete studies.

that the distinction between identity-neutral and identity-sensitive mechanisms does not correspond simply to economic and non-economic, for the identity-sensitive processes also influence economic capital, for example, gendered assumptions regarding men and women's economic roles.[23]

This insistence on the contingent nature of the interaction between class and gender and race goes against the grain of many contemporary cultural analyses of class; for example, Gary Day writes: 'Ultimately, of course, race, gender, sexuality and culture cannot be separated from class' (Day, 2001, p. 200). This seems correct as regards behaviour: how could one, for example, clearly distinguish which aspects of the behaviour of male professionals or female cleaners derive from their class and which from their gender? But it would be a mistake to suppose that class could not possibly exist without gender (or race or other social divisions) and vice versa. Moreover, as we have seen, the origins or causes of class and gender differences are radically different. Even associations which appear to be universal may be contingent. One of the roles of theory is to grasp the necessary conditions of existence of objects, as distinct from their contingent associations. When confronted with associations between x and y, we need to ask counterfactual questions of the form: could x exist without y, and vice versa?; what difference would the absence of y make? In answering them we learn about their conditions of existence.[24]

By asking the same kinds of theoretical question, we can adduce that the subjective experience of class is not a *necessary* condition of the (re)production of economic class^S in capitalism (though it contingently affects its course). By contrast, subjective experience and identities are necessarily constitutive of gender because gender differences are ascriptive in character.

In emphasising that some of the key mechanisms that generate inequalities in holdings of economic capital are indifferent to identities, I am countering a kind of vulgar culturalism or culturalist imperialism which assumes ascriptive, cultural definitions 'go all the way down', so that, for example, poverty is ultimately a product of a culture of poverty. As long as

---

[23] A further distinction might be introduced between the formal capitalist economy itself and the informal non-capitalist economies, most importantly of the household, with which it articulates.

[24] John Frow objects: 'The very act of *listing* the "factors" that make up social positionalities (age+gender+race+sexual orientation+ . . .) assumes, as Judith Butler puts it, "their discrete, sequential coexistence along a horizontal axis that does not describe their convergences within a social field"' (1995, p. 102). They do indeed converge and interact but it does not follow from this that they cannot exist independently of one another. The task of abstract theory is to assess whether their relationship is contingent or necessary through abstraction, and to define their conditions of existence, structure and powers. The task of concrete analysis is to examine how they contingently interact, possibly producing emergent effects (Sayer, 2000a and b).

the identity-neutral processes of capitalism continue unchecked, changing how we treat people of other classes will make only small differences. Contrary to the impression given by social constructionist accounts of class, which blur the difference between concepts of class and what they are about, thereby rendering the former voluntaristically performative, people are not simply members of this or that class because of how others define their class and behave towards them, though these do have some effects. It should also be noted, incidentally, that while ignoring culturally generated problems – many of them economic – is far from progressive, nor is the converse tendency of neglecting identity-neutral sources of problems, or reducing the latter to the former. The British government (and many others) prefers to treat unemployment as a problem of the identity of individuals who are unemployed and their inability to make themselves marketable, rather than of the inability of the economic system to provide sufficient employment. This concealment of identity-neutral influences upon economic processes and economic class is a form of mystification. As we shall see in the following chapters it is also common in lay views of class and helps to legitimise class differences.

Conclusions and implications

Though people's class antennae – their practical sense of class – are usually highly sensitive to social differences, their discursive consciousness of class is generally less well defined, conflating inequalities of different kinds and origins.[25] If we are to make sense of the lay experience of class and assess its adequacy we need to identify its various components and how it differs from other sources of inequality, as well as how it interacts with them.

If by 'class' we mean an abstract concept of economic class which ties it to identity-neutral mechanisms then it cannot be said to be a product of misrecognition or symbolic violence, though it tends to stimulate these. If we use a more inclusive, concrete, concept of class such as that of Bourdieu or common lay senses, which already subsume identity-sensitive mechanisms, then of course it has to be acknowledged that class in this sense is partly a product of (mis)recognition. Although class in the abstract economic sense is itself normally produced partly regardless of identity and (mis)recognition, it is, of course, like gender, hugely important for *forming* subjective identities and the habitus (Charlesworth, 2000): class is certainly a cause of 'misrecognition', in the sense used in

---

[25] It is not unusual for our feel for a game to be highly proficient while our attempts to represent it discursively falter.

chapter 3. Bourdieu's approach to class has many strengths and I shall draw upon it in subsequent chapters. However, I have argued that it needs modifying to take account of gender and the various sources of economic capital.

Thus, there are both similarities and differences between class and 'race', for example. Interactions between people may in both cases express fear, distrust, contempt, disgust, loathing, derision, and senses of inferiority and superiority, but class differences would exist even in the absence of these responses, whereas the inequalities of 'race' are fundamentally dependent on them. Were it not for the popularity of cultural reductionism, in which all differences are treated as products of cultural representations, it would not be necessary to state the obvious: racism is a necessary condition for the reproduction of 'race', but 'class-ism' is not a necessary condition for the reproduction of class. There is a danger here of an inadvertent three-way complicity between such reductionist accounts of class, lay views of class as merely a regrettable product of class prejudice, and Thatcherite and Blairite views of class as a product of old-fashioned political attitudes. Whereas individual actors of egalitarian outlook can do something about racism and sexism by eliminating it from their own behaviour, they can do little on an individual level about class inequalities. Living in a class society and hence depending on others with different incomes, education and tastes, we cannot avoid being complicit in the reproduction of class inequalities.

The fact that differences in objective social position may be produced by the operation of both identity-neutral and identity-sensitive mechanisms has important implications for the moral significance of class and for what can be done about class. To the extent that class inequalities come about through the operation of identity-sensitive mechanisms, they can be reduced by attacking discrimination, though this may have only limited effect. To the extent that class differences arise from identity-neutral causes, such as the effect of demand and supply on numbers of jobs and pay, they can only be countered through different kinds of measure, ones which are indifferent to identity but regulate economic activities, including prices, for example through minimum wage legislation and employment rights, progressive taxation and restrictions on the mobility of capital.

5   Struggles of the social field

Introduction

Class inequalities involve not merely differences in wealth, income and
economic security, but differences in access to valued circumstances,
practices and ways of life – 'goods' in a broad sense – and in the recognition or valuation of those goods and their holders. They produce and are
shaped by struggles and competition, domination and resistance, as well
as compliance, whether willing or reluctant. What is the nature of these
struggles? What are they about? What are the goods that are being struggled for? What is the relation between the valuation of particular goods
and the social position of the groups with which they are associated?
The purpose of this chapter is to answer these questions. As we noted in
chapter 1, lay moral sentiments and norms regarding how people should
treat one another and how different behaviours should be evaluated imply
assumptions about the nature of goods and the good life. We will deal
with the latter first, moving on to moral sentiments and evaluations of
behaviour in subsequent chapters.

I shall begin with the general nature of the struggles in question, what
they are over, for and about, and what broad forms they take. To what
extent are they instrumental struggles for power *per se*, or struggles over
access to valued ways of life? To what extent do they involve contestation
of the definition and evaluation of goods or competition for goods whose
value is agreed upon but which are unequally distributed? We then examine the nature of goods themselves, distinguishing between those which
are seen as valuable in themselves, and those which are valuable primarily for advantages which they bring their holders vis-à-vis others. More
specifically, I argue that the distinctions between use-value and exchange-
value and internal and external goods bring into view the respects in which
the inequalities and struggles of the social field go beyond the pursuit of
interests and power. This affords a far richer understanding of struggles
for goods and recognition. As we shall see, these distinctions are of considerable normative significance but are elided in Bourdieu's concept of

capitals. Although recognition is important, I argue that it is the unequal distribution of goods which are valued in themselves which is the most problematic feature of class inequalities. Next, by reference to the relationships between the posh, the good, the common and the bad, we examine how the valuation of goods is affected by their uneven distribution across the social field, and their association with particular social groups which tend to monopolise them. Finally, in order to demonstrate just how important and difficult are the problems that arise from inequalities in the distribution of goods and differences in their valuation, we analyse some empirical examples drawn from the work of Annette Lareau, Diane Reay, Valerie Walkerdine and Helen Lucey concerning childrearing and education in working class families. They involve dilemmas concerning their parents' commitments, in particular their pursuit of goods and valued ways of life and futures for their children. They demonstrate that the struggles of the social field are not just about power and distinction but about how to live.

What are the struggles of the social field?

The struggles of the social field in question here are not those of formal, organised, public politics or old-style 'class struggle', but the everyday, informal micro-political struggles and competitions such as those analysed by Bourdieu, though the two can be linked. They involve 'capillary' power as well as 'arterial' power. The struggles and competitions are not only against others but *for* certain 'goods' – by which I mean not just commodities, or indeed recognition, but valued circumstances, practices, relationships and ways of life.[1] They involve not only inequalities in the distribution of material goods but the 'soft forms of domination', the innumerable minor and often subtle and unintended acts of symbolic domination of everyday life, and the resistance these engender. They have several dimensions, and the question of what should be sought after and struggled for is itself one of the subjects of the struggles of the social field. Material resources are scarce and as one group or individual strives to make a living, then, whether they realise it or not, they are in competition with others. Symbolic resources can also involve a similar logic, for in their pursuit of symbolic goods such as education, actors can hardly escape competing with others, even if they do not see themselves as doing so, and the value of their capital – for example, their educational

---

[1] In terms of the philosophical distinction between the right and the good, the micro-political struggles are primarily about the good, struggles over rights being more a feature of organised, macro-politics.

qualifications – will be judged[2] through comparison with those of others. Moreover, many goods – both material and symbolic – are positional and therefore cannot be universalised, and many competitions are zero-sum games or net positive-sum games which also produce some losers.[3] Struggle and competition in this sense may therefore be more a by-product of the ordinary business of individuals and groups going about their lives than a goal or strategy. Generally people do not plan and strategise very much; most of the time their action involves 'protension' rather than planning, that is, an orientation to the future based on a feel for the game and an openness to contingency.

There is competition to gain inclusion into certain groups and access to the goods they currently monopolise. These may be pursued so that those currently excluded can then exclude others, or in order simply to be equal. Of course, it is tempting for the excluded to start off pursuing the latter and then switch to the former when they have been included; egalitarianism is always more attractive when looking up the social hierarchy than when looking down. Nevertheless, self-interest is not necessarily always dominant, and much action is neither simply self-interested nor altruistic.

Even with these qualifications, talk of the 'struggles' of the social field may seem exaggerated, and in danger of devaluing the term to the point of meaninglessness. Quite simply, not all is struggle, for there is also a great deal of peaceful coexistence, compliance, cooperation, solidarity, sympathy, respect and generosity, and mutual indifference. To understand how far social life involves micro-political struggles we have to acknowledge how far it does not involve them. This is important because we need to recognise the moral dimension of social life, not only in itself and as a basis of social order, but as a source of resistance to the existing order. Insofar as resistance is directed towards achieving more just and better ways of living the two are related. Dismissive views of morality, particularly common in radical academia, therefore help to occlude both consent and resistance. To be sure, sometimes what actors consider to be moral is highly questionable, as in the morality of the traditional patriarchal family: to acknowledge morality is not to endorse every form it takes. Sometimes, too, even appealing moral qualities such as generosity and openness to others can have the effect of allowing oppression to persist, as in the common case of the generosity of the dominated towards the privileges of the dominant. Regardless of whether we agree with lay moral sentiments and

[2] As before, in practice, 'judgement' may be too strong and rationalist a term for a process of selection and semi-conscious evaluation strongly influenced by the habitus.
[3] This need not imply that inequality is unavoidable, for the competitive games are not natural fixtures but contingent social products capable of being changed.

norms, they are, as E. P. Thompson famously demonstrated (Thompson, 1963, 1991), central not only to consent and compliance but to resistance to domination and injustice. Resistance does not stem merely from the pursuit of power for power's sake, but from the pursuit of goods in the broad sense.

Equally, to claim that there is a moral dimension to the dispositions, dynamics and micro-politics of the social field is not to deny that there are also amoral, selfish, immoral and indeed evil dimensions too. As we argued in chapter 2, motives are typically mixed and inconsistent. It is not unusual for people both to resent the snobbery of those with more cultural capital than themselves while being snobbish about those with less cultural capital. It is often in people's self-interest to behave in a way that is ethical. (What is ethical or unethical is not a matter of its relationship to self-interest.) It is not that domination and injustice are abnormal interferences in an essentially moral order but that everyday life is a complex mixture of just and unjust, good and bad.

Bourdieu usually portrays the struggles of the social field relating to both material goods and the symbolic order overwhelmingly in interest-based terms, as pure power-play. Actors strive to defend, and where they can augment, their capitals. Their ability to do this varies according to their position within the social field. Some are well placed to augment their economic capital but not their cultural capital, and vice versa. Competition for capital affects the profits that can be gained from them, and the rates of exchange among different forms of capital. Increased access to formerly exclusive kinds of goods, such as university degrees, tends to devalue them.

Frequently the actions whereby each class (or class fraction) works to win new advantages, i.e. to gain an advantage over the other classes and so, objectively, to reshape the structure of objective relations between the classes . . . are compensated for (and so cancelled out ordinally) by the reactions of the other classes, directed towards the same objective. (Bourdieu, 1984, p. 157)

Even those who attempt to avoid competing inadvertently have to invest in strategies that defend their capital from devaluation. On this view, in other words, whether they are aware of it or not, or like it or not, everyone is caught up in a Hobbesian zero-sum competition for power and advantage relative to others – 'a perpetual and restless desire of power after power, that ceaseth only in death' (Hobbes, cited in Singer, 1993, p. 37).

Ironically, a wholly interest- and power-based view of struggle de-politicises it for it ignores its normative content and implications; although Bourdieu's use of critical terminology like 'misrecognition', 'symbolic

violence' and 'domination' implies injustice, the struggles are not represented in much of his early work as being *about* justice, even from the side
of the dominated, but as a neutral competition for capital, with winners
and losers, albeit a competition which is played on a sloping field, and
in which yesterday's winners and losers are likely to be tomorrow's. To
understand inequalities, domination, competition and resistance we need
to examine why they should *matter* to actors.

This might seem unfair as Bourdieu stresses the desire of the dominant
to secure not merely power but legitimacy, but then he avoids any discussion of whether any such struggles for legitimacy are themselves legitimate, leaving the impression that this is merely a way of further increasing
their power. In crypto-normative style, it is implied that the legitimacy
is questionable, but no direct argument is presented as to why it might
be. The views of the dominated about the legitimacy of their domination
are treated largely in terms of their effects – for example, regarding the
way in which rejections of authority by the dominated have the effect of
legitimising the dominant's worst feelings about them and justifying their
social exclusion. This leaves the actors' normative grounds for the resistance unclear. Without knowing these we cannot assess whether it was
justified – and we cannot justify judging the negative judgements of the
dominant as wrong. (That many would see such judgements as outside
the scope of social science does not alter the fact that we cannot justify
using terms like 'domination' and 'symbolic violence' without explaining in what respects the social relations involved are bad.[4]) Logically, we
could react to the references to domination by saying, 'Yes, why not? –
what's wrong with domination?' That few readers are likely to respond
in this way reflects the fact that in such cases description and evaluation
are inseparable.

The oppressed people interviewed in *The Weight of the World* (Bourdieu
et al., 1999) had a great deal to say about the legitimacy of their situations and the dominant discourses about them and they offered reasons
for their evaluations. These were not necessarily complete or particularly coherent but they indicate something that can easily be forgotten
in using concepts like 'habitus' and 'feel for the game': that people are
evaluative beings; that what befalls them matters deeply to them; and that
they cannot develop a comfortable or contented feel for just any game,
or accept just any rationale, or submit to just any 'interpellation'. No
struggle is reducible to striving for power or advantage, because power
or advantage can only exist in relation to goods, that is, valued things,
practices and ways of life. Having a monopoly of something which is

---

[4] These issues are discussed further in chapter 9.

a matter of indifference to others does not give you power over them. The dominant claim that their goods are superior to others both (1) for *non-instrumental* reasons – because they believe (often rightly) it to be the case – and (2) for *instrumental* reasons – because the more these goods are desired by others the greater the profit that the dominant can derive from monopolising them; it is in their interest to universalise their goals without universalising the conditions for their achievement.

At one level, Bourdieu recognises this in emphasising how the struggles of the social field are not only for goods but over the very definition of what counts as a good, thereby emphasising the symbolic aspect of the struggles. But this latter dimension also tends to be seen in Hobbesian and instrumental terms – whatever definition of the good best fits with the habitus of a particular social group, or whatever best increases the value of its capital (explanation 2 above), will be struggled for. The amoral analogy of the game, with its 'stakes', encourages us to think of the contestation of goods as mere power-play. This conceals the fact that while it is indeed possible for groups to do this, they also struggle for things which they value for their own sake, regardless of whether they bring them advantage vis-à-vis others. Egalitarian dispositions and strivings are defined out of the picture by the amoral Hobbesian framework. If the dominated resist it is implicitly only because they too want to be dominant, not because they want equality and an end to domination. Similarly, the advantaged can only want to maintain or augment their advantage; no advantaged person or group could possibly want their advantages to be shared equally. Unless we acknowledge their moral-political content, we will fatally misunderstand the nature and normative significance of the struggles of the social field. Thus the micro-politics of the social field include patriarchal, feminist, conservative, socialist, racist, anti-racist and many other elements, none of which are merely instrumental. These alternative orientations are not stakes in the competition but normative agendas in their own right. They are not merely about getting to the top of the pile but about changing the nature of the social order.

Bourdieu tends to acknowledge these as only occurring exceptionally, through politicisation leading to the de-naturalising of social determinations, and argues that otherwise the struggles of the social field will be limited to 'competitive struggle', that is '. . . the form of class struggle which the dominated classes allow to be imposed on them when they accept the stakes offered by the dominant classes . . . [and] . . . implicitly recognize the legitimacy of the goals pursued by those whom they pursue . . .' (Bourdieu, 1984, p. 165). They therefore struggle for position, but not to change the nature and structure of positions themselves. One of the effects of the reduction of normativity to the struggle for power is that Bourdieu does not consider the possibility that the goals pursued by the dominant might be legitimate, so that the dominated are not misguided in also pursuing them.

Arguments can be conducted in order to find the truth (or at least to find out what seems to be the case, or 'for the best', beyond self-interest). Alternatively, they may be conducted in order to gain victory over others ('eristic' arguments), in which case any means will do. Attempts to persuade others of the superiority of certain values and practices generally face others who have not only different beliefs and dispositions, but interests dependent on the practices or situations which are being opposed, and who will therefore be inclined to treat the matter not as one of accepting the force of the better argument but of using any means to win. Any argument against sexism faces this problem, for example. Bourdieu would no doubt have had reservations about this description of social interaction as if it were an ongoing, grand, dispassionate public seminar, but ordinary conversations – including internal ones – occur about such matters and can involve this tension between instrumental and non-instrumental, moral-political criteria.

These tensions between interest and reason or ethics raise problems similar to those experienced by oppositional groups in far-left politics in the 1970s, regarding whether to emphasise seizing power or persuading people of the need for change. Too much emphasis on the former led to corruption, self-repression and loss of sense of purpose, while emphasis on the latter was naive in overestimating the impact of speaking truth to power; socialists, feminists, greens and so on may win arguments but still fail to make much impact against established interests.

The micro-politics of everyday life involve not only the pursuit of capital but the search for the good life. They are not necessarily merely differences between people with different interests and with self-serving rationalisations of those interests. In a modern plural society, there are many competing value systems, some of which may be internalised as 'divided habitus', and it need not take a political education to confront them. The elderly woman who was a full-time housewife, and invested heavily in that identity, is faced with the contrast with her employed daughter's lifestyle, which incorporates greater autonomy, more involvement in public life, a relative devaluation of domesticity, and different expectations of men. Mother and daughter might each wonder about the pros and cons of these ways of life, and how their own lives might have been different if they were of a different age. (Neither might think of feminism as such but both might reflect on issues that have very much to do with feminism.) Insofar as the mother comes to accept and value her daughter's way of life, she can hardly avoid devaluing her own lifelong investments. But unlike mere financial investments they concern her whole being in terms of her commitments and character. Similarly, in *The Weight of the World*, Bourdieu et al. provide an excellent analysis of the dilemmas of elderly farmers facing the combined loss of economic capital consequent upon the decline of small farming and the loss of recognition of their way of life, which is only too apparent in their sons' wish not to inherit their farms. While such crises certainly involve a devaluation of actors' capital, they are also about what constitutes a valuable life (Bourdieu et al., 1999, pp. 381–91 and 507–13).

Difference and conformity

Given that inequalities operate on several axes and involve several different kinds of capital, the struggles of the social field are not reducible to competition for the same goods but are also over how goods should be valued. Nevertheless, as we saw in chapter 4, the relations between different forms of capital are not random; there is a partial co-variation of different forms of capital, and the relations between them differentiate the social field. The struggles are characterised by a tension between striving for difference so as to be 'different-but-equal' by pursuing different goods from those valued by the dominant, and striving for advantage on terms set by the dominant, by pursuing the same goods that they value.[5] They are not merely about access to goods but about distinction from others; they involve struggles not only to be included but to exclude others. Many groups outside the most dominant attempt to do both, though in different proportions. Some are more conformist than others. The space of possibilities in this 'choice' is limited. If those in subordinate positions rely too heavily on competing on the terms of the dominant, both economically and symbolically, by striving for more of what the dominant currently monopolise and value, the odds are stacked against them. The dominant are likely to resist any potential devaluation of their capital by restricting access to it or by switching to more exclusive goods. The subordinate who compete in this way also forgo the small but significant opportunities for degrees of autonomy from the pressures to accept the terms set by the dominant. On the other hand, the risks of relying too much on striving for difference are that this may lead to self-exclusion from the goods enjoyed by the dominant (which are unlikely to be mostly illusory) and invite the dominant to disparage the 'alternative' goods and marginalise

---

[5] There are parallels here with the sameness/difference debate in feminism and with Elizabeth Gross's argument for feminists to pursue autonomy rather than equality, given the dangers of the latter being geared to male expectations (Gross, 1986).

their holders, hence making them different-and-*unequal*.[6] Furthermore, as Bourdieu argues, the attraction of the different-but-equal strategy for downwardly mobile members of the middle classes indicates its nature as a doomed attempt to resist classification (1984, p. 370).

This tension between inequality and difference is both cause and effect of the correlation in holdings of different forms of capital. It is unusual for a group to have large holdings of just a single kind of capital, not only because holdings of one form of capital tend to convert into another, but because, with the partial exception of economic capital, the risk of marginalisation limits strategies of relying heavily on a very limited range of capital or of valuing goods in an unconventional, counter-cultural manner. For these reasons the struggles of the social field are characterised by a tension between difference and conformity, in which difference offers the promise of escape from inequality but is threatened by conversion into indicators of inequality through marginalisation.

We can clarify the implications of the dual nature of competition by reference to two hypothetical extremes:

> Scenario A. Total agreement between different social groups on what constitutes goods – hence competition or struggle is purely over their distribution.
>
> Scenario B. Total disagreement between different social groups on what goods are.

Under scenario A one would expect inequalities to be keenly felt. Scenario B could have contrasting implications. Provided there is no expectation of a need for agreement about goods, so that different groups are happy to agree to disagree, there need be no direct competition between them for goods. Liberalism and markets encourage us to treat the definition of goods as a matter of mere preference rather than as binding for all as members of society. This need not be a situation in which all are 'equal but different', however; there may still be inequalities in wealth and power, in which case the dominant classes will have more chance of getting what they define as goods than the subordinate classes have to get what they define as *theirs*. Insofar as the different goods required the same resources, competition would remain.

While this may be so, the above discussion offers a purely instrumental and strategic view of the matter: it says nothing about the propriety of the struggles. Difference may be good, indifferent or bad; it all depends

---

[6] One ethical implication of this tendency for difference to be limited in societies based on inequality and domination is that a significant reduction of domination and inequality should allow an increase rather than a decrease in diversity, since there would be no dominant class to feel threatened by challenges to its norms. This reinforces Tawney's arguments against those who imagine that an egalitarian society would lack diversity.

on what the practices involved are like, and the same goes for conformity. We therefore need to return to the matter of the evaluation of goods, including valued practices and ways of life – which is itself central to the struggles of the social field. It is not merely an academic matter but one which is relevant to people's well-being, and therefore contributes to the moral significance of class.

People may regard others' conceptions of the good – be they conventional or unconventional – with indifference or with a mixture of alarm and contempt. The latter may derive from an unexamined fear of difference, in the shape of ills such as class contempt, racism or homophobia, but it may alternatively derive from a more examined (if not necessarily justifiable) fear of particular ideas, behaviours and ways of life which are felt to be dangerous and unethical for all. Some differences may be mutually inconsistent or exclusive. Ethical norms such as those regarding treatment of animals are inherently universal in their claims, rather than matters of individual or group preference. Many goods are common rather than individual, not only by virtue of those respects in which people are similar, but through the interdependence of all groups, at least through participation in the social division of labour. Such similarities and interdependences imply that the struggles of the social field will pull towards scenario A. To the extent that there is a common culture and to the extent that even members of different cultures are part of the same social division of labour, the tendency to pursue the same goods as others is bound to be strong.

Thus far we have outlined some of the key structures of the competitions or struggles of the social field from a largely strategic point of view. In effect, we have elaborated what is implicit in Bourdieu's analysis, but gone beyond it a little by beginning to counter his predominantly Hobbesian view, by recognising that actors do not merely strive for what is instrumentally advantageous, but for what they consider to be good. But there is still far to go in escaping the Hobbesian framework by exploring the normative content of the struggles of the social field. It is to this task that we now turn through an analysis of *goods*.

The nature of goods

We have used the term 'goods' in a very broad sense to include not only consumption goods but all those things which are valued, be they institutions, milieus, circumstances (such as good health and security), or valued practices, relationships and ways of living. If we are to understand the significance of social inequalities and the struggles of the social field we need to analyse their normative implications further. In this section I shall do this by exploring the nature of goods and valuations themselves, introducing some distinctions which illuminate their normative significance regarding class inequalities. In so doing, I hope to resolve certain ambiguities concealed by the use of the Bourdieuian concept of capital in explaining the struggles of the social field.

At the most general level, it is important to distinguish between goods as valued in themselves, and goods as valued for advantages which they bring their holders vis-à-vis others.[7] Examples of the former are being well nourished and free from illness or belonging to a supportive community. In other cases – as most obviously illustrated by status symbols such as Rolex watches – goods are valued mainly for the advantages over others that they bring or symbolise. Many things can be valued for both. A university degree may be valued both for the intrinsic satisfaction of the study involved in obtaining it and for the competitive advantages it gives one in the labour market. A house in a pleasant neighbourhood may be valued both in itself and for the status it implies. From both egalitarian and sociological points of view, it would be useful to know how these types of goods and valuations vary across the social field.

In a Bourdieuian approach, a focus on the habitus tends to suggest goods of the first kind, which people feel comfortable or uncomfortable with, according to their habitus. While there is some truth in this, as I argued in chapter 2, it is reductionist, for it ignores the influence of discourses which transcend particular habituses and the possibility of actors resisting and thinking beyond their own particular situation. A focus on capitals and the struggles of the social field suggests mainly the second kind of instrumental and strategic valuation of goods that are essentially positional. Where capital takes an embodied form, as is the case with some kinds of cultural capital, we could, like Bourdieu, fuse these two aspects together, but it is important to distinguish the two kinds of valuation and goods.

Distinctions of this kind are far from merely academic; they identify differences that are crucial for people's well-being, and for the character and political culture of their society. For example, as we see all too clearly in education, neoliberal trends towards the introduction of competition for resources amongst both individuals and institutions produces a pressure to emphasise the pursuit of educational goods for the advantages they bring vis-à-vis others rather than for their own sake. In the process, educational goods, like research and teaching, become a means to the end of earning money and prestige rather than an end in themselves, and they may suffer as a result.

---

[7] I am indebted to John Baker for suggesting this way of framing the discussion.

I shall attempt to justify these claims by introducing and exploring two more specific versions of this distinction, the first between use-value and exchange-value, the second between internal and external goods. The former distinction concerns normative judgements that are mainly of the functional value of objects and practices; the latter concerns the ways in which investment in practices and relationships bring different kinds of satisfactions, skills and achievements. I shall then sketch out the kinds of inequalities in the distribution of the goods identified in these distinctions and draw out their implications for the phenomenon of relative deprivation.

Use-value and exchange-value

Use-value and exchange-value involve two radically different kinds of valuation. We assess use-values qualitatively and according to different, often incommensurable, standards – be they qualities of films, food, houses or banking services. Hence disagreements over their valuation refer to and sometimes dispute different criteria for different use-values (Anderson, 1993). These qualities have particular associations or meanings for users, or in more recent terms, following Baudrillard, 'sign-value', though there is nothing new about this.[8] Valuation invokes and evokes meanings of the thing valued for the valuer, and since meanings are always social, valuations have a social dimension (Anderson, 1993), indeed the associations are part of what we value about the objects.[9] In contrast, exchange-value is quantitative: in determining how much one thing will exchange for another we commensurate the incommensurable and compare them on a single scale regardless of qualitative differences in the objects exchanged. Thus while the use-values of different kinds of activity – such as painting and engineering – are incommensurable, the exchange-values of the corresponding forms of capital – of artists and engineers – are effectively treated as commensurable.

Aristotle's related distinction between production for use and for money-making (in which a means to the economic end of consumption – money – becomes the end of economic activity) was described by Polanyi

---

[8] Although, after Baudrillard, sign-value is often seen as superseding use-value, this is implausible, for what commodities signify is generally not unrelated to their use-value. Commodities can have both use-value and sign-value, and of course it remains the case that they would soon cease to be produced if they didn't yield exchange-value.

[9] These associations may be strongly attached to the character of the object and subject, such as that between a sofa and relaxation, while others may seem arbitrarily related, such as the association between a certain brand of jeans and a particular youth sub-culture. Although as Baudrillard argued in his discussions of 'sign-value' the latter situation may be becoming more common, this can be acknowledged without imagining that use-value is no longer important, or that it is always detached from sign-value.

as 'probably the most prophetic pointer ever made in the history of the social sciences' (Polanyi, 1944 [1957], p. 53; see also Booth, 1993). It anticipated the shift later summarised in Marx's notation as a move from C-M-C (the sale of commodities for money in order to buy commodities) to M-C-M' (the advancement of money capital to produce commodities for sale in order to make a profit) (Marx, 1867:1976). With the rise of capitalism, what was merely an incidental aberration or vice in Aristotle's time – the direction of economic activity towards the accumulation of money – becomes an imperative (Booth, 1993). Marx used the use-value/exchange-value distinction to distinguish capital from mere machines, materials or buildings. The latter have use-value, but only become capital when they are acquired in order to command the labour of others and to earn exchange-value.[10] If we apply this to Bourdieu's non-economic forms of capital, we can see that, in effect, it is the exchange-value or symbolic profits that they bring which are primary.

It is hardly surprising that in a capitalist society, not only the production of goods but their use should come to function as a means to the acquisition of an abstract, convertible form of social power – though not necessarily intentionally. Further, as Bourdieu argues, competition for exchange-value and its symbolic equivalents extends to phenomena such as culture, education and social relations. Apparently disinterested actions such as socialising, expressing tastes, or learning can affect individuals' social, cultural and educational capital. They can all function as forms of capital and bring their possessors various forms of advantage. They have exchange-value, though the rates of exchange between the various forms of capital are always contested through the struggles of the social field. They can yield profits, and generate soft forms of domination. Thus cultural capital can be signalled not only by formal representations such as an arts degree, but by subtle indications of social location – a certain bearing and social ease, an assured, relaxed command of appropriate cultural goods – which bring the holder advantages, whether intended or not. Actors can enhance their social capital by developing networks of contacts that are useful both practically and in terms of reputation. They may be able to transform these forms of capital into others, including economic capital. Note that actors do not necessarily intend to defend or

---

[10] Ironically, Bourdieu does offer an explicitly Marxist definition of his forms of capital as 'accumulated labour (in its materialized, or its "incorporated", embodied form), which when appropriated on a private, i.e. exclusive, basis by agents or groups of agents, enables them to appropriate social energy in the form of reified or living labour' (1984, p. 241). However, he fails to take note of Marx's connection to the use-value/exchange-value distinction.

augment the exchange-value of their capital, but this symbolic valuation happens anyway and structures the competitions of the social field. Bourdieu treats the pursuit of capital as being primarily about making profit, albeit usually in non-pecuniary form ('symbolic profits'), rather than for the use-values involved in the capital.

While the insights produced by Bourdieu's use of the concept of capital are considerable, it shares with capitalist culture itself a tendency to prioritise exchange-value and to overlook how it differs from use-value. However, the difference is crucial, both for explaining the nature and structure of the inequalities and struggles of the social field, and in relation to their normative significance for both actors and observers. We should, for example, insist on the difference between 'investments' – say in education – made for their own sake or use-value (for example, learning German) and investments made in order to enhance the holder's social standing and yield economic or symbolic profit (e.g., educational qualifications). Of course, the use-value of education includes an instrumental dimension – enabling one to communicate with people who speak a different language, or whatever – as well as a possible intrinsic interest, but this is different from instrumentalisation in order to gain social advantage vis-à-vis others. In relation to all Bourdieu's forms of capital – economic, cultural, educational, linguistic, social – the distinction between them and the practices or goods to which they relate is vital for both an explanation and a critique. Getting an education, enjoying music, making friends may contingently give one educational, cultural and social capital, but to treat the former as the same as the latter – even where the latter arise unintentionally from the former – is a disastrous mistake.

A further important difference between capital and the goods or activities to which it relates is that capital is a positional good, that is, one whose value is depleted the greater the number of people who come to have it (O'Neill, 1999), whereas the same is not necessarily true of the activities to which capital relates.[11] Thus, educational qualifications – as educational *capital* – are devalued as more people come to have them, though the use-value of their education is *not necessarily* devalued too. A particular maths lesson has a certain quality no matter how many other maths lessons of the same kind are given. Conversely, scarcity may enhance exchange-value but it does not give something greater use-value unless it is strictly a positional good. The fallacy is evident in the phenomenon of 'limited editions'. Conversely, the assumption evident in the double meaning of the term 'common', that whatever is widely available and

---

[11] Some use-values are positional too. As road congestion becomes serious, the use-value of cars declines with the number of people using them.

hence of limited exchange-value must be inferior, is equally fallacious, yet, as Bourdieu shows, it is a key illusion of the struggles of the social field.

While there is no necessary relation between the exchange-value of something and its use-value, from a normative point of view we might expect them at least to correlate positively, so that high exchange-value indicates high use-value. I may buy a BMW to show I have arrived, but it won't function as an object of envy unless others can be convinced that it is worthy of envy. If BMWs were unreliable and awful to drive they would not bring their owners any distinction. In other words, BMWs wouldn't have the exchange-value they have – in the sense of either price *or* status – if they didn't also have a high use-value. Without such a connection the exchange-value or prestige of goods is threatened by their lack of foundation and, like the emperor's new clothes, is vulnerable to ridicule. Although Bourdieu demonstrates how particular characteristics of objects or practices resonate with a particular kind of habitus so that people of that type tend to want and feel comfortable with them, he excludes evaluations of quality or use-value from his explanation of preferences and actions and symbolic domination. This abstraction from the question of whether particular objects and practices are good or bad is problematic. It is not simply that what the poor value fits with their habitus and what the rich value fits with theirs. *Generally*, things with more exchange-value tend to have more use-value, and in many cases, as we discussed through the thought-experiment of scenario A (see above, p. 103), those in different parts of the social field *agree* on the nature of goods but have differential access to them. The poor do not live in poor housing because it fits with their habitus but because they cannot afford better, and the rich do not live in spacious, well-heated housing simply because it fits with their habitus, but because its use-value is superior and its exchange-value is no object. Nor is the preference of the rich for such houses simply a matter of displaying advantage or symbolic profit, for, as the BMW example shows, the latter would not be sustainable if the use-value of the housing was poor. The poor are not fools, duped by symbolic domination through dominant discourses, for envying them. Of course it is possible that the status of poor quality goods may be 'talked up' or gain added exchange-value by their association with a dominant group; and sometimes, as Bourdieu emphasises, it is possible for a lack of apparent utility to become stakes in these struggles and indeed for this to be a marker of distinction – superfluity signifying superiority, the absence of the pressure of necessity. In such cases, rival and subordinate groups may attempt to deflate others' capital by exposing the spurious nature of their investments' assumed quality, showing that their exchange-value bears no relation to their use-value. Therefore we cannot explain how the struggles of the social field work out without acknowledging the role of judgements of intrinsic quality or use-value. Struggles over distinction are also contestations of the intrinsic worth of objects and practices, and the fact that that worth is contested does not make it simply arbitrary. The *contestation* of use-value differs in kind from that of exchange-value: whereas the prime consideration in the latter contest is instrumental – whatever will fetch the best 'price' – arguments about the use-value of the goods refer to the qualities of the goods themselves, such as the particular ideas and skills taught in a degree course: if it's a good course in these terms, then it is so *regardless* of its exchange-value in the educational and job markets.

That the relation between the use-value of an activity and the exchange-value of the corresponding form of capital is contingent is of vital importance. While we may tend to assume that exchange-value is or should be a reasonable measure of different use-values, exchange-value can also vary independently of use-value – not surprisingly in view of the interests at stake. There is, for example, no necessary connection between the splendour and superfluity of an ivy-clad university college and the quality of the education that goes on within it. The claimed or assumed qualities used to defend the value of the educational capital may even be bogus, as in the case of the Oxbridge MA. (Students who have an Oxbridge BA can get an MA just by waiting a certain number of years and paying a fee – that some people make excuses for this is a reflection of the cultural privilege enjoyed by Oxbridge.) The exchange-value of an Oxbridge MA as educational capital is undeserved for it lacks any corresponding process of education. Its market value depends on the success of the illusion that Oxbridge MA students have done something more than a BA, and on the associated exchange-value (prestige) of the symbolic capital of Oxbridge, which serves as collateral, so to speak.[12] If we failed to note the illusory character of the recognition we would mis-describe the situation. In other words, in failing to be critical we would fail to explain.

To treat exchange-value as a substitute for use-value is to imply that recognition is purely a subjective matter having no justification in what those who are recognised do (the 'boo-hooray theory of value'); the famous can only be famous for being famous, not for doing anything worthy of fame, and the good is whatever happens to be praised. In Oscar Wilde's words, it amounts to knowing the price of everything and the value of nothing. In terms of use-value we try to evaluate things in terms

---

[12] That many people know that it is purely tokenistic does not excuse it. Many do not and are fooled by it. Those who excuse it in this way would presumably object to other universities doing the same thing.

of their qualities, whereas the exchange-value of capital can be influenced by irrelevant associations. Bourdieu's reluctance to acknowledge disinterested judgement restricts him to exchange-value, but his apparent critical intentions imply the need for references to use or intrinsic value. In refusing this, he weakens his own critique. Moreover, in view of Bourdieu's enthusiasm for market economy concepts, we might note how this is complicit with the tendency, noted by Rousseau, Smith and Marx, for identity in commercial society to become a matter of appearance which is divorced from the qualities a person actually has, a complicity shared by postmodernism (O'Neill, 1999).

A *critical* analysis of material inequality and symbolic domination cannot evade judgements of the use-value or intrinsic quality of the goods associated with the various kinds of capital, such as the quality or use-value of learning in educational capital. It has to distinguish between deserved and undeserved recognition or misrecognition. Of course, any attempt to make such a distinction is likely to invite suspicion that one is trying to establish an authoritative, indeed authoritarian, basis for judgement, an absolute set of values. However, I fully accept that judgements of (use-)value are contestable. But this does not mean either that all claims to recognition are of equal merit, or disqualified by being associated with particular social positions, or that there must always be some ulterior motive behind the judgements and contestations such that critical distinctions can never be rationally justified. A 'critical theory' that evades normative judgements is a contradiction.

Internal and external goods

While adding the distinction between use-value and exchange-value to Bourdieu's economic metaphors of capital and symbolic profit is useful, we can further illuminate the struggles of the social field and the normative significance of inequalities for actors by reference to a broader but related distinction between *internal and external goods*. Alasdair MacIntyre introduces this distinction in his critique of modernity (MacIntyre, 1981, pp. 187ff.).[13] While MacIntyre does not explore the sociological implications of the distinction, his ideas can benefit from such an exploration (McMylor, 1994).[14]

Internal goods are those that are internal to a practice in which one takes part, such as the specific achievements or 'excellences' and satisfactions of doing complex skilled work and other activities well, whether

---

[13] Something similar is also implicit in Adam Smith's distinction between praiseworthy acts and praise, which we will encounter later (Smith, 1759:1984).

[14] For commentaries on the implications of the concept for commodification and the arts, see Keat, 2000.

mental or manual. They may be found in activities such as sports, music and other arts, academic study, cooking, which allow learning and the development of complex skills. While I may achieve and enjoy internal goods through these activities, they may also bring me external goods of approbation, fame, prestige and money. Whereas the internal goods such as those of making music, intellectual work, friendship or cooking, etc., are detailed and specific to each, the external goods which one might achieve through them are more indifferent to their character, particularly in the case of money.

MacIntyre uses a specialised definition of practices (hereafter practices*), defining them as social activities which are governed by their own standards of excellence and conducted and organised in such a way that these – rather than external goods of money and status – are of prime concern to participants (Keat, 2000). The practitioners themselves take the lead in defining their internal goods, though this does not rule out internal contestation of their definition and identification, indeed contestation may be intrinsic to the vigour of the practice*. The disputes are themselves constrained by shared acceptance of certain internal norms of the practice*, and if this common ground is lost, the practice* splits or dies. The internal evaluation of goods need not exclude possible influence from those who are outside the practice* yet affected by it. Where practices* constitute activities within a wider division of labour rather than a self-sufficient activity, considerations of service and accountability to outsiders are likely to figure in the definitions of internal goods, though of course there is usually scope for tensions between producers' and users' interests here. Thus, one might expect doctors to take account of patients' views in defining the internal goods of the practice* of medicine.

In some cases the pursuit of internal and external goods may be compatible, for example, as in making music or consuming luxury goods; in others they may be mutually exclusive – trying to befriend someone as a way of making money is likely to undermine the friendship. While some practices* may involve competitive behaviour, success may enrich and extend the practice's internal goods in ways that benefit others. For example, the contributions of Bourdieu to the practice* of social science have enriched the internal goods from which others can benefit. However, as with exchange-value, competition for external goods is a zero-sum or positional affair, in that it is impossible for all to benefit simultaneously; for example, it would simply not make sense to call all academics 'leading academics'.

MacIntyre tends to choose 'elevated' examples of practices*, such as architecture and chess, and ones which involve projects and easily recognisable achievements, thus reproducing philosophy's usual somewhat

middle class and masculine model of the individual who is primarily concerned with pursuing his 'projects' and is relatively free to do so. In using
the concept of practices* I want henceforth both to broaden its scope to
include less socially elevated and less traditionally masculine ones, and
to extend the category of internal goods to include those internal to relationships, such as friendship or parenting.

This distinction partially overlaps with that between use-value and
exchange-value, and they share certain properties and normative implications, but the differences between the two distinctions are several.
First, whereas the use-value/exchange-value couple is characteristic of
commodities, internal and external goods may also be unrelated to
commodities; indeed, they may be related to things that can't be commodified, such as friendships. Secondly, internal goods are about not so
much what one might get from things (such as the mobility we derive from
a car) as the skills and excellences we develop through participating in a
regular and committed way in activities. Although their achievement is
generally satisfying, 'internal goods' refer primarily to the achievements
or excellences themselves. Thirdly, one might sometimes want to argue
that the use-value of something includes its possibilities not only for providing access to internal goods, but for promoting external goods too,
as in the case of a prestigious car, in which case use-value would cross-
cut the internal/external goods distinction. Fourthly, while internal goods
may enable people to earn external goods, including money, they differ
from most use-values in that they cannot generally be alienated through
exchange. In some respects, then, the concepts of internal and external
goods are broader than those of use-value and exchange-value insofar as
they refer to activities, skills, achievements, relationships and recognition,
and are not associated only with economic goods. On the other hand, in
other respects, being simpler, the use-value/exchange-value distinction
is the broader insofar as it goes beyond practices* and can be applied
to simpler activities such as market exchange and the use of mundane
goods. In the light of these differences I shall sometimes, according to
context, use the concept of internal and external goods in preference to
those of use-value and exchange-value, though there are some contexts
in which both apply.

Although they are not always incompatible, the normative implications
of the pursuit of internal and external goods are very different. Like Adam
Smith, MacIntyre acknowledges that external goods are genuinely goods
that 'no-one can despise . . . without a certain hypocrisy' (1981, p. 196),[15]

---

[15] As Lichtenberg (1998) also notes, we would generally regard anyone who was completely
indifferent to what others thought of them as psychologically suspect.

but again, like Smith, he argues that they are properly tied to and parasitic upon internal goods (see also O'Neill, 1999). When we assess a research project in terms of its internal goods, we focus on things like the quality of its methodology, its use of theory and so on. In assessing it in terms of external goods we ask how big the grant was, how much publicity it has had, and so on. We expect the latter to be proportionate to the internal goods; a sloppily designed, under-theorised bit of data-bashing should not be rewarded with praise or money, while one that is carefully designed and theorised, etc., should.[16] Smith's point was that the internal goods (or 'praiseworthy acts') would be good even if no-one happened to praise them (Smith, 1759:1984). When a teacher manages to teach a child to read both have achieved internal goods regardless of whether either gets any praise for it, though of course one hopes that they would be praised. In these respects, the normative implications of internal and external goods parallel those of use-value and exchange-value. We are social beings and we need the recognition of others: the question is what the recognition is for, or, to put it provocatively, whether there is any problem with having unearned income or status unrelated to any genuine internal goods.[17] The fear of many commentators was that the rise of capitalism and a highly commodified culture would lead to the prioritising of external goods over internal goods.

It also matters from whom the recognition or external approbation comes: praise which comes from those who themselves excel in the practice* is valued more highly than praise from those who are novices or ignorant of it (O'Neill, 1999). We want to know whether what we have done is 'really' special or whether we are just being flattered or patronised: giving a gold medal to someone who has achieved little, on the basis of ignorance of the practice* in question, devalues the award. To win external goods without matching internal goods would be a hollow victory, enabling one to bathe in others' disingenuous, or sincere but misplaced, praise, knowing that one had done nothing to deserve it, and in addition lacking the satisfaction of having achieved internal goods. This means again that internal goods are seen as more fundamental than external goods. We want the latter, but we also want to deserve them.

---

[16] Some may want to protest that descriptions such as 'carefully designed' are themselves just external descriptions, but this misses the point, for of course all descriptions are in a sense 'external'; the point is that the goods in question (to do with learning) are internal to the practice of research, whereas those of fame are not: although the latter may be pleasing, research can be done without it.

[17] The micro-politics of the social field often involves challenges to the external goods associated with practices* by attacking the qualities of their internal goods. Thus, feminism challenges the qualities or internal goods claimed for masculinity and femininity.

This simple but important point about the expertise of the valuer or provider of recognition of achievement has been widely overlooked in the social theory of recognition. Given the localisation of particular practices* in the social field and their association with particular habituses, those who are qualified to pass judgement on others often come from similar social groups. The mutual recognition which goes with shared involvement in such localised practices* helps create solidarity within class and gender cultures. In other cases, where the experts occupy a more socially elevated position, their judgements are likely to have overtones of condescension. Occasionally, the experts may occupy a lowly position: in the case of football, which has a predominantly working class location and knowledge-base, the relative ignorance of more middle class supporters is a common source of amusement and derision among more traditional supporters. However, notwithstanding these sociological aspects, from the point of view of recognition of achievements it is the expertise rather than the social position of the valuer that matters.

A partial exception to the dependence of external on internal goods is the external good of money. Its acquisition does not even require any kind of achievement or excellence, or approbation, even though these sometimes do prompt payments or gifts of money. In capitalist economies, the distribution of gains and losses made by people in markets has much to do with luck in relation to patterns of scarcity and demand rather than merit and contribution. Secondly, money is also special because it is so colourless, liquid or transferable, so that even if we receive money as a reward or payment for some praiseworthy service, it carries no trace of what it was honouring. This is why competitions and awards usually don't award just money but trophies which cannot be cashed in, and whose specificity and non-transferability unambiguously mark the particular achievements for which they were awarded. Anybody can get money, only very special people can win a Nobel prize or an Olympic medal.[18]

Given the growth in importance of money and the orientation of capitalism to making money rather than producing use-values (the latter being only a means to the former), it is not surprising that many commentators feared that external goods would become valued regardless of internal goods, and the management of appearances and impressions would become more important than doing worthwhile things. Some authors, like Smith and Veblen, may have been overly pessimistic in assuming that

---

[18] 'In the realm of ends everything has either a *price* or a *dignity*. Whatever has a price can be replaced by something else as its equivalent; on the other hand, whatever is above all price, and therefore admits of no equivalence, has a dignity.' (I. Kant, *Groundwork of the Metaphysics of Morals*, quoted in Lewis White Beck (ed.), *Kant Selections* (New York: Macmillan, 1988), p. 277.)

consumption would be driven overwhelmingly by the desire to win envy, prestige and status. Much consumption is driven by the desire to facilitate access to internal goods: the would-be cook buys cooking equipment that will enable a wider range of dishes to be made; the new parent invests in toys that will involve the child and enrich her experience (Sayer, 2003).

In addition to internal goods it is common for practices in MacIntyre's sense to have certain hazards, 'necessary evils' or other negative features. Not all negative features may be avoidable. Work that is satisfying may also involve health hazards. Parenting famously involves not only internal goods but tantrums and loss of autonomy. Often the quality of internal goods relative to such negative features depends on how much of a particular activity an individual does. As the example of caring shows, the desirable features become increasingly offset by negative features of self-abnegation and loss of autonomy for the carer, the more caring he or she has to do (Sevenhuijsen, 1998). In some cases, unless activities are shared, their internal goods may be negated. Given the typically gendered pattern of activities and relationships in practices*, their distribution is one of the concerns of critiques of gender orders.

Practices* may be evaluated either from within or in comparison with others in terms of their contribution to social life. While it is customary to give examples of practices* that are likely to win wide approval, it is possible for contentious and repugnant activities to meet the formal criteria of practices* as MacIntyre defines them.[19] (An extreme example is paedophilia; its immorality and injustice and the inadequacy of practitioners' justifications of it are easy to identify.) Hence it is essential to note that use of the term 'internal goods' does not imply endorsement of any particular claims about the value of substantive instances of such goods. Further, in comparing different practices*, externality effects, and how individuals and societies balance their priorities, come into play. Even where a particular practice* is widely valued, there may still be problems of how it fits into both individual lives and social life more broadly. Individuals' attitudes to practices* may be affected not only by evaluations of their internal goods but in terms of the opportunity costs of getting involved in them, including taking into account their responsibilities to others. They may consider what they are entitled to relative to others or egotistically maximise their own self-interest regardless. Though mundane, these are important issues of personal politics which can impact on individual and social well-being. As Aristotle argued, the pursuit of the good life involves not only maximising a particular kind of internal good or the overall quantity of internal goods but attempting to find a

---

[19] My thanks to Nick Crossley for pointing this out.

satisfactory balance between different kinds of practices* and other activities and relationships. Failures to find such a balance are evident in recent concerns about workaholism and time-poverty, and about the tendency of many social policies to aim at a male breadwinner norm. It is not only inequalities in access to particular goods – and in burdens of necessary evils – that matter, but inequalities among individuals and social groups in the possibility of achieving balance. In this context, policies for limiting excessive working hours are crucial.

Bourdieu only occasionally distinguishes the two kinds of goods in his definitions of capital, although it is sometimes implicit in his detailed analyses of particular goods (for example, in discussing educational capital he occasionally distinguishes the competences acquired through education from the external rewards which contingently attach to them (e.g., 1984, p. 88)). One of the most important features of the struggles of the social field is that they are not just for dominance or about relative position in the status hierarchies, but about the struggle by people to live as they want to. Inequality and domination rest on control of access to internal as well as external goods, for without the former, not only would symbolic domination be vulnerable, but there would be little point in competing and struggling. Or, to put it in Weberian terms, there would be little point in struggles of social groups to achieve closure, if it didn't give them privileged access to some internal goods and use-values. Even where it is primarily driven by the pursuit of the external good of money, this in turn is primarily a means for providing access to use-values and internal goods, some of which are likely to be ends in themselves.

Having examined how internal and external goods are differently valued, we can now turn to how they are distributed across the social field.

Inequalities and the distribution of internal and external goods

Involvement in practices* tends to be strongly differentiated by class, gender, race, age, and other social divisions. The sociological dimensions of practices* are important precisely because of their significance to actors as a source of internal and external goods. While simple inequalities in resources are important, inequalities matter to people most in terms of their impact on the lives that they seek to live and the things, relationships and practices* which they value. They affect what Amartya Sen calls their 'capabilities' to engage in ways of life they have reason to value (Sen, 1992; 1999). Hence the significance of use-value and internal goods. Income and wealth inequalities are only a rough guide to inequalities in access to internal goods, for while many do require some expenditure, others depend more on time and relationships: to some extent, people create them through their own efforts. In this respect, there is something in the folk wisdom that 'the more you put in the more you get out' (in terms of *both* internal and external goods). However, there are likely to be major inequalities in access to the activities and institutions in which this relationship works. Their distribution is likely to correlate with that of cultural, social and educational capital.

Some kinds of work, paid or unpaid, can be a source of both internal goods and external recognition, but many offer neither and may be stultifying rather than satisfying. Not every kind of work can be made into a practice* and provide satisfaction, though this, of course, does not legitimise the confinement of some to boring work and others to interesting work. It is noteworthy that research suggests that these inequalities affect individuals' cognitive capacities themselves: the capacities of people doing interesting work tend to grow while those in boring work decline. This means that the effects of the quality of work carry over into individuals' capacities in leisure time too, thereby further widening inequalities in terms of capacity for enjoyment of internal goods (Murphy, 1993). In other words, this highlights the importance of the *qualitative* division of labour, that is, the distribution of different kinds of work (both paid and unpaid) and the access to internal goods (if any) which they afford, and which in turn tend to elicit the external goods of recognition. Some authors have argued that, with the exception of the poor, for whom the priority is of course more money, differences in the quality of work have a bigger impact on individual happiness and well-being than differences in income. In other words, above a certain level, it is internal goods which make the most difference to our well-being. As Robert Lane has shown in his major review of empirical research on markets, increased wealth is only correlated with increased happiness for roughly the poorest fifth of the population of rich countries (a conclusion which Smith conjectured in *The Wealth of Nations* (Smith, 1776:1976)) (Lane, 1991, 1998; see also Murphy, 1993).

The tastes, preferences and valuations of particular goods or practices* by different groups are not a result of mere propaganda, dominant discourses or historical accident, but are related to their respective habituses, which predispose them to some practices* and not others, as Bourdieu showed. The differentiation of practices* by class and gender is both a major cause and effect of social inequalities. The distribution of internal goods across the social field therefore varies qualitatively as well as quantitatively. However, while there are certainly differences in what is valued, the struggles of the social field are intense precisely because there is a great deal of overlap or commonality in the evaluation of goods and practices* which (a) matter a great deal for people's well-being, whatever their class or gender, and (b) are nevertheless very unequally distributed. Trying to pass off the effects of these inequalities as mere differences in lifestyles – as if they were freely chosen and as if they were differences to be celebrated – is one of the most transparently disingenuous rhetorical strategies of conservatism.

At the same time, the empirical results reported in *Distinction* show that the correspondence between particular practices* and certain parts of the social field is only approximate (Bourdieu, 1984). This is to be expected. Actors may be able to change their habitus by immersion in a new context. They may sometimes want to transgress the social boundaries associated with a particular practice*. It is not unknown for a working class teenager to want to become a doctor despite the social distance that she would have to overcome. Bourdieu would have presumably said that this was not at all inconsistent with her position but entirely predictable. The phenomenon of children from poor families having 'unrealistic' ambitions might be interpreted as consistent with their social location which, unlike that of middle class children, lays out no clear career paths before them, and therefore prompts either resignation to limited prospects or 'unrealistic' aspirations. However, unrealistic or not, the teenager might still, despite all the social barriers, be attracted to the internal goods of the practices* to which she aspires, and she might have some sense of what these goods might be, regardless of whether she underestimates the barriers of class (and gender) or recognises them but wants to challenge them. As usual, sociologically-reductionist explanations of such behaviour which fail to allow the possibility that the disadvantaged might understand and want to challenge their disadvantage are likely to be demeaning and lead us uncomfortably close to elitist mockery. Even if, as is likely, she fails to get access to the practice*, the desire to do so is significant for it would suggest that actors' own evaluations of practices* and their internal goods are not completely sociologically-reductionist. Precisely because such practices* involve goods which can provide fulfilment, social usefulness and moral purpose, some individuals from unlikely backgrounds are likely to seek them. This in turn provides the basis for some of the micro-political struggles of the social field. Actors' evaluations of practices* normally located in other parts of the social field from their own are not necessarily negative; if they were, the dominance of those who monopolise them would be weakened, as we saw earlier.

Three important implications follow from this discussion of the distribution of internal and external goods. First, given the asymmetric relation between internal and external goods (the latter being properly parasitic upon the former, but not vice versa) and their different normative implications, the distribution of internal goods can be said to be more important than that of external goods.

Secondly, since the achievement of internal goods is only partly dependent on income and other external goods, many who do not have much economic and other kinds of capital but who have enough income and time to enjoy some internal goods may be content, and perhaps justifiably so. One of the problems of Bourdieu's reduction of internal goods and use-values to their exchange-value in the form of capitals is not only that it produces a picture which is thoroughly bleak in missing the pleasures and sources of fulfilment in working class culture, but that in doing so it fails to acknowledge one of the reasons why resistance to inequality is not greater. As Angela McRobbie notes in her review of *The Weight of the World*, there has been extensive research in cultural studies on such matters (McRobbie, 2002), and they can be acknowledged without lapsing into a complacent excusal of inequality or a patronising idealisation of working class culture.

Thirdly, it has implications for the critique of consumption in capitalism as being based on vanity and status-seeking, as noted first by authors like Smith and Hume and later in more developed form by Veblen, for much consumption is oriented to use-values and to practices* which it supports and which are pursued primarily for their own sake. To be sure, it is in the interest of producers and sellers to treat exchange-value as a good measure of use-value, and in the interest of the vain to pretend that their personal value is reflected in what they own and consume, as early commentators such as Smith and Rousseau feared. Yet the struggles of the social field over consumption are not just about exchange-value, or the rate of exchange of different types of capital. Even insofar as there is a status-seeking aspect to consumption, as Judith Lichtenberg (1998) has pointed out, consuming because others consume may not necessarily be driven by a desire to demonstrate superiority over them but rather to avoid shame and achieve equality with them. What looks like status rivalry from Veblen's position looks different in terms of the theory of relative deprivation.[20]

The valuation of goods and practices* is generally made in relation to particular reference groups who either have or lack them: lacking something the other members of one's reference group lack is less troubling than lacking something which they have (Runciman, 1966). *Which* others are implicitly or explicitly involved in our valuations is likely to vary with the specificity of the goods in question. Some are pervasive, common

[20] In practice, as style fascism implies, things may be more ambiguous in that being equal to peers may be a way of suggesting superiority relative to non-peers.

to many cultures, others specific to particular sub-cultures or practices*. There is thus a kind of sociology and social geography of reference groups in relation to the valuation of goods. By changing our horizons and reference groups we change our feelings of relative deprivation or advantage. The excluded may feel torn between envying the better off and associating with others with whom they have more in common to avoid feeling a sense of lack. The struggles of the social field involve both. Although we have multiple, overlapping reference groups in modernity, we have varying degrees of freedom to choose them – this being a source of inequality in itself.

As Bourdieu emphasises, it is common for those who are refused certain goods to refuse what they are refused. What he fails to note is that they not only invite the scorn of the dominant in so doing, they also *confirm their refusal of internal goods which are valuable regardless of whether the dominant happen to value them.* The distributional inequality is more important than the symbolic domination accompanying it. The inequality means that the subordinated objectively lack the basis for esteem. Any esteem that they are given in the face of this inequality therefore either lacks foundation or has to be qualified by reference to social and economic handicaps. Either way, it is bound to seem patronising.

To say that an individual group objectively lacks the basis for esteem may seem curiously judgemental and out-of-keeping with the relativist and idealist tenor of popular culture and some types of sociology, which tend to see all judgement one-sidedly as a reflection of the social position of the judge and as having nothing to do with the qualities of what they are judging. Faced with the choice of criticising the class-generated inequalities in the distribution of internal goods, which imply unequal distribution of external goods, it is as if many have decided that it is preferable to give equal esteem rather than face up to the fact that inequalities in access to internal goods make this spurious. It is as if noting class disadvantage and advantage was itself a kind of snobbery rather than a recognition of the immorality of class inequality. (This is a familiar jibe directed at egalitarians by the Right.) It is as if, in some spheres, we prefer to give a spurious kind of equal recognition to all rather than develop a fairer system of distribution which would actually enable people to achieve the internal goods that warrant such equal recognition. Meanwhile in other spheres, where meritocratic ideals hold, we seek ever finer ways of ranking people according to performance, again without reference to their unequal access to resources for participating in such competitions. Although the ideologies of spurious equality of esteem and meritocracy seem to be utterly opposed, both share a reluctance to face up to inequalities in access to internal goods and the resources needed to support them.

The posh and the good

The social field is characterised not only by an unequal distribution of commodities and internal and external goods, but by certain biases in the valuation of use-values, practices*, internal goods, and the people associated with them, according to their social location. These involve over-valuing anything associated with the dominant and under-valuing whatever is associated with the subordinate, though sometimes the bias may be inverted. This applies both to class and to gender, as well as other divisions such as those of age and ethnicity. Thus manual skills and work gendered as feminine are under-valued relative to mental skills and 'men's work'. The effects of this are double-edged: on the one hand, it would seem to imply a tendency to exaggerate the inequalities in the value of what different groups are able to do, since if we realise this we can see that things are not as bad as they seem, for the inequalities in the distribution of use-values and internal goods are not as extreme as that of external goods reflecting recognition; on the other hand, given that recognition matters to people, it can be seen as worsening the effects of inequalities in the distribution of use-values and internal goods by adding to them the effects of misrecognition.

As regards class, we can illuminate the effects of this tendency by examining the meaning of the word 'posh'.[21] Posh is a marker of high class position, be it in the form of a posh accent, posh car, posh wedding, or whatever. It is vital to understand that the posh only contingently corresponds to the good but its use often conceals this through a double slippage of meaning, first from associations of upper/middle classness to ones of quality and worth, and secondly from quality and worth back to their owners, so that the posh is not only equated with superior goods but with people who are in some way supposedly superior. Both might be termed 'aura effects'. The first slippage is not surprising given that expensive versions of particular commodities are generally better than cheap ones, and only affordable by the affluent. The second slippage, from the superior quality of goods to the supposed superiority of their owners, is central to capitalist consumer culture and relentlessly exploited by advertising.[22] Even though many may be sceptical about it, it is still tempting to

---

[21] The word supposedly derives from the days of steamer ships from Britain to India when the upper classes would select cabins on the Port Out and Starboard Home in order to be in the shade. 'Classy' is an interesting synonym.

[22] To refuse such slides by, in effect, denying (correctly) that the posh is necessarily good still leaves the class hierarchy intact, merely challenging the support it gets from symbolic domination. The rich might lose some of their respect but they would keep their disproportionate wealth. Once again, where class is concerned, distribution is only secondarily influenced by recognition.

indulge in the illusion, and peer pressure may push one to do so. While it was sharply criticised by Smith and Hume as a form of vanity, it is significant that today the charge of vanity is rarely heard – it seems both dated and unnecessarily 'moralistic'. Nevertheless, encouraged by advertising, plenty of consumption is influenced by the desire to become an object of envy. The lie is also given by the recent popularity of questions such as: 'What do your clothes/car/etc. say about you?' Here aesthetic judgements are taken as an indicator not merely of 'lifestyle' but of individual worth, in terms either of competence, priorities and character, or more simply of position in the social field, which we are invited to take as an indicator of all those things.[23]

Equivalent ambiguities and slippages are found in the use of the word 'common', as if whatever was widely distributed was automatically inferior, indeed vulgar, and whatever was rare (exclusive) was automatically superior. Many euphemisms for class, such as 'well-spoken' and 'from a good family' or 'rough', function by concealing status behind an apparently neutral judgement of merit.

The spoken and unspoken interactions of the social field are pervaded with subtle and not so subtle sentiments of 'class contempt' (Reay, 1998a) and 'othering' which are extraordinarily sensitive to indicators of accent, demeanour, appearance, clothing and possessions. Although these may be triggered by differences in style and aesthetic tastes, they chronically spill over into judgements of moral worth, as is perhaps clearest in the case of middle class judgements of working class women's appearance (Skeggs, 1997). Descriptions of people as 'common' or 'rough' carry moral connotations. If we ignore the hierarchically structured nature of the competitions and struggles of the social field, we may misread them, confusing the struggle for respect or respectability[24] of the subaltern with a struggle for advantage driven by vanity, or alternatively as simply an expression of 'difference' or 'lifestyle'.

The striving for recognition that the dominated feel pressured into when they find themselves talking posh in the company of people of higher class, spending more than they can afford on weddings, not wanting to look 'cheap', etc., are all understandable but doomed ways of trying to win respect and prove that they 'are as good as them'. 'The construction of identities' is not merely about the aesthetics of lifestyle but about moral worth and recognition. The struggle is doomed because it is one which the subaltern are not allowed to win, and it is in any case irrational to

---

[23] However, as we noted earlier, not all struggles of the social field are driven by the pursuit of advantage over others.

[24] As I shall suggest later, the pursuit of respect and respectability are not the same.

judge people's moral worth according to whether their vowels are flat, what they wear at weddings, where they can afford to live, etc. It is nevertheless understandable because we all need recognition – of equality if not superiority.

Of course the contingent relation between the posh and the good does not mean that the posh cannot indeed be good; social theory is posh, for example, but it can also be good (though it is worth asking if it is not sometimes merely posh!). Equally, the common might indeed be bad. To challenge the symbolic domination involved in the conflation of the posh and the good and the common and the bad is not to deny such possibilities. In the case of culture, an optimistic interpretation of the weakening of the hierarchical distinction between high and low culture, and the rise of cultural omnivorousness, is that they suggest a growing willingness to evaluate cultural goods regardless of their class associations, although this may have more effect in terms of broadening the range of goods available to the middle classes than in reducing symbolic domination and inequalities.[25] This latter possibility reminds us that the struggles of the social field are often not intended by actors to assert or dispute symbolic domination. They are in part about the pursuit of things and ways of life which actors value regardless of their effect on the reproduction of inequality and symbolic domination, though inadvertently their actions may confirm, accentuate or weaken these. Bourdieu emphasised the way that domination is inadvertently reproduced, but it may inadvertently be reduced as well.

As noted earlier, it is irrational to devalue and reject things simply because they are valued by the dominant, not only for the consequentialist reason that it is likely to confirm rather than challenge one's exclusion and subordination, but because such a reaction by-passes the question of whether those things actually are worthwhile. The 'lads', in Paul Willis's celebrated book *Learning to Labour,* who rejected dominant norms regarding the value of education, damaged their own prospects not merely because they invited the dominant to reject them, but because they missed out on the internal goods of education (Willis, 1977). Education is worthwhile in itself because it enriches our capacities to flourish, regardless of whether it brings us exchange-value. It is rational not to value things which the dominant value only if their use-value or internal goods are indeed worthless or over-rated. The same applies to rationales for rejecting things associated with the subordinated.

---

[25] An empirical study in the UK of cultural omnivorousness by Warde et al. (2003) shows it to be primarily restricted to privileged classes rather than a tendency applying across the whole population. See also Skeggs, 2004.

It has to be acknowledged, however, that it may be difficult to avoid such associations, on either the side of the dominant or the subordinate, even if we want to approach the goods dispassionately. For example, my appreciation of classical music or political discussions on Radio 4 is often marred by the posh voices usually accompanying them, which grate on me because of their association with superiority, arrogance, pomposity and condescension. As Bourdieu demonstrated, these characteristics are not merely accidentally and conventionally associated with different positions in the social field but are effects of the formation of the habitus, which in turn reflect position within the social field. This means that insofar as the good is (falsely) equated with the posh it will be associated with distance from necessity. Thus, history and classics are valued more highly than engineering or geography, and within social science, theoretical work is valued more highly in terms of cultural capital than policy research, and indeed, as Bourdieu shows, there are corresponding differences in the social background of students and academics in these fields (Bourdieu, 1988).

Despite – and because of – the continuing importance of class and other inequalities, some people may want to break free of status markers and live in ways which they imagine escape these associations. For Bourdieu, the idea that we can escape the markers of our social location through our consumption choices is entirely illusory – a 'dream of social flying, a desperate effort to defy the gravity of the social field' (Bourdieu, 1984, p. 370). Of course, there is indeed a high probability that such attempts will fail. This is both because it is hard to change one's habitus and because symbolic domination involves multilateral relations of recognition and misrecognition that are unlikely to be changed unilaterally. Even those who do not wish to compete are treated as competitors. Nevertheless, from a normative point of view (which may be present in lay motivations), the dream of escape from the influence of the distortion of judgements of people by class and other relations of domination remains central to egalitarianism (Tawney, 1952). It amounts to a desire to distinguish the good from the merely posh and to pursue internal goods regardless of these distortions.

Equivalent arguments to those regarding the posh and the good apply to gender, where we need to distinguish the merely masculine or feminine from the good, in order to avoid double standards. Just as the posh may sometimes be good, so certain behaviours regarded conventionally as masculine, or feminine, may be good. Hence, when we value behaviours which are gendered in a particular way, it need not necessarily be *because* of gender (indeed from a normative view it should not). Thus hospitals value caring behaviour in their nursing staff, and they do so not because caring is gendered as feminine, but because caring is what they need to provide. Similarly, accountancy businesses favour formal rationality not because it's gendered as masculine, but because formal rationality is their business.

From a normative point of view the important question is not whether X is posh, common, masculine or feminine, but whether X is good regard-less of such associations.[26] Further, those things and behaviours which are judged in this way to be good but are monopolised by one class or gen-der should be redistributed or de-gendered, while those things which are judged to be bad and correlated with a particular class or gender should be stopped rather than redistributed. The hope of egalitarians with respect to class must be that inequality can be reduced to the point where the classing of behaviours is no longer significant and people can be judged without such distortions. Note that such a radical reduction of inequality need not prejudice the scope for difference; on the contrary, it would allow voluntary differences to develop without the restraining effect of dominant values which penalise difference by exclusion and marginal-isation. We can thus elaborate and strengthen Tawney's argument that equality can allow enhanced rather than reduced scope for variety and difference, because whole classes of goods would no longer be devalued simply by reference to their sociological coordinates.

Commitments and the posh and the good

In chapter 2 we emphasised the normative significance of actors' commit-ments, whether to causes, practices* or to other people, or various combi-nations of these. Commitments are more durable than mere preferences; people invest in them emotionally and pursue and defend them even when it brings them disadvantages (Archer, 2000). For example, the usual com-mitment of parents to their children is radically different from their pref-erences for this or that kind of decor or make of car, strong though these may be. (Children are not fashion accessories.) The emotional quality of such commitments attests to their seriousness in terms of their implica-tions for well-being. They involve valuing things for their own sake, not merely for individuals' own satisfaction (they may even be prepared to die for them) or for external goods or profit. Commitments are constitutive of individuals' characters, such that adults who lack any, lack character (O'Neill, 1999). In this sense, commitments are what our lives are about.

---

[26] Relativist and sociologically reductionist approaches according to which all beliefs are purely a function of social position and experience can never grasp the significance of these normative issues.

The normative implications of social inequalities for individuals' abilities to form and pursue commitments are therefore of much greater importance than their ability to meet their preferences regarding use-values, though some resources are needed to support the pursuit of commitments. The most important struggles of the social field concern those over commitments.

Commitment to children has an obvious importance from the point of view of any moral-political vision of the future of society. The vulnerability of children and the fact that they are so dependent on adults means that they are a prime focus of moral concern and commitment. Equally, it is no surprise that there are strongly held views on children's upbringing and education. Practices of childrearing and attitudes towards education also differ strikingly by class, and are a key site of difference and conflict between people, and of course they are fundamental to the intergenerational transmission of class and the development of the habitus. Parents can hardly avoid considering whether middle class childrearing practices are better than working class ones. In effect, they have different attitudes to the internal goods and standards of education and parenting. Thanks to the dominance of those with high economic and cultural capital in defining good practice, the distribution of external goods – prestige, rewards and qualifications – is skewed towards those groups (Bourdieu, 1996a; Lynch and Lodge, 2002), and ironically the elision of the difference between the posh and the good is particularly strong in education. Education's internal goods are not positional, but its external goods clearly are. Though some may value their child's education for its own sake (a view now likely to be regarded as quaintly naive and hopelessly passé), education is increasingly oriented towards external goods, to the extent that the internal goods are becoming just a means to the end of achieving external goods. In this situation parents and children find themselves locked into an overwhelmingly competitive process. Given that children are strongly influenced by their peers as well as their parents, there are pressures among the advantaged to segregate their children from others so as to avoid unwanted influences. This tendency reinforces and is reinforced by residential segregation by class and, in countries such as Britain, by selection policies of schools.[27] Arguments for countering deprivation hold much greater force in the case of children than adults. We might feel that it is none of our business how other adults live, provided they do not harm us, but if we feel they are bringing their children up badly we may be tempted to comment or intervene for the children's sake. Childrearing and education therefore present telling illustrations of the struggles of the social field and what they are about, and I shall use

[27] I shall discuss feelings about this segregation in chapter 8.

them to illustrate the importance of the distinctions I have been making in this chapter.

Research by Annette Lareau (2003) and Valerie Walkerdine and Helen Lucey (1989) on differences between working and middle class parenting and by Diane Reay on parents putting their children through school highlights not only class differences in childrearing and attitudes to education, that is, differences regarding how goods are to be valued, but competition for some of the same goods (Reay, 1998a; see also Walkerdine et al., 2003, Thomson and Holland, 2003). In Britain, Walkerdine and Lucey note how middle class mothers tend to take every opportunity to turn the time they spend with their children into lessons, in contrast to the more arms-length, non-interventionist relationship of working class mothers. The latter are more authoritarian in disciplining their children, the former more likely to give elaborate explanations for the restrictions they impose. Similarly, in the USA, Lareau describes middle class childrearing as a process of 'concerted cultivation', in which children are expected to talk to adults and reason with them, and to undertake an exhausting round of activities – typically music lessons and organised sports – outside school. The attention these parents give to their children gives them a sense that they are entitled to the attention of others, including, crucially, that of professionals who act as gatekeepers to the goods they seek. In contrast, the 'natural growth' approach of working class childrearing allows children to play freely with others and have little interaction with adults. Working class parents do not see it as their role to intervene in this sphere, beyond setting certain strict, non-negotiable limits, which their children generally accept without question. Thus, on the one side the middle class child enters the adult world not only with a strong curriculum vitae, but already accustomed to operating as an entitled subject, and with communication skills acceptable to middle class gatekeepers; on the other, the working class child is likely to have not only fewer educational qualifications but a habitus that is ill attuned to interacting with such gatekeepers and unresponsive. Lareau found that children from the poorest working class families tended to avoid eye contact with others, this being regarded as threatening in their communities. In sharp contrast, middle class children were taught to look adults in the eye, give a confident handshake, and talk as equals. The implications of these differences for their respective subsequent performance in the labour market hardly need to be stated.

For the working class children, development of toughness in the face of domination prefigures lives in which there is likely to be little room for reasoned negotiation. For those who attempt upward mobility, toughness in the form of willingness to sacrifice the approval and support of their family and peers who refuse or fail to achieve educational advancement is also an asset. Middle class children are less likely to require this toughness, not only because they are in a position of advantage, but because pursuing educational goods will strengthen rather than weaken their bonds with their peers.[28] Not surprisingly, as Simon Charlesworth notes, working class young people tend to regard middle class students as immature and frivolous, lacking an appreciation of how hard the world is (Charlesworth, 2000).

Lareau notes positive and negative aspects of both middle class and working class childhoods. The middle class children may have acquired the ability to operate as entitled subjects in middle class occupations, but they were frequently exhausted by the unrelenting round of improving activities, and generally less happy than the working class children, and were inclined to whine when they didn't get their way. The working class children were able to enjoy unsupervised, unstructured, creative play and interaction, they learned how to get on with older and younger children and to manage conflict, and were more respectful to adults (Lareau, 2003, p. 85). Walkerdine and Lucey, coming from a working class background, viewed similar contrasts in childrearing with strong but mixed feelings – both wanting to defend their own upbringing, expressing anger[29] at the disparagement of working class childrearing by the middle classes, and yet also acknowledging some of the advantages of middle class approaches and resenting what their own childhoods had lacked (Walkerdine and Lucey, 1989). These mixed feelings – which are shared by many others – are responses to the structure of the struggles of the social field: they involve a contestation of both the class distribution and the class valuation of goods (who has or achieves these goods and what are they really worth?), and they represent a difficult discernment of the posh from the good, the common from the bad.[30] They do *not* merely affirm what the habitus disposes them to affirm; they are negotiations of normative issues which are crucial for who children become and the quality of their lives.

In becoming academics, Walkerdine and Lucey gained the advantages of hindsight from upward mobility, but similar kinds of normative concern and contestation are evident in the working class mothers studied by

---

[28] Although this is a relatively comfortable position, the recent rise of concerted cultivation reflects, and is likely to intensify, uncertainty generated by increased competition for middle class jobs and fear of failure. For the middle classes, parenting itself has become deeply competitive.

[29] '. . . we write out of anger, an anger in which working-class child-rearing practices have been either systematically pathologised or patronised . . .' (Walkerdine and Lucey, 1989, p. 2).

[30] For example, many people in Britain would regard the posh practice of sending one's children away to public school as far from good.

Reay (Reay, 1998b). These women were worried about how best to help their children do well in a school environment dominated by middle class values. While they felt under a middle class gaze, and resented this, they wanted their children to be academically successful not merely to achieve respectability or approval but because their children would benefit from it as people. In other words, they were concerned with the internal as well as the external goods of education. Their meetings with teachers were frequently frustrating and stressful for them, but reading their accounts of how they pursued their commitments to their children's education, I would suggest that the reasons for this lay not only in the relations of condescension and deference, or in differences in educational, cultural and economic capital, but in difficulties in assessing the goods of education.

In both these cases I would suggest that the sensitivity and painfulness of such issues derives from the combined presence of the following normative elements:

(1) Justified resentment of others' undeserved advantages, and anger at being (or having been) denied them. Note this presupposes that the advantages are real and not illusory – worth having, not spurious. The proper target of criticism here is not the goods but the undeserved monopolisation of them by the dominant classes.

(2) A less justified (though hardly surprising) temptation to refuse to acknowledge that the goods that the dominant classes have monopolised include some that really are worth having. This can result in a kind of self-exclusion, which of course is the most effective means by which inequality and domination can be maintained.

(3) Justified suspicion that some values, behaviours, goods are actually *not* worth having, but merely required or valued by the dominant, so that there is a justified resentment at having to defer or conform to them; i.e., this is a resistance to some norms because they're *merely* middle class or posh and nothing more. For example, speaking in a posh accent is merely posh; there is no good reason why a posh accent should be seen as any better than a regional accent.[31] Here, in contrast to the previous point, the scepticism concerns the 'goods' – hence not their monopolisation, but rather the expectation that all should conform to them.

(4) Despite the inclination to seek what seems best regardless of its class (or gender) associations, there may be an awareness that as a matter of tactics it is worth going along with norms whose only justification is that they enhance individuals' chances of success in the competition.

---

[31] Regional accents are not necessarily less clearly articulated than posh ones, even though they may be unfamiliar outside their regions.

By contrast, 'being true to yourself' may carry a heavy price. These norms are not limited to those of the dominant classes. There are cases of goods whose instrumental value differs according to position within the hierarchical structure of symbolic and material domination. Thus, given the way that gender and class pressures interrelate, it is easier for middle class boys than for working class boys to accept schooling without being seen as effeminate. These class- and gender-related characteristics may either simply be accepted uncritically or be negotiated more or less covertly. Academically oriented working class children, especially boys, may try to conceal their interest in school work from their peers.[32] They face an intense conflict between the pursuit of what they consider to be worthwhile, and masculinity and class identity (Reay, 2002), that is, between what they consider to be good and what will bring them status, whether on the basis of gender or class identity.[33] While education is less likely to be coded as unfeminine than as unmasculine, working class girls who pursue educational goods may nevertheless also meet classed and sexist opposition to their efforts (Skeggs, 1997). In either case we see a tension between individuals' norms and those of their social positioning which eludes sociologically reductionist analyses. The socially mobile may find themselves acting as social chameleons, changing their accents and behaviour according to who they are with. While these class- and gender-differentiated norms may be valued in their own right, they may also be valued tactically as appropriate strategies for people placed in different parts of the social field.

(5) On top of all this, as often happens with internal goods and practices* and is surely the case with the evaluation of childrearing and schooling, there are large areas of uncertainty where it's hard to know what is for the best. Moreover, the unequal distribution of cultural and social capital means that the uncertainty is greatest for dominated or socially excluded groups, who in any case will have most difficulty getting access to educational goods.

(6) More generally, as we noted at pp. 111–17, there is a broader question of how to value the practices* and internal goods of being educated in comparison to *other* internal goods, such as those of developing friendships and a sociable nature. The relative values given to these tend to vary by class, with working class people often valuing the

---

[32] Being able to pass as one of the lads while also being able to get one up on them is one of the most successful strategies of masculinity, and not just in youth or among the working class.

[33] Note again that the good may sometimes *coincide* with the posh, or indeed the masculine or feminine.

latter more than education, and the middle class giving more importance to education. On the one hand this reflects the lack of educational prospects of the working class and might be seen (as Bourdieu would no doubt have proposed) as a way of refusing what they are refused and making a virtue out of necessity; on the other hand, we might question the middle classes' scramble for qualifications and their valuing of competitiveness over sociability, and defend the working class choice. There is also a difficult question here of how to balance ideals against immediate tactical imperatives; many middle class people wish there wasn't so much competition for qualifications and want their children to be well socialised and not merely academically successful, but their fear of downward mobility prevents them from withdrawing from the educational competition. Again, these are questions of how to live.

Analysing such judgements in this way creates a picture of the dispassionate deliberations of an observer whose standing is equal to that of others, which is precisely not the case in class societies. There are not only likely to be questions about the worthiness of the features of the social situation which they're considering entering, such as those noted above, for individuals may also worry about whether they themselves are worthy, or at least whether, to use a common euphemism, it's 'for them'. Reay quotes one working class mother as saying regarding her daughter: 'I do think it would be nice for her to go to Royden Girls'. I know it's got a very good reputation but then again I thought what if the other girls think she's not good enough to be there' (Reay, 1998a, p. 271; see also 1998b, p. 62).

The possible suppressed meanings of 'not good enough' are worth lingering over, especially in light of the fact that individuals can hardly make judgements of self-worth independently of their reception by others. It seems easy to acknowledge that middle class people will choose places and institutions which they regard as appropriate for their standing, but shocking to be reminded that working class people may feel unable to attempt to enter those places not only because they will experience prejudice but because they feel that indeed they might not be worthy of them.

All of this reminds us that the micro-politics of class, the struggles against the 'soft forms of domination' identified by Bourdieu, are not only over access to existing goods but over the definition of what is good; they are about who people want to be, what they want and can expect to make of their lives, part of which, as the case of parenting shows, is a struggle to form and pursue commitments and to get access to the means for doing so.[34] In the process, they are simultaneously struggles to establish self-worth.

Conclusion

The aim of this analysis of the struggles of the social field has been to probe how inequalities are structured in relation to actors' normative concerns. By treating actors as evaluative beings and examining the relation between the structure of inequality and symbolic domination and different kinds of valuation and goods we can gain insight into how inequalities matter to them. At the same time we have developed a normative perspective on social life that is both continuous with the normative content of the struggles of the social field themselves and yet goes beyond them and thereby affords a critical view of them. As usual, evaluation involves a re-examination of existing judgements.

This has been an analytical approach to the normative dimension of the struggles of the social field over goods. No doubt Bourdieu would have warned about the dangers of the scholastic fallacy – i.e., project-ing a contemplative, analytical relation to the world onto actors who, by and large, have an unexamined practical sense of or feel for the practices in which they live. I recognise that, in practice, inequality and symbolic domination are experienced primarily emotionally and with only limited reflection. In some situations, such as those described in the previous section, actors are likely to experience powerful but mixed feelings of envy, pride, resentment, anger and – in extreme situations as a conse-quence – consternation. While acknowledging the danger of the scholas-tic fallacy, I would argue that there is more rational discrimination and judgement in lay action, including in emotional responses, than Bourdieu claimed. (Paradoxically, they are evident in the actors' accounts recorded in *The Weight of the World*.)[35] Furthermore, as I argued in chapter 2, emo-tions are not to be counterposed to reason but are evaluative judgements about circumstances beyond people's control which are likely to affect their well-being and their commitments. What the above analysis was

---

[34] Many of the interviewees in *The Weight of the World* emphasise the importance not of appearances or material possessions but of their commitments, to others and to causes or practices, and the disappointment and loss of sense of self that follows from inability to carry these through. This is in line with arguments in philosophy which place lasting commitments and relationships as central to the development of character (O'Neill, 1999, pp. 84ff.).

[35] On the other hand, if I am guilty of reading too much into lay actions, I hope that the analysis may nevertheless be of some use in engaging with readers' normative views.

attempting to do was to take them seriously and articulate their rational content.[36]

Of course, lay actors do not use terms such as 'use-value' and 'exchange-value', internal and external goods' or 'practices*' (though they do use terms such as posh and common), but the concepts behind them are implicit in much of what they do, including how they contest symbolic domination. The struggles of the social field are driven not only by actors seeking to attract external goods and to maximise the exchange-value of their capital, not only by their pursuit of the posh and avoidance of the common. They are also about seeking use-values and internal goods and pursuing commitments for their own sake, regardless of whether they affect their standing relative to others. Insofar as they seek external goods of approbation and grant approbation to others they do not necessarily only seek advantage over others, they also care about whether the external goods are deserved. Thus the struggles of the social field are partly about whether status (and indeed class in the narrow sense, as distinct from status) is deserved or warranted. Resistance to symbolic domination and inequality can involve both scepticism about the valuations of goods made by the dominant and a struggle for access to those things that they monopolise that do seem genuinely worthwhile. I have been arguing that this double-sided struggle is implicit in the everyday micro-politics of class and gender. To pursue just one side of this strategy invites failure: for example, if actors accept the judgements of the dominant class or gender without question, they under-value the goods associated with the subordinate class or gender (as in the case of the skills involved in 'women's work'); if, on the other hand, they refuse to believe that anything the dominant have or do is worthwhile, and uncritically validate whatever is associated with dominated groups, then this leaves the dominant free to retain their monopoly of many worthwhile goods without challenge and merely withdraws approval for their judgements. In the latter case, the dominant could reasonably conclude: 'If you don't value what we have, then you can't complain about being unequal.' (Again, it is hard to see how the dominant could be dominant if they did not monopolise the best goods.) In normative terms the important evaluative issue is not whether X is posh, common, masculine or feminine, but whether it is good or bad.

We have taken two steps beyond most descriptive work on class and inequality: first in relating inequality and domination to goods and what people care about, and secondly in treating their evaluations critically, acknowledging possibilities for rationalisation, for prioritising

---

[36] Compare Bourdieu's analyses in *The Weight of the World* (e.g., pp. 510ff.).

exchange-value and external goods over use-value and internal goods, and for allowing their evaluative judgements to be distorted by class associations, as in the conflation of the common and the bad. As we shall see in chapter 6 these two steps are also mirrored in the need for ethics both to be grounded in social being and to go beyond its current forms. In making the second step we have gone beyond description of lay normativity to prescription of alternatives, though, as we have argued, these are basically developments of selected tendencies already implicit in lay practice.

These arguments jar with the view that what is good and bad is not something that can be judged independently of gender or class, but is relative to them. But it is one thing to acknowledge that our judgements are influenced by gender and class, quite another to regard those influences as carrying some authority (or indeed lacking any worth). The danger of this assumption is that it essentialises gender and class. Gender and class dispositions do not have essences; they do not derive from differences in natural causal powers but depend on the contingent though powerful ways in which individuals are socialised.[37] Nor are they necessarily good: even if those dispositions become deeply engrained in our habitus, and therefore seem 'authentic', we can critically evaluate and attempt to override them if we wish. To be sure, given our habitus we can hardly help but favour some things over others, but the habitus can be changed, albeit over a long period of time. Feminism has developed a critique of the feminine and masculine habituses, such as the former's self-abnegating tendencies and the latter's disposition towards dominance, and has had some impact in changing men and women. There is no reason why the class dimension of habitus should be spared a similar critique. For example, to have an embodied taste for ease and for being deferred to and served by others without reciprocating, on account of a privileged upbringing, is, I would argue, unhealthy for both the individuals themselves as well as others. Our dispositions can be challenged so that they become more than just reflections of our position within the social field, perhaps even becoming at odds with it, though ultimately one would hope to change the social field so that it is conducive to the formation of habituses which allow a better social order in which all can flourish.

This radical attempt at judgement independently of class and gender or other social divisions might seem to imply a view from nowhere, or worse, its universalism might be accused of covertly being based on a

---

[37] As argued in chapter 2, social constructions are constrained and enabled by the causal powers and liabilities of the materials they use. But in this case these properties are not themselves differentiated by class, or indeed by gender, even though the latter, unlike the former, is socially constructed around or by reference to real and imagined biological differences (Archer, 2000; New, 2004; Sayer, 2000a).

specific social location. I would argue, however, that it implies a view from
the basis of *interactions between* classes and genders, between individuals
who of course are always more than just bearers of class and gender,
whose behaviour cannot be judged purely in those terms. As I argued in
chapter 2, ethical sentiments and norms are less socially localised than
aesthetic ones, and have, in part, universalising tendencies deriving from
the reciprocal character of social relations, from their responsiveness to
our human as well as our more specifically cultural being, and partly
from experiences of good and bad treatment which are not reducible to
effects of class and gender or other social divisions but cross-cut them. As
before, I invite those who are still sceptical to put forward an alternative
normative approach.

I recognise that my argument here is strongly anti-relativist, and there
may be not only relativists but readers who are in general anti-relativist
who find it too strong: they may want to say that judgements regarding
goods are always going to be relative to actors' situations; or they may say
that judgements may differ with respect to the same situation, if different
discourses about it are available. Both points are correct, but normative
arguments about how we should live, about distribution and recognition
and the nature of the good, need not only be restricted to questions of
what is best given existing patterns of inequality and difference, but can
be extended to questions of whether those patterns should exist at all.
Egalitarianism is not merely about how people should act but about the
legitimacy of the positions from which they act. Moreover, the position
I have advanced does not propose a single vision of the good but rather
leaves this open; I have not said which kinds of use-value, internal goods,
practices* and commitments are good – only that they are more fundamental than exchange-value, external goods and preferences. But then
the search for the good is part of what the strivings and struggles of the
social field are about.

Such matters take us beyond the politics of distribution and recognition
by raising the questions about what kinds of goods matter and hence
what kinds of inequalities are most important, and also for what kinds
of characteristics or behaviour recognition is being sought. Though it is
important to combine the politics of distribution and recognition, it is
not enough, at least in terms of how they are normally defined, for they
do not address very clearly what people can do and how they live but
instead focus on some of the preconditions of such matters, whether to
do with material resources or the recognition of others.[38] The categories

---

[38] In Amartya Sen's terms they do not address people's capabilities, but merely some of
the factors contributing to them (Sen, 1992).

of recognition and distribution are simply too thin on their own to enable us to get far in understanding the significance of inequalities, and of material and symbolic domination. Those of internal and external goods and commitments get us closer to what people value in life.

Exploring the sociological implications of concepts such as that of internal and external goods helps not only to clarify the structures within which domination operates, it also helps us see that if we are to understand much about inequality, domination and how to counter them, then we need to discuss lay and other concepts or senses of 'the good', 'well-being', etc. Without clarifying our ideas on the latter, we are likely to be unclear about where our criticisms of existing arrangements are coming from, what exactly they are criticising, and where any policies for change should be headed. In feminism it has been recognised that attempts to change gender orders need to decide what kinds of norms and objectives should be set, for example, whether employment policies should aim at a male breadwinner norm or a female caregiver norm or some other norm (Fraser, 1997). If one starts thinking about the third option, we quickly run into complexities, for example concerning the distribution of responsibilities for care of others when people have made different choices about whether to have children, and people differ in their own needs for care. The complexities affect individual and social well-being, by influencing the choices that people can make and the responsibilities they bear. Unless one tackles such issues, it becomes difficult to defend critiques of the status quo let alone work out what changes are needed. Though usually having roots in different theories and philosophies from those drawn upon here,[39] much feminist literature addresses matters to do with the nature of the good (e.g., on the ethics of care, the public and the private, sexuality, capabilities theory) (*Feminist Economics*, 2003; Segal, 1999), but there seems to be no equivalent of this in relation to class. 'What do women want?' – which always means what should they want? – is regularly asked in the popular media without expecting the answer to be 'To be like men'. No-one asks 'What do the working class want?', although if they did many middle class people might assume the answer ought to be 'To be like us'. Diane Reay argues that '. . . the solution to class inequalities does not lie in making the working classes middle class but in working at dismantling and sharing out the economic, social and cultural capital which go with middle-class status' (Reay, 1997b, p. 23). In addition, I would argue, it involves re-assessing how practices – both in the narrow sense defined by MacIntyre and in a broader sense – and goods are valued as well as how they are distributed, by disentangling the

---

[39] But see Nussbaum's neo-Aristotelian feminism (Nussbaum, 1999).

good and the bad from the posh and the common. At what norms and goals should attempts to reduce or eliminate class differences aim? One of the many reasons socialism ran out of steam could be that it stopped considering such matters, so that as it was succeeded by neoliberalism and 'The Third Way', the questionable goal of attempting to extend middle class ways of life to others became the implicit target by default.

6 Moral and immoral sentiments and class

Introduction

We are evaluative beings. Our streams of consciousness have an evaluative dimension which ranges from spontaneous, unexamined, unarticulated feelings about other people, objects and practices, and about what to do, through to more considered evaluations of those things (Archer, 2003). As we argued in chapter 2, emotions or sentiments should be taken seriously as they often provide highly sensitive evaluative judgements of circumstances bearing upon people's well-being and what they care about (Nussbaum, 2001). In using the term evaluation I shall henceforth stretch it beyond its normal scope to encompass the whole of this range. The intensity of these responses also ranges from the subtlest differences in ease or unease, preferences and aversions, through to strong identification and approval or revulsion and disapproval. They are central to the subjective experience of class and it is the purpose of this chapter to examine their normative structures.

In dealing with forms of inequality such as those of class, or gender or 'race', it is customary to focus on phenomena such as snobbery and elitism, sexism, racism, contempt, disgust, 'othering', and the like, that is, on sentiments and practices which are in various ways oppressive, immoral or, in more old-fashioned language, vices. This is understandable given social science's emphasis on the study of social problems; indeed, many – myself included – would have doubts about the point of social research that did not deal with social problems of some sort. However, from the point of view of understanding the subjective experience of class this is unsatisfactorily one-sided, for it fails to do justice to the complexity of lay normativity. It is not only that there are also sentiments of mutual respect, benevolence and compassion, alongside contempt and disgust and the like, but that the struggles of the social field make little sense if we ignore the virtues and moral sentiments and focus purely on the bad, for the former incline actors towards both maintaining social order and resisting oppressive relationships. Moreover, in many cases the vices and virtues cannot be understood separately, for they are interlinked; for example, shame and humiliation are internally related to their opposites – pride and respect. In addition, from the point of view of a supposedly critical social science, any critique of social life, even if only implied, presupposes the possibility and desirability of a better social order. If such an approach ignores the elements of moral or virtuous behaviour, then its critique has no point of purchase in lay practice from which it can attempt to lever social improvement.

In contrast to sociology and other social sciences, moral philosophy tends to be far more interested in virtues and the good than vices and the bad, often treating the latter merely as the absence of the former.[1] It also tends to discuss virtues and sentiments at the level of individuals and in abstraction from relations and structures of inequality, producing a somewhat optimistic picture of social life. As Margaret Urban Walker comments: 'One moral philosopher says "The human form in others invokes deep-seated patterns of projection, identification, and sympathy" . . . Well sometimes. *Very* often the human form in some people prompts in others indifference, suspicion, fear, aversion, contempt, xenophobia, and more than occasionally, hatred' (Walker, 1998, p. 177, emphasis in original). Sociology and moral philosophy therefore have complementary shortcomings. We need to steer a course between the optimism produced by moral philosophy's abstraction of moral sentiments from relations of inequality and the pessimism of sociologically reductionist treatments of all evaluation of others as nothing more than the reproduction of class contempt, sexism, racism and the like. Moral philosophy is indeed weak in acknowledging such phenomena, but it would be absurd to reverse the problem and ignore benevolence, compassion and the like, as if inter-class relations were purely mutually contemptuous. As usual, the most cynical interpretation is not necessarily the best, and cynicism should not be mistaken for scepticism, for we can be sceptical about cynicism.

Understandably, sociologists have been particularly interested in how actors' moral judgements and distinctions vary according to their social position, and are sometimes used for drawing boundaries (Kefalas, 2003; Lamont, 1992, 2000; Southerton, 2002a and b; Tilly, 1998). Our social positions tend to be stable and to shape our experience, and hence our evaluations of others and their actions. But we occupy several different positions, not only according to class, gender and race, but in terms of age and relations to parents and dependants, as teachers or students,

---

[1] See Alexander, 2003.

doctors or patients, producers or consumers. An individual may be in a subordinate position in some of these and a dominant position in others, though some may find themselves predominantly on one side, so that their experience is overdetermined rather than diverse. Everyone is likely to experience the major emotions at some time in their lives, but the dominant patterns are likely to vary somewhat according to social position (Bartky, 1990).

Despite this social differentiation of experience, including emotional experience, lay morality is not simply differentiated in a way which corresponds to the boundaries of social groups. Actors use moral and other evaluative distinctions not only to draw boundaries between themselves and others but to discriminate among behaviours across and within class and other social divisions, for they can hardly fail to notice that they can be well or badly treated by members of any group, including their own. While this might seem either too obvious or simply less interesting sociologically than moral boundary-making, I want to argue that it illuminates both the normative character of lived experience and the experience of and responses to class. In fact, unless we *also* acknowledge the scope for moral behaviour and evaluation to vary *independently* of major social divisions such as class, we cannot make sense of lay understandings of such divisions. An indication of the significance of this fact is the tendency of workers to be more concerned with how they are treated regardless of rank, than about rank itself (Lamont, 2000). Some may regret this from a political standpoint, but equally many more political commentaries fail to notice such moral concerns and their importance to people for their sense of well-being. Much political quiescence – and also much resistance – depends on such experiences.

Actors' evaluations (in the sense defined above) are not merely kinds of commentaries on others but are crucial in influencing their own actions towards them. In this chapter I shall therefore discuss both moral and immoral sentiments and attempt to analyse their normative structures. I shall also provide some preliminary comments on their probable relation to class inequalities in terms of how these evaluations affect the experience of class, and conversely how class affects those evaluations. This focus on the normative monitoring of conduct of self and other as a basis for action and social order was the prime focus of Adam Smith's remarkable analysis in *The Theory of Moral Sentiments* (Smith, 1759:1984), and I shall draw upon this in part. I shall first make some preliminary general remarks on evaluation in relation to the social field. Next, taking the lead from Smith, I outline a selection of moral sentiments or emotions that are important for understanding the experience of class, giving special emphasis to one which is only implicit in Smith's work – shame. I shall then proceed to the more negative sentiments involving contempt and 'othering' before summarising the conclusions of the chapter.

Preliminaries

As Smith argued, judgements of self and of how to act are refracted through the imagined and actual judgements of others. *Which* others people take as their reference point is important, and they may of course consider how several differently positioned others would judge their conduct. As Bourdieu reminds us, judgements of self and other are made from within situated social relations, and the relation between the evaluator and the evaluated and their positions within the social field are usually reflected in the evaluation, though many such relations occur among people occupying the same position: they are not limited to relations among unequals. Many actions are implicated in more than one social relation and moral dilemmas often arise where acting considerately towards person A involves acting inconsiderately towards B, and relative harms have to be weighed.[2] Further, as neither Bourdieu nor Smith adequately acknowledged, in making judgements actors draw upon available ways of thinking about such matters, including not only moral norms and narratives, but discourses such as those of racism, sexism and class which expect different behaviours from people according to their social position. Mixed, indeed contradictory and confused, evaluations are common, but if we take them seriously we often find that they are indicative of contradictory pressures, including ones that might not be apparent were we not to take lay normativity seriously.

Actors' evaluations of self, others, conduct and objects can relate to three different kinds of qualities, though the boundaries between them are fuzzy:

(1) Aesthetic: regarding matters such as decor, clothing and personal appearance.
(2) Performative: regarding competence and performance, such as that of a doctor or teacher.
(3) Moral: regarding moral qualities or propriety.

It is important to appreciate the possibility for overlap and slides among these three forms of evaluation, and, from a normative point of view, whether such slides are legitimate. Thus, it is common for appearances to be taken as indexes of competence and moral worth. Although the rationale for this slide is weak, being little different from style fascism,

---

[2] See Smart and Neale for an analysis of lay morality and such dilemmas in relation to marital breakup (Smart and Neale, 1999).

fear of such judgements disciplines people, for example, inclining those whose work relies on the trust of others to dress smartly. Competence (2) and probity (3) may also be more legitimately related: a professional who is incompetent is not necessarily excused their incompetence just because they happen to be well-intentioned rather than malicious, for it might reasonably be considered part of the moral duties of a professional to ensure that they become competent in their work. More generally, moral qualities are also a necessary element of competent performance of most jobs and tasks. These three kinds of judgements are commonly intermixed with judgements relating to class, gender, 'race', sexuality and age, etc., *but they would need to be made – and are made – even in the absence of such social divisions.* They may be thoroughly inflected by these social differentiations but they are not wholly reducible to them. The ongoing self- and mutual monitoring necessary for social life requires them, whatever the types of social division present.

Moral sentiments and class

I now identify some key moral sentiments and emotions and analyse their distinctive features, commenting on some of their more typical relations to class differences. This is more in the nature of an abstract, critical philosophical analysis of sentiments and emotions than a description of lay sentiments in practice. These are, of course, 'vague concepts', and in practice, one sentiment may shade into another – benevolence into compassion, humiliation into resentment and rage, for example. Sometimes they may be provoked by the expression of an opposite sentiment by an other, such as shame by contempt or fear by anger. Again, any of these sentiments and related emotions can be evoked by a wide range of social settings, and not only within and in response to relations of domination, whether of class or whatever.

As we noted in chapter 2, Smith argued that while aesthetic judgements varied considerably according to social position, moral judgements were less influenced in this way, though he also clearly identified the possibility of class differences distorting moral sentiments: to some extent they cross-cut class and other social divisions but they can also be refracted by them. His analysis of moral sentiments begins by abstracting from social class (or the 'orders' of society, as he called them), implying that they were primarily grounded in common features of human socialisation, and possessing characteristics that are more or less universal. Only then does he proceed to discuss how social inequalities affect moral judgement. His approach thus acknowledges sociological variations and influences but avoids sociological reductionism. This is not to say he avoided the trap of generalising from parochial bases, and hence of underestimating cultural differences; one could hardly expect anything else in eighteenth-century Britain. But he and other philosophers also provided ways of understanding the fellow-feeling and moral sentiments that cut across differences of culture, gender, class, 'race' and so on, and hence why there can be not only cultural chauvinism, sexism, class contempt and racism, and so on, but their opposites, including cases of opposition to these things from those, such as white anti-racists or middle-class egalitarians, whose own social group have benefited from them.

The extent to which people have these sentiments depends on their situation, and experience; it is not only that ethical dispositions and moral norms influence practice, but that ethical practices encourage the development of such dispositions and norms. Further, it has to be recognised that the attribution of ethical dispositions to people as part of their 'humanity is only partly an empirical claim. It remains also partly an aspiration'[3] (Glover, 2001, p. 25). This applies not only to the attributions of ethical theory but to the role of moral norms in everyday life; precisely because they are norms – whether external or internal(ised) – they are about what ought to be rather than what is. As anthropologists rightly point out, there may be substantial differences between norms and actual practice, and sometimes these differences may be sustained by tacit collusion. While it would be naive to imagine otherwise, at least some norms are likely to be sincerely believed in and earnestly followed, indeed they may be central to actors' commitments, even if attempts to act on them are sometimes frustrated by overriding contingencies.

Sympathy or fellow-feeling

In Adam Smith's specialised usage, 'sympathy' is not limited to the sentiment of commiseration, but applies to any kind of fellow-feeling with any kind of emotions and situations of others (Smith, 1759:1984, I.i.i.5, p. 10) as 'beings like us' (Griswold, 1999, pp. 55, 85). It can thus involve feeling something of another's joy, contentment or anger as well as sorrow.[4] It is not so much an emotion as the means through which emotions are intersubjectively conveyed and understood (Griswold, 1999, p. 79). It allows actors to develop moral imaginations. It can range from spontaneous sharing of emotions to a cooler, more distanced and considered understanding of the meaning or significance of situations for

---

[3] This identifies the weakness of simple dichotomies of the positive and the normative with respect to ethics. (See chapter 9.)

[4] Despite this it has to be said that Smith does also sometimes use 'sympathy' in the more common sense.

others.[5] Expression or acknowledgement of fellow-feeling in this sense also produces important psychological and social effects, such as enlivening happiness or easing grief. However, the spectator's understanding of the other is fallible[6] (it may be 'illusive', as Smith put it), and Smith went to great lengths to argue that even where it is not mistaken the spectator's response is not the *same* as the other's own response, for there is an unbridgeable, though variable, distance between them.[7] Equally, actors' responses to their own situations are fallible (they may be mistakenly contented or angry, for example). Nor need fellow-feeling signal approval; one may understand that someone is angry or happy but feel that such sentiments are unwarranted (Griswold, 1999, p. 55, n. 34). For these reasons, understood in this specialised way, sympathy or fellow-feeling does not entail or guarantee unity. Nor is it necessarily moral; one might empathise with the joy of the greedy, or delight in another's misfortune. Further, as many have noted, fellow-feeling often declines steeply with geographical and social distance, though this does not *necessarily* occur and there are many important exceptions.[8]

This capacity for intersubjective understanding and feeling, and the accompanying 'contagious' nature of sentiments, is fundamental for Smith, in that it provides the means by which individuals evaluate both the behaviour of others and, through this, their own behaviour. They do so, not from an Archimedean point, but from within the social relations which they experience, though they may try to generalise from and moderate[9] such experiences. The understanding ranges from pre- or non-discursive responses to discursive, hermeneutic relations.

---

[5] In light of more recent developments in the philosophy of social science and social ontology, we might now want to fill out the notion of fellow-feeling by including a hermeneutic dimension in which actors' frames of meaning overlap, although it would be important not to reduce fellow-feeling to a purely linguistic mode, for Smith clearly included pre- or non-linguistic forms of communication.

[6] Although Smith invoked the imaginary figure of the 'impartial spectator' in analysing how people judge behaviour he saw the impartiality more as a goal than as an achievement. He also saw this figure as ordinarily imagined by ordinary people, not as a moral philosopher or other authority.

[7] Smith has a very rich and nuanced account of the tensions between the capacity for fellow-feeling and the unavoidably self-centred character of actors' perception of others.

[8] It is possible that such exceptional cases could be a response to a common humanity, though this is something contemporary sociology would generally be reluctant to concede. While I am sure sociologists are as capable of cross-cultural fellow-feeling as anyone else, it could alternatively be explained as itself a learned, culturally specific, capacity. If it is the latter, we should ask if it is a good one to have acquired. If it does not exist, then ethics, being a matter of both empirics and aspiration, leaves us open to aspire to that which is lacking.

[9] By the verb 'moderate' I intend here an analogy with university examiners' work of moderating,

I realise that from a contemporary point of view it is tempting to be sceptical about such claims: it is hard to explain how the phenomenon develops; it takes for granted the role of discourse, which is reduced to a neutral medium having no effects of its own; individuals may differ in the extent to which they have this capacity; and some forms of social order encourage it more than others.[10] However, no matter how unsatisfactory or incomplete the explanation, to deny that it exists would imply denying our own powers and would render the social nature of everyday life incomprehensible. As Griswold puts it, 'We could not demand anything from each other . . . unless we were somehow aware of each other as subjects of experiences like our own . . .'[11] (Griswold, 1999, p. 84). Sceptics need to ask themselves if social actors, in any culture, could be completely devoid of the capacity for fellow-feeling: would human society be even possible on that basis? Ironically, one of the most fundamental flaws of neoclassical economics, which mistakenly likes to invoke Smith as its forebear, is its use of a model of 'rational economic man' who has no need for or notion of fellow-feeling, and hence is radically socially inept or autistic (van Staveren, 2001).

Benevolence and generosity

Though much discussed by Smith, these are sentiments that are rarely acknowledged in sociology, with its understandable emphasis on the bad features of social life and its less understandable scientistic tendency to purge social action of its affective and normative aspects or reduce them to interests. In mainstream economics, rational choice theory can also see them only as anomalous. But in our everyday life they are of course hugely important to our sense of well-being and happiness and hence are highly valued, and we certainly notice when they are absent. They are properly regarded as social virtues – neither reducible to self-interest nor necessarily opposed to it. They make a difference to the experience of class, though often in ways that excuse rather than condemn it.

[10] Once again, as Glover notes, claims about moral sentiments and virtues are partly empirical and partly matters of aspiration. Severe lack of fellow-feeling can exist, but, as in autism, it is likely to be seen as a problem. Even the Ik, of central Africa, studied by Colin Turnbull, who famously lost the moral sentiment of compassion after losing their land, continued to require sympathy in the Smithian sense, for it is a precondition of social life (Turnbull, 1972). Part of the difficulty for sociologists is that an explanation of the phenomenon would properly take us into psychological processes.

[11] I don't think this requires any exaggerated notion of either the unity (coherence) or the uniformity of subjects; it merely presupposes some degree of similarity. Neither does it assume that fellow-feeling is infallible.

Compassion and pity

As we noted earlier, to understand sentiments such as those of compassion and sympathy we need to avoid counterposing emotion to reason and acknowledge that emotions are about something and have cognitive content. Martha Nussbaum argues that the emotion of compassion involves a certain kind of reasoning directed at someone's suffering (Nussbaum, 1996, 2001). It involves 'the belief[12] that the suffering is serious', a belief 'that the suffering was not caused primarily by the actor's own culpable actions . . . and that the pitier's own possibilities are similar to those of the sufferer'[13] (Nussbaum, 1996, p. 31). Compassion involves moral imagination and presupposes a conception of human flourishing and the vulnerability of people to social and natural events beyond their control. As Nussbaum and others have noted, the third element, regarding the pitier's imagination of her own similar possibilities, also implies her difference and separateness. The pitier's beliefs are of course fallible, as are the pitied's own beliefs about their condition (they may rationalise their suffering, for example). Compassion gives the compassionate a reason not merely for wanting to nullify the suffering of the dominated but to resent and nullify its causes (Griswold, 1999, p. 98).[14] It can therefore lead to a social critique and not merely to individualist responses.

However, there are also problems with compassion: being based on the observer's own, often limited, understanding of the sufferer's situation, it may insult their dignity; and do more to ease the pitier's conscience than the pitied's suffering. As Smith pointed out, pity can easily slide into contempt (1759:1984, III.3.18, p. 144).[15] Where expressions of compassion are about suffering caused by foreseeable and avoidable social processes, but are not accompanied by similar concern about their causes, or where the pitier is complicit in those causes, compassion is likely to be experienced as humiliating and unwelcome, and indeed as hypocritical. According to Nussbaum, it is probably for such reasons that, from the Victorian era, the term 'pity' became associated with condescension and superiority.

[12] As before, beliefs – along with 'conceptions' – may be a feeling rather than something on which the actor has deliberated.

[13] These possibilities may be purely hypothetical but nevertheless vivid; the pitier may feel confident that the misfortune will never affect her, but that were she in that situation, perhaps in another society, she would also be vulnerable. Charities such as Oxfam rely on this.

[14] Such claims come with a *ceteris paribus* clause for such sentiments may be overridden by other considerations.

[15] On this slippage from compassion to (ashamed) contempt and disgust, see also Nussbaum, 2001. It is perhaps easiest to appreciate in the case of attitudes to the elderly infirm.

The relative social positions of the pitier and pitied make an important difference here. Where compassionate relations exist among people of similar position in the social field, there need be no overtones of condescension. Where, as occasionally happens, compassion is felt towards the suffering of someone of a higher social position – as in the 'Diana syndrome' – there is obviously no condescension either. But in the more common situation where the compassion is directed 'downwards', to the suffering of those whose social position is weaker, and where the suffering is a product of their social position rather than a random misfortune, pity is likely to be seen as condescending and humiliating; indeed, realisation of this may deter the pitier from expressing their compassion publicly. Moreover, it is likely to be experienced as not only condescending but hypocritical if the pitier's own relative good fortune is connected to the suffering of the dominated. This may be true of compassion of the dominant for the dominated in the cases of all the major axes of inequality – gender, race and class. To the extent that the pitier in this situation recognises his or her own complicity in the processes producing the suffering it may be accompanied by feelings of guilt. To the extent that the suffering is a product of social structures irreducible to interpersonal relations, and is recognised as such, it may be accompanied by a more political anger about such structures.

Envy and resentment

'I have no respect for the passion for equality, which seems to me merely idealizing envy.' (Oliver Wendell Holmes, Jr, cited in Hayek, 1960, p. 85)

Envy is often regarded as an immoral rather than a moral sentiment – for example, Smith regarded it as 'an odious and detestable passion'[16] (Smith, 1759:1984, p. 243), but I wish to argue that in some circumstances it may be justified. Hayek and other anti-egalitarians assume that the accusation of envy provides a knock-down argument against egalitarianism. They imply that far from being based on elevated criteria of justice and fairness, egalitarianism has its origins in a low and unworthy motive. The appeal of the accusation for the dominant is that it invites them to assume that the enviers are unworthy and that they, the envied, are worthy, when of course the opposite may be the case. (Interestingly, unlike Smith and Hume, Hayek does not criticise those who seek to be envied.) It cannot explain how there can be middle class egalitarians. For the egalitarian, the jibe exposes the complacency and lack of moral vision of

---

[16] At the same time he wrote of the need for 'proper indignation' at 'insult and injustice' (Smith, 1759:1984, p. 243).

the dominant, indeed the contempt of those who have benefited from an unfair and unjust system for those who have been dispossessed or blocked by it. For those who believe that most wealth is created by workers and appropriated by the bourgeoisie the jibe is akin to thieves dismissing the complaints of those they have dispossessed as based on envy. For those who believe that economic inequalities come about through a range of mechanisms that have little to do with responding to need, effort or merit, the accusation is also a cheap shot.

Nevertheless, egalitarians may find the accusation discomforting because it appears to involve a double bind:[17] to deny it seems implausible, for if there's nothing to envy about the ways of life of the rich and powerful why should one want to redistribute what they have?; on the other hand, to acknowledge envy appears to invite dismissal because it is widely seen as a low motive. To get past this dilemma we need to reconsider the meanings of envy.

Envy can be resentful or unresentful. In the former case it can either prompt the envier to seek to seize that which is denied to them, or alternatively to destroy it. In the latter case ('benign envy' as Rawls calls it) it may reflect the envier's regret about what s/he lacks, rather than antipathy towards the envied, who may indeed be seen as admirable (Rawls, 1971, p. 532). The envy of those who have won through a fair competition ('on a level playing field'), whether through luck or effort and skill, does not warrant resentment. It may even be combined with a generous acknowledgement of the envied's entitlement to their advantages. In some cases, it can be acknowledged that envied skills and talents can also benefit others, though insofar as the acquisition of these skills may have been assisted by unearned, undeserved advantages, this praise may be qualified. The association of envy with resentment may be something some actors want to avoid since feelings of resentment may reduce their own happiness, and they may prefer to be generous and unresentfully envious and hence content. Even when perfectly justified, resentment can be more painful than acceptance for those who have been exploited or excluded. By expressing a generous kind of envy they may also win the approval of the envied and appear to retain the moral high ground.[18] By this means, the attempts of the dominated to maintain goodwill can help

---

17 Of course, the double bind is itself disingenuous in the context of a society which worships wealth and power and nurtures envy in order to encourage consumption (Baker, 1987, p. 142).

18 Smith notes these possibilities but regards this 'magnanimity' as disingenuous and as liable to give way to shame (Smith, 1759:1984, p. 244). This too seems to involve a double bind – envy is 'detestable' but attempts to avoid it through such strategies must fail.

to maintain their domination. In this case, far from being associated with egalitarianism, envy may indicate class deference towards the dominant.

While Aristotle uses 'envy' pejoratively – the envious are pained at all good fortune (1980, p. 43) – he also refers to the 'righteous indignation' in response to 'undeserved good fortune' (ibid.). Similarly Runciman (1966, p. 11) distinguishes 'between a feeling of envy and a perception of injustice' (see also Baker, 1987, pp. 141–2). It is the latter sentiment which I would argue amounts to what Carolyn Steedman has called 'proper envy': '. . . by allowing envy entry into political understanding, the proper struggle of people in a state of dispossession to gain their inheritance might be seen not as sordid and mindless greed for the things of the market place, but attempts to alter a world that has produced in them states of unfulfilled desire' (Steedman, 1985, p. 123). This, I would argue, is right. The kind of envy associated with egalitarianism is less to do with possession of material goods than a product of systematic exclusion from things which are held to be valuable for all.

Justice

Actors' sense of justice and fairness may be selective but it would be bizarre to deny its existence, whatever its imperfection. For Smith, the sense of justice derives from resentment at injury done to others as would be judged by an imagined other or impartial spectator.[19] It therefore derives from the capacity for fellow-feeling, from imagining the suffering of the one who has been harmed. This encourages the 'negative virtue' of abstention from harm and inclines the observer to resent harm by others. Smith also invokes another sense of 'justice' – one which is often overlooked in moral and political philosophy but which is essential to the ongoing evaluations that actors make of their situation and others: this is the sense of 'doing justice to' the particular qualities of a person, object or circumstances. It is thus far removed from abstract principles of justice such as those of Kant or utilitarianism.[20] It implies that what is morally required in our dealings with others is that we pay close attention to these particularities, so that our responses are appropriate: for example, evaluating others and how we should act towards them in terms of need, desert and situation (Griswold, 1999, p. 233). When we feel that

[19] Recall that the imaginary figure of the impartial spectator is not regarded as infallible, nor does he or she have to be detached from the social field, indeed were they to be so, they would lack precisely the moral imagination required of them.

[20] As many commentators have pointed out, such abstract principles presuppose for their persuasiveness the existence of actors already equipped with moral imagination and sentiments.

we or someone else has been unjustly treated it may not necessarily be simply because we or they have been treated unequally, but because the treatment has failed to take into account relevant specificities that bear on the situation. This conception of justice therefore need not imply equality of treatment of others. It could imply avoiding the harm done by treating unequals equally, for example, the elderly and young, or able-bodied and disabled. Alternatively, in societies in which class and status differences are naturalised, as they still were in Smith's time, it implies treatment according to those differences. Through its linkage to the lay moral imagination, which itself develops through everyday social inter-action and reflexive monitoring, Smith's conception of justice fits more readily with the lay sense of justice than those more oriented to normative ethics.

There are at the same time other senses of justice which would tie it to equality, whether of treatment or outcomes or via unconditional recognition. In everyday practice, the different logics of these concep-tions are not necessarily a problem. Lay moral sentiments derive from everyday interactions among sentient actors having familiar susceptibili-ties for suffering and capabilities for flourishing,[21] and mediated by avail-able discourses. As usual there are cultural variations, in this case in the particular definition of harms and qualities susceptible to harm, often supplying apologetic explanations for relations of domination, but it does not follow from this that a sense of justice and fairness of some kind is of no consequence or mere fantasy or only found in western liberal societies. Actors' mixed and often inconsistent evaluations and motives invariably include it in some form. As we shall see, one of the virtues of Smith's 'bottom up' analysis of morality is that he is well aware of the imperfections of lay morality, and seeks to locate its sources in everyday practice rather than abstract principles formulated in the pursuit of logical perfection.

Toleration . . . and mutual indifference

Respect for others and their autonomy is also a common moral sentiment. On its own, this liberal sentiment emphasises our need for autonomy at the expense of our dependency on others and our need as social beings for connection. Liberal ideals can imply a bleak, misanthropic and lonely society in which individuals, tacitly assumed to be adult males unencum-bered by dependants, avoid each other in order to respect their individual

---

[21] The susceptibilities and capabilities vary but mostly within recognisable limits, as for example between those of infants and adults, the sick and the healthy.

autonomy (Baier, 1994). It need require no appreciation of others' qualities, no active contribution to their well-being, no enjoyment of social virtues, merely the avoidance of harm to others and their property. In their everyday actions, people do not generally knowingly limit the freedom of their class others, but 'respect' – in this minimal, negative sense – their autonomy.[22] Respect for others' autonomy and rights and tolerance of their ways of life can thus range from a feeling of the sanctity of individuals through to mutual indifference or contempt.[23] As Norman Geras argues, in modern societies, the flawed liberal ideal too often reduces to a 'contract of mutual indifference' (Geras, 1998).

Shame . . .

Shame has been described as the most social of the emotions, as it has often been assumed to be an important mechanism of social integration, making individuals conform to external judgements and norms (Barbalet, 2001; Scheff, 1990). Although Smith did not single it out for discussion in his analysis of moral sentiments, it is occasionally mentioned[24] and is implicit in his emphasis of the way in which people monitor their own actions by viewing themselves from the standpoint of others. At the same time, it is a particularly private, reflexive emotion, in that it primarily involves an evaluation of the self by the self.[25] Shame is a complex emotion evoked by failure of an individual or group to live according to their values or commitments, especially ones concerning their relation to others and goods which others also value, so that they believe themselves to be defective. It is commonly a response to the real or imagined contempt, derision or avoidance of real or imagined others, particularly those whose values are respected (Williams, 1993). While the negative judgements may be verbalised, they can also be signalled intentionally or unintentionally through expressions and comportment, and in the way the shamed person is generally treated. To act in a shameful (or contemptible) way is to invite such contempt, including self-contempt. It

---

[22] However, they may limit it unintentionally through minority private property ownership of resources like living space, land and other means of production, which restrict the liberty of non-property owners (Cohen, 1995).

[23] Smith recognised both the moral sentiment of the respect for the sanctity of the individual, seeing it as central to justice, and 'the horror of solitude' (1759:1984, II.ii.2.3, p. 84).

[24] E.g., 1759:1984, pp. 84–5.

[25] Shame is usually prompted by some experience in relation to others, imagined or real, but primarily concerns the self: 'Shame is the most reflexive of the affects in that the phenomenological distinction between the subject and object of shame is lost' (Tomkins, in Sedgewick and Frank, 1995, p. 136).

may be prompted by inaction as well as action, by lack as well as wrong-doing. Particularly where it derives from lack rather than specific acts, shame may be a largely unarticulated feeling existing below the threshold of awareness – one that is difficult 'to get in touch with', yet still capable of blighting one's life, both in terms of how one feels and the impression one makes on others and hence how they respond to us. As we shall see, this 'low-level shame', which shades into low self-esteem, is particularly common among subordinated groups. It has somewhat different characteristics from the more intense, sometimes burning, shame that follows from specific actions. At the extreme shame can be an extraordinarily powerful emotion involving endless reflection and self-condemnation, sometimes tormenting people to the point where they commit suicide or violently attack others (Gilligan, 2000). Its power is evidence of the importance of recognition by others. To be ashamed is to feel inadequate and shrink from the gaze of others. Because of its seriousness as an index of ill-being and failure and the fact that we can feel ashamed of our shame, it is generally only acknowledged through euphemisms by those who experience it, for to admit shame publicly is humiliating (Scheff, 1990).

Like all emotions, shame is *about* something: it has referents. It may relate to failure to achieve valued appearances, for example in looks or clothing (aesthetic shame), failure to carry out some task to an expected standard (performative shame), or – more importantly – failure to conduct oneself in ways deemed proper, and to live in ways considered acceptable (moral shame). It may also be a product of internalisation of others' contempt for one's identity. All of these kinds of shame are common in the context of class inequalities. Like other emotions, shame is a fallible response in the sense that it can be unwarranted or mistaken.[26] The person who through no fault of their own has a despised body shape or who cannot afford fashionable clothing has done nothing shameful, but might still feel shame. Equally, the complementary feeling of contempt may be unwarranted, if it is unrelated to any shameful or contemptible behaviour for which the despised can reasonably be held responsible. This is the case with class contempt. Thus, as with other moral sentiments, we can acknowledge the existence of shame without endorsing every instance of it as appropriate. We may even deem some sentiments of shame to be misjudged or *im*moral, for example, the shame of married men of my father's generation whose wives went out to work, which supposedly indicated that they were unable to 'keep' them.

---

[26] This is less obvious than in the case of its opposite, pride, instances of which are often described as 'false'.

Shame may also be engendered by invidious comparison with others who have done better than ourselves in competition for goods which we value, such as educational achievements or moral behaviour (Tomkins, in Sedgwick and Frank, 1995, p. 161). This source of shame is particularly important in relation to class. Within the educational systems of class societies, the shaming of those who fail is a structurally generated effect, as Bourdieu's extensive research on such systems demonstrates, even though it is felt as an individual failure (e.g., Bourdieu, 1996a). Those who believe that society is basically meritocratic are most vulnerable to shame. Whereas gender ideology prescribes mainly different standards for men and women, class ideology prescribes both similar and different standards for different classes; the working classes are both imagined or expected to be able to compete on equal terms with others and expected to fail.

To the extent that the things we come to value are shared so that we identify with others, shame may derive from vicarious sources, through empathy or fellow-feeling (Tomkins, in Sedgwick and Frank, 1995, p. 159). We may share the shame experienced by other members of our own group, or take on the shame we feel they should feel, even where they do not. As members of many groups we can experience shame in relation to any group that we identify with: 'I may feel shame at the indignity or suffering of any human being or animal to the extent to which I feel myself identified with the human race or the animal kingdom, and have reverence for life as such' (Tomkins, in Sedgwick and Frank, 1995, p. 160).[27] Given that we belong to a number of different groups it is possible to feel both contempt and shame in response to another's behaviour, depending on which group is being considered. Members of the British middle classes may feel contempt for working class football hooligans for their behaviour and in relation to their class, but shame as fellow Britons.

Shame is often associated with guilt, and in popular usage the distinction between them is sometimes fuzzy and unstable (Bartky, 1990), but, broadly speaking, shame is primarily inner-directed, and need not be tied to harm to others, whereas guilt is more related to specific failures (real or imagined) in the treatment of others. While both involve responses to the real or imagined feelings of others, in the case of shame the others' feelings are ones of contempt, derision or avoidance, whereas in the case of guilt the others' feelings are assumed to be ones of anger, hurt or indignation (Williams, 1993). In addition, whereas shame can concern aesthetic and performative matters as well as moral issues, guilt is

---

[27] Many vegetarians cite shame in response to the suffering of animals reared for food as one of the influences upon their vegetarianism.

aroused only by awareness of moral failings in relation to others The two emotions are often combined; one may feel both guilt at having failed to honour a promise to someone and shame about having let oneself down in this respect. What is often called 'middle class guilt' appears to involve shame as well as guilt insofar as it implies both regret about belonging to a society based on unfair inequalities and regret for specific actions of their own which help to reproduce middle class advantages at the expense of the working class.[28] However, they can also be distinct; an adult who is unable to read may feel shame about this, but not guilt.

Shame is in some ways the opposite of self-respect and pride, but they are also related. To experience shame is to feel inadequate, lacking in worth, and perhaps lacking in dignity and integrity.[29] Self-respect derives from a feeling that one is living a worthwhile life and a confidence in one's ability to do what one considers worthwhile. Although deeply private, self-respect is also a profoundly social emotion: it is impossible for us to maintain the conviction that how we live and what we do is worthwhile if there are no others who appreciate our actions (Rawls, 1971, pp. 440–1), and the approval of others is crucial for well-being, albeit particularly those we respect. Rom Harré suggests that actors continually seek out situations where they risk contempt and hence shame, in order to win respect, implying that unless we take such risks, we shall achieve little respect or self-respect (Harré, 1979). In this way, shame and self-respect are linked. Those who never risk contempt because they never put their beliefs 'on the line', whatever the situation, are likely to be seen as lacking the courage of their convictions, or having no convictions or commitments and hence lacking character. This strategy fails because it too invites contempt. One might also feel shame about not having any convictions. Maintaining integrity in the face of pressures to bend is a prime source of respect and self-respect but it is buttressed by fear of the contempt and shame which failure would bring. Thus, the chief sources of self-respect among the American working class men interviewed by Michèle Lamont derived from their self-discipline, their ability to work hard, provide for and protect their families, and maintain their values in an insecure environment (Lamont, 2000). They could hold up their heads, and define themselves as morally superior to managers, who, they felt,

---

[28] Middle class guilt and shame is usually very limited and mixed with a good deal of self-justification. There are often only the barest traces of these sentiments because class inequalities are normalised, if not naturalised, and in any case responsibility for class inequalities lies with social forces that are not reducible to individual actions.

[29] 'If distress is the affect of suffering, shame is the affect of indignity, of defeat, of transgression, and of alienation . . . While terror and distress hurt, they are wounds inflicted from outside which penetrate the smooth surface of the ego; but shame is felt as an inner torment, a sickness of the soul.' Tomkins, in Sedgwick and Frank, 1995, p. 133.

lacked integrity, failed to value people properly and generally dissembled in their pursuit of money, power and status.[30]

On the one hand there are forms of shame in which the shamed person has high self-regard and which derive from situations in which she has let herself down according to her own standards. In these cases she accepts the real or imagined judgements of others insofar as they accord with her own views. Conversely, if she feels badly regarded by others for whom she has no respect, and with whom she profoundly disagrees, she will not feel ashamed, because she doesn't feel she has done anything to be ashamed of. In such cases, as the psychologist Sylvan Tomkins argued, the negative feeling of shame is dependent on a positive valuation of the behaviours, ideals or principles in question (Sedgwick and Frank, 1995, pp. 136ff.). It is because they are positively committed to certain standards that their failure to meet them causes shame. In these cases, 'shame is far from requiring diminished self-regard as its essential backdrop' (Nussbaum, 2001, p. 196).[31] It is only if we have certain expectations of ourselves that we can be shamed. This central feature of shame is commonly overlooked by sociological accounts whose disciplinary inclination to emphasise external social influence leads them to treat shame as merely the product of external disapproval (e.g., Scheff, 1990). If one has high self-regard, to be treated with contempt by others for whose values one has no respect might induce sadness and anger but it need not induce shame. The worst kind of disrespect, the kind that is most likely to make one feel shame, is that which comes from those whose values and judgements one most respects. Hence the stronger the commonality of values, the greater the possibilities for shaming.

On the other hand there are also forms of shame in which the shamed person lacks self-regard and therefore either lacks the confidence to disagree with even unwarranted disrespect, or else still feels shame even where she does disagree with the criticism or contempt of others. The low self-regard derives not from a single episode but from the habitus as a result of years of subtle or unsubtle forms of disrespectful treatment by others. These are evident in gendered and classed behaviour in which the subordinate are not listened to, interrupted, not taken seriously, patronised, or viewed in a way which is insensitive to their social disadvantages. The disrespect need not be verbalised, but may be evident in subtle forms of comportment, and may be confirmed by differential access to

---

[30] See also Kefalas, 2003. Presumably the managers were not shamed by this contempt because they did not regard the workers as worthy judges of their character and because they had other sources of self-respect, particularly achievement.

[31] Unlike Tomkins and Nussbaum, however, I don't believe this applies to the low-level shame of members of subordinated groups.

internal and external goods, and in the unequal distribution of material wealth.

Sandra Lee Bartky describes her experience of teaching middle-aged female students who, despite being in the majority on the course and despite being aware of generally performing better than the male students, nevertheless still felt inadequate. The shame they experienced was not so much an emotion or a belief as 'a pervasive affective attunement to the social environment . . . a profound mode of disclosure of self and situation' (Bartky, 1990, p. 85).[32] Their failure to resist being positioned as inferior was a product of their limited confidence in their own self-evaluations. Where the shamer has higher social status relative to the shamed person, their opinions are likely to be socially authoritative (Calhoun, 2003). The power to shame is therefore disproportionately concentrated among the dominant.[33] Cheshire Calhoun, citing Lehtinen, argues that 'women are less likely than men to defy shamers' judgements of them because they have internalized a low self-evaluation' (Calhoun, 2003, p. 10). Low-level shame as a product of subordinate class position is similar, except that, as we argued in chapter 4, the inferior positions which invite condescension and low expectations from others are partly a product of identity-neutral processes. Low-level shame may be less intense than episodic shame, but it is more durable and probably more sociologically significant in relation to the reproduction of class and gender.

Calhoun argues people are most likely to feel shamed even by judgements they disagree with in situations where they have some regard for those who judge them negatively, where they have to cooperate with them on a regular basis, and where they are in a minority, or perhaps a silenced majority. We are participants in 'social practices of morality', such as those of workplaces, which for us are likely to be 'the only moral game in town', and even though we may feel our co-participants are sometimes mistaken in their particular negative judgements of us, their views can carry weight and shame us – especially if they are *significant* co-participants and if we respect many of their other views. We would have doubts about anyone whose self-regard was such that they were oblivious to all negative judgement from co-participants, even if the latter were sometimes mistaken, because it would suggest that they did not take social practices of morality seriously (Calhoun, 2003). Morality is not simply an epistemic matter but a product of the social character of being.

Low-level shame often cannot be articulated, indeed it can *lead to* withdrawal and inarticulacy in terms of a feeling of lack of authority to speak,

---

[32] Bartky attributes this specifically to women, though I suspect it also occurs in men, albeit less commonly.

[33] This is another instance of the questionable association of the good with the posh.

and hence lack of practice in articulating one's situation, at least in the presence of class others (Charlesworth, 2000). This in turn is likely to be interpreted by others as sullenness or evidence of low intelligence. The poorest are thus not only materially deprived but linguistically dispropriated and hence disempowered as subjects. The deeply embodied nature of low-level shame is evident in the fact that it also tends to be peculiarly resistant to demonstration of its lack of warrant, so that it is common for those members of subordinated groups who are upwardly mobile to continue to feel that they are not good enough, and that one day they will be 'found out'. It can be reduced by sharing experiences with other sufferers, hence bringing it to discursive consciousness and gaining the self-regard and confidence to refuse disrespect. Thus, as James Scott has shown in relation to slave societies, the oppressed often develop their own 'hidden transcripts' which defend their moral worth and have the potential to be made public and serve as a rationale for resistance (Scott, 1990). To remove low-level shame can also require years of repeated practice in the sense of drilling new behaviours into the body and mind, and gaining access to the practices* and goods that provide both self-respect and respect in the eyes of others.

We can summarise these variants of responses to contempt in similar fashion to the last chapter's summary of judgements regarding the posh and the good in relation to schooling:

(1) feeling shame because we accept that our behaviour has been genuinely defective (warranted shame);
(2) rightly feeling confident that the other's contempt is misplaced and hence feeling no shame (warranted refusal of the other's contempt);
(3) mistakenly thinking the other's judgement is unwarranted and hence feeling no shame (shamelessness, arrogance);
(4) feeling shame because we mistakenly accept unwarranted judgements by others (misplaced shame);
(5) feeling shame despite disagreement with the other's negative judgements (unwarranted but overriding shame).

Responses 4 and 5 are most common among the subaltern. While these variants can be distinguished analytically, in practice it may be difficult to decide whether we should feel ashamed, first because many judgements about conditional recognition and moral matters are extremely difficult, secondly because of the social nature of moral practices which make going against the majority difficult, and thirdly, in the case of low-level shame, because it is deeply embodied and resistant to analytical influence.

The shame response is an important mechanism in the production of social order, indeed it is hard to imagine how there could be much social order without it, for through it people internalise expectations, norms and

ideals, and discipline and punish themselves. Discourses may give people scripts, but people can care about some parts of these scripts and feel
indifferent about others according to how they bear upon their well-being;
they are not merely programmed by discourses. (Recall that discourses
cannot voluntaristically construct just anything: even though they can
try to define well-being they may fail to do so and be resisted by actors
drawing upon conflicting parts of the same and other discourses.) Under-
neath the remarkable variety of cultures, the universal human capacity
for shame is one of the mechanisms by which people are ensnared by
discourses and norms, in all their diversity. But the metaphor of being
ensnared is also too passive, for the human need for recognition, whose
pursuit always carries the risk of failing and being shamed, drives us to
seek out ways of acting virtuously from among the many possibilities
offered and defined by our culture. All this is not to deny the common
presence of power in social settings involving shame, but on their own,
concepts of power, whether in capillary or arterial form, cannot explain
the internalised normative force and selectivity of shame responses. Thus,
although not directly acknowledged by Bourdieu, a capacity for shame is
a necessary but rarely acknowledged condition for symbolic domination;
indeed, the latter is scarcely intelligible independently of these
emotions.

However, it is superficial to regard shame merely as an emotion which
produces social conformity, for this fails to do justice to its normative
structure, and therefore fails to explain the full range of its effects. The
desire to avoid shame may promote *resistance* rather than conformity.
Those who are fervently anti-racist, for example, may speak out against
racism in situations where doing so might put them at some risk. If we
had no normative commitments, then it is hard to see why we would
ever want to resist and how we would ever be shamed, because we would
simply 'go with the flow', accepting whatever the pressures of the moment
required. However, the anti-racist who keeps silent when others make
racist remarks is likely to feel shame for conforming instead of resisting.
Shame can therefore produce either conformity or resistance, but we
cannot make sense of this if we reduce it to no more than a product of
fear of external disapproval.

Which behaviours are worthy of pride, and which are the proper cause
of shame, is of central importance normatively, and traces of such concerns may be apparent in internal conversations. They are especially likely
in modernity, given the plurality of value systems and the emphasis on
the project of the self. There are different sources of value and respect –
for example, domesticity, vocational achievement, parenting, masculinity and femininity – many of which are partly mutually incompatible.

Unequal societies which nevertheless have widely shared or hegemonic norms have a greater capacity to generate shame than more normatively diverse ones because so many are denied the means to live according to such norms. Thus the more that working class parents are ambitious for their children and the more they accept dominant values regarding education and meritocracy, the more vulnerable they become to shame if the school system rejects them.[34]

When faced with objective conditions which are shaming, that is, which give people little alternative but to live in ways they do not consider acceptable, there is always a temptation to reconsider the valuations giving rise to the shame, devaluing what was valued, and valuing what was despised. To the extent that working class people refuse what they are refused, they avoid the shame that accompanies lack, indeed this may be a motive for their refusal. By contrast, the desire to be respectable and recognised as such is a shame response dependent on some degree of positive feeling towards what is lacked. At times people may simply be ambivalent about such matters. The struggle of subordinated groups for self-respect is particularly likely to lead to contradictory dispositions and opinions. They may try to make a virtue out of their position and their toughness and fortitude in bearing burdens, at the same time as they feel shame about having to bear those burdens. These are simultaneously responses of resistance and compliance. An example of this was found in a study of working class people in West Cumbria, an isolated and oft-forgotten part of north-west England, with high unemployment and an economy dominated by the notorious Sellafield nuclear power complex. Attitudes and dispositions towards the latter indicated both resistance and resignation and rationalisation, both criticism of the industry's secrecy and dominance and – in response to outsiders' criticism of the industry – defensiveness towards it. They both wanted to know more about the hazards and did not want to know. They both celebrated the toughness implied by living so close to hazards, and felt shame and anger that they should have allowed their area to have become the recipient of nuclear waste from other regions and countries (Wynne et al., 1993).[35]

Such mixtures of shame and defensiveness and defiant pride are typical of situations in which people have to seek self-respect in circumstances that are not of their choosing. Concrete situations typically confront us

---

[34] This is borne out by Diane Reay's research on working and middle class mothers' experience of putting their children through school, discussed in the last chapter (Reay, 1998a) and also the experience of academics of working class origin (Reay, 1997a).

[35] Thanks to Bronislaw Szerszynski for drawing my attention to this research.

with competing pressures and value systems and though we don't necessarily have to resolve many of the resulting tensions in order to get by in
daily life, they are likely to produce emotional ambivalence. The subaltern in particular are likely to be torn between envy and rejection of dominant values and the associated goods lying beyond their reach, and hence
between acceptance and refusal of shame. That shame can sometimes
be a product of situations beyond actors' control is vitally important for
understanding the experience of class. It is all the stronger where actors
have individualistic explanations of inequalities. Thus the black working
class youths studied by Jay Macleod who believed in the American dream
of individual responsibility for one's own fortune were more vulnerable
to shame than their white counterparts who rejected it (Macleod, 1995).
By the same token the French working men studied by Lamont were less
likely to feel shame than their US counterparts because they had a more
structural and politicised understanding of class (Lamont, 2000).

. . . and Humiliation

Closely associated with shame is the production and experience of humiliation. This is occasioned not merely by the attribution of deficiency to
an individual or group, but by public affirmation of this inferiority, in its
most extreme forms requiring the humiliated to confirm it by debasing
themselves (Glover, 2001). Humiliation ranges from particular acts, such
as the denigration of a child by a teacher in front of classmates (which
might be for their social class, 'race', gender, body shape or sexuality, or
reasons unconnected to these), to mild, implied forms of humiliation such
as speaking for others who can perfectly well speak for themselves. The
very presence of wide disparities of wealth, coupled with the tendency for
advertisers to invite consumers to see their consumption as a measure of
their worth, could be said to have the effect of humiliating the poor.[36] This
might be termed 'structural humiliation'. Fear of humiliation encourages
the dominated to hide their poverty or other forms of lack, and to conceal
anything which signifies their low status. It can also prompt superfluous
conspicuous consumption (at personal cost) to conceal the lack. (It is
interesting that critics of capitalist culture tend to notice the conspicuous
consumption more often than the related concealment of lack, reading it
as evidence of profligacy.)

Humiliation may also be caused by benevolent acts. Targeted redistribution based on means-testing, for example, may be well-intentioned but

---

[36] Tawney referred to the 'moral humiliation that gross contrasts of wealth and economic
power necessarily produce' (Tawney, 1931, p. 41).

provokes resentment and lack of response because of its humiliating character, for it publicly draws attention to the recipients' lack.[37] Especially where specific goods, rather than money, are distributed on the basis of means-testing, it implies a lack of respect for the recipients' autonomy, for it involves intruding in decisions which for others are private. In this way, despite its intentions, charity can be humiliating (Wolff, 2003). It is possible – though rare – for members of the dominant classes to realise the danger of redistributing in ways which humiliate and demean the poor. Just as generosity on the part of the dominated towards the dominant ('if they've earned it they're welcome to it') legitimises and perpetuates inequality, so the moral desire on the part of some members of dominant groups to avoid humiliating the poor may deter them from doing anything about the inequality (Anderson, 1999; Wolff, 2003).

The humiliation of means-testing illustrates the structural nature of class. The old arguments of egalitarians against mere charity appealed to reasons that can help us understand symbolic domination. Even if it is argued that the poor are not poor through any fault of their own and therefore should claim the benefits without feeling humiliated, the enduring, structural nature of economic inequality, and its close correlation with inequalities of cultural, educational and other forms of capital, are likely to make acceptance of such a position difficult. It would be different if redistribution on the basis of means-testing were compensation for a rare, one-off disaster, but against the backdrop of the structural inequality, the exceptional and palliative nature of the policy is bound to undermine its legitimacy in the minds of its potential beneficiaries. Where the dominated are confident that their disadvantages derive not from personal deficiency but from injustice – in terms of both distribution and recognition – redistribution is more likely to be understood as affirming entitlement rather than repairing lack.

For Smith, these and other moral sentiments have their basis in moral psychology, in our vulnerability and our physical, psychological and emotional dependence on others: 'All the members of human society stand in need of each other's assistance, and are likewise exposed to mutual injuries' (Smith, 1759:1984, II.ii.2.4., p. 85). The 'assistance' may derive from actors' sense of justice, gratitude and benevolence or from a sense of utility, prudence and enlightened self-interest, especially in the case of market relations (ibid., p. 86; see also Smith, 1776:1976). The universalising component of morality derives not simply from an abstract principle but, as Smith argued, is implicit in the psychology of social interaction. The need for 'the pleasing consciousness of deserved reward' encourages

---

[37] Of course it can be introduced as a way of policing and regulating the poor.

actors to treat at least some others fairly, and indeed well. That actors can gain such recognition from within their own group may mean that they have less need for it from others, but they still need it from somewhere. That the desire for deserved recognition is often overridden by more anti-social dispositions and motives (of which Smith was well aware), which are often encouraged by inherited inequalities and injustices and their associated legitimising discourses, does not contradict this claim. Unexercised powers or powers which are exercised but overridden by others are the normal stuff of open systems such as those of society (Bhaskar, 1979; Collier, 1994; Sayer, 1992, 2000a). It is these counteracting or overriding tendencies to which we now turn.

Immoral sentiments and class

Class contempt[38] (Reay, 1998b), like other kinds of 'othering', ranges from visceral revulsion, disgust and sneering, through the tendency not to see or hear others as people, to the subtlest forms of aversion. In its mildest forms it may merely involve a slight feeling of unease when in the company of others, and may merge into a sense of not belonging rather than hostility towards the other. Even at its mildest, class contempt can, on certain occasions, such as job interviews, make a major difference to people's life-chances. It responds to accent, language, appearance, comportment, demeanour, values, actions, possessions and lifestyle. These correlates of class differences are minutely acknowledged in literature, in every soap opera, and lampooned in comedy.[39] Class contempt thus includes but goes beyond snobbery and can be felt 'up' as well as 'down' the social scale. Like racism or sexism, ageism, or homophobia, it lacks any rational moral basis. Yet it is striking that while sexist and particularly racist language has become taboo in official discourse, the language of class contempt has not, so that, for example, the *Times Higher Educational Supplement* could report without critical comment that the chief executive of the Council for Industry and Higher Education referred to students from lower social groups as 'the unwashed', needing to develop their social skills (*THES*, 17.5.2002).[40]

Others may be derogated or privileged simply by virtue of their class or gender, etc. Who is this person? What's their background? Anyone who is

---

[38] I use Reay's term in preference to Bourdieu's 'class racism', which obviously carries unwanted baggage.

[39] Indeed it is a measure of the pervasiveness and significance of classed behaviour that in theatre or films an actor who failed to act as befits the class of the role they were playing would be judged a very poor actor.

[40] See Skeggs, 2004 for discussion of many other examples.

out of place is likely to be regarded with suspicion: how can this working class person be stylish?; how can this person with a working class accent be a professor of politics?; how can this female plumber be competent?; and so on. Such cases illustrate how signifiers of class, gender or race serve as prompts for judgements of worth. Doubts about the capacities and sometimes even the propriety of the out-of-place individual reveal the kinds of expectation and valuation held regarding those who are in-place; working class people are not expected to be capable of intellectual work, or women of being plumbers. Class contempt is typified by illegitimate slides from aesthetic to performative and moral disapproval. It is complemented by approval of self and those of the same class and projection of all that is bad and immoral onto the other, which reciprocally confirms the goodness of one's own class (Skeggs, 2004). This is evident in the criminalisation of the black working class and more recently the poor white working class, and the condoning of middle class crime. Further, working class women in particular are in many cases treated as objects of disgust focusing on 'excessive artificial appearance' which 'immediately signifies moral worthlessness' (Skeggs, 2004, pp. 99ff.). This bolsters the upper middle classes' impregnable sense of superiority, and a less secure sense of superiority in the petits bourgeois.

Like many emotions, contempt can be betrayed by facial expressions – the raising of the upper lip into a sneer – even if it is not expressed verbally. As Tomkins points out, this is a physical drawing back from the object of disgust – or distaste (Tomkins, in Sedgwick and Frank, 1995). As usual such expressions tend to take more subtle forms in the upper classes, given their avoidance of strong facial expression and displays of emotion. Being in a position of dominance they do not need to send out any stronger signals and to do so would only indicate that they cared. Hence the slightly grimaced smiles rather than aggressive sneers. They do not have any need to resent others, even if others disgust them, whereas for dominated groups resentment is more likely to be the stronger feeling. Class contempt was famously evident in Margaret Thatcher's facial expressions when answering questions from interviewers about things and others that she found distasteful, particularly people she regarded as inferior. Her answers would often be preceded by a short pause to indicate the irksome nature of the question and the inferiority of the questioner, then an intake of breath through the mouth during which the upper lip would be slightly pulled back by the cheeks. Her mouth movements would suggest an unpleasant taste, and as she drew herself up to speak she would half close her eyes and look downward and then up again. She would tilt her head to one side patronisingly with a withering look as if talking to a disobedient child, her distaste again displayed by her mouth movements and swallowing while she spoke in measured phrases, theatrically alternating these with fierce denunciations in which she would glare at the questioner. She positively oozed class contempt and condescension, provoking either admiration or loathing in her audiences according to their class affiliations.[41]

Pervasive though class contempt undoubtedly is, it does not of course exhaust the bases on which self and others are evaluated, for such judgements are also made of particular behaviours and characters. From both positive and normative points of view, it is important to appreciate that not all contempt for the behaviour of class others is class contempt, for one might feel equal contempt for such behaviour when it is found in members of one's own class.[42] The same applies to gender; not all disapproval of the behaviour of someone of the opposite sex need be a product of sexism, for one might condemn the same behaviour in one's own sex. By class contempt we mean contempt for people and their behaviour by virtue of their class position, not their behaviour, or alternatively contempt for their behaviour simply because it is associated with a particular class, because it is posh or common rather than good or bad.

Like sexism, racism, ageism and homophobia, etc., class contempt forms a background against which aesthetic, performative and moral judgements are made. They tend to act as modifiers of these judgements, introducing double standards into them, so that the same appearance, achievement or behaviour in people of different groups are evaluated differently; what is acceptable in a man is unacceptable in a woman, what whites can get away with blacks cannot, and so on.[43] Adam Smith recognised this effect in relation to class: 'This disposition to admire, and almost to worship, the rich and the powerful, and to despise, or, at least, to neglect, persons of poor and mean condition, . . . is . . . the great and

---

[41] Of course, one of the extraordinary features of Margaret Thatcher was her appeal to some strains of *working class* authoritarianism, to those who wanted to distance themselves from people they considered below them. This reminds us that while relations of domination and condescension and deference typify inter-class relations, they are also to be found in other sites, including members of the same social class.

[42] The distinction between condemnation of others and condemnation of particular behaviours is an important one and sometimes evident in lay thought. See below, chapter 8.

[43] Deciding what would be fair and justified judgements in the context of these forms of difference is often *not* a matter of disregarding difference and attempting to impose a single standard; thus the differences between the young and the elderly may not all be false ascriptions but may require judgements which take them into account. In other words, the issue of deserved and undeserved recognition takes us into the debate over equality and difference, explored particularly in feminism (e.g., Phillips, 1997).

most universal cause of the corruption of our moral sentiments' (Smith, 1759:1984, I.iii.2.III, p. 61).[44] Smith's focus on everyday relationships rather than on perfecting a normative philosophy of ethics enabled him to recognise such 'corruptions' as a common feature of social life. They are fundamental to the subjective experience of social divisions, producing distortions not only of moral sentiments but of evaluations of non-moral qualities too. But actors may also recognise the illegitimacy of such slippages and distortions, especially if they themselves are negatively positioned in relation to them, and respond – either by inverting the privileges and derogations or by rejecting them.

At the same time, judgement of others is not wholly a form of othering which operates completely irrespective of what others actually do, though it certainly is in part. Insofar as we are dependent on others we cannot normally afford to grant or refuse them recognition completely unconditionally. We also need to judge how they are behaving, including how they are treating us and others; in other words we need to make recognition conditional. This opens up the possibility of having our prejudices contradicted by their behaviour; in other words, people's aesthetic, moral and performative evaluations can sometimes conflict with prejudices relating to class, gender and other divisions. Thus class contempt coexists with, and can check and be checked by, more moral sentiments of sympathy and generosity; indeed, this is a prime source of challenges to class contempt, and similarly with sexism, racism, homophobia and so on. Those who refuse to acknowledge these conflicts and who refuse recognition to others regardless of what they do, purely on grounds of irrelevant indicators such as 'race', gender or class, age, sexuality or disability deprive themselves of relationships or assistance from which they could benefit. Conversely, those who grant recognition unconditionally to favoured groups and hence refuse to believe they are capable of failing to live up to expectations expose themselves to risk through gullibility.

A common ploy of progressive playwrights and novelists who deal with social divisions such as class, gender or 'race' is to counterpose the moral prejudices of their characters with examples of moral others. Thus the white supremacist, snob or sexist is shamed and humbled by the superior moral behaviour of a black or working class man or woman. The characterisations of moral others may themselves be patronising, and inadvertently perpetuate stereotypes (for example, the moral but nevertheless *simple-minded* other), and intellectuals may enhance their own cultural

---

[44] Those familiar with Smith will know that the omitted parts of this quotation are important for understanding Smith. However, delving into this would require a substantial digression which does not affect my argument.

capital by developing critiques of such work, but it identifies the essential contingency of the relation between moral conduct and such social divisions. Moreover, if this were not the case, it is hard to see why we should think there was anything wrong with hierarchical divisions such as those of class, 'race' or gender.

In addition to these ways of evaluating and differentiating people, which imply conditional recognition (whether distorted or not), there may also be a moral feeling that people have a right to be respected simply as human beings, i.e., unconditional recognition, though clearly in practice, this idea(l) of an inclusive human moral community is often not acted upon, and many kinds of 'others' are in varying degrees excluded from it. Among the French and US black and white working class men interviewed by Michèle Lamont the few that expressed anti-racist attitudes did so by appealing to such universal qualities.

Conclusion

Morality here figures not as formal norms or teachings based on religion or on ethical theories tenuously linked to our sentiments, but as grounded in the social psychology of emotional responses as evaluative judgements, shaped by the dialectic of autonomy and dependence and the need for goods and recognition. I have emphasised how moral and immoral sentiments relate to class, but, as we noted at the outset, *all* social relations have a moral dimension to them, be they between parent and child, men and women, workmates, friends, neighbours, strangers, traders, people of different cultures, and more. Both moral and immoral sentiments can arise in all of these. Actors gain the main part of their moral education by living in these relationships. Thus it might be from having suffered disrespect or some other source of pain within one kind of relation that they come to imagine their effects on others in similar or different relations, including class relations.

Dispositions and sentiments towards unequal others are typically mixed and inconsistent, combining class contempt (and/or sexism, ethnocentrism, etc.) of various strengths with sympathy and generosity. Sometimes moral sentiments of compassion may cross over into condescending pity and aversion. The situation is further complicated by the fact that feelings towards class others are not necessarily simply in response to their class, but can be to other characteristics which have some independence from class influences too, such as stature and beauty. Lay evaluations of self and others may often be misguided in various ways – they may be 'moralistic', hypocritical or sometimes immoral and unjust, and they may ignore social conditions, so that problems are always attributed simply to individuals. However, these sentiments and evaluations, be they tacit or considered, cannot be ignored because: (a) they matter greatly to individuals; (b) regardless of whether we agree with them, they help to reproduce our social reality; (c) they tell us something about class relations, and (d) they represent rival normative stances to those of moral and social theory, to which the latter must answer, if it expects a hearing beyond academe.

Many contemporary sociologists are likely to be sceptical about the attention I have given to moral sentiments. If so, I would appeal to their reflexivity and ask whether they could live without these sentiments or dispositions – without being aware of the difference between friendliness, compassion, shame, guilt, hatred, revulsion, etc., without continually monitoring their own and others' conduct, and whether they could avoid trying to distinguish between deserved and undeserved recognition (for example in marking essays). If other accounts cannot acknowledge these, and hence are contradicted by our own practice, then as I argued at the outset, we should reject them. If we ignore moral sentiments we are likely to reduce the analysis of class to a one-sidedly bleak account of prejudice and hostility which not only misses much of the picture but gives no means for understanding sources of resistance other than the pursuit of power.

7   Responses to class I: egalitarianism, respect(ability), class pride and moral boundary drawing

Introduction

As we saw in the discussion of the micro-political struggles of the social field, the ways in which people act towards class others involve varying mixes of pursuit of advantage, deference, resistance, and pursuit of goods for their own sake. But they are also influenced by their moral sentiments and norms, which are only partially inflected according to class and other social divisions. They can operate (not necessarily intentionally) within the terms of class hierarchy or without regard for it. Yet, even actions which are not driven by struggle for advantage over others, indeed, even those that have egalitarian motives, are likely to be twisted by the field of class forces in ways which reproduce class hierarchy.

In this chapter I focus on four responses to class: egalitarian tendencies, the pursuit of respect and respectability, class pride, and moral boundary drawing. There are overlaps and tensions among all of these. Wanting to be equal can be coupled with wanting respect. Class pride claims and asserts what the pursuit of respectability merely seeks, and is usually coupled with moral boundary drawing. The subaltern, in particular, are likely to slide from one response to the next. In the context of structural class inequalities, all of them are likely to provoke condescension. They are most easily described in terms of intentions, but they may all also exist below the threshold of consciousness as dispositions, as part of the habitus.

While all these matters concern the subjective experience of class, they are responses to objective social structures, distributions of capitals, hierarchies and differences, discourses and cultural values. They are intertwined with other axes of inequality, particularly gender, but they reflect the distinctiveness of class. As we saw in chapter 4, the determinants of class, in the broad senses used by Bourdieu and in lay discourse, encompass both identity-sensitive mechanisms, such as those involving responses to actors' cultural capital and status, and identity-neutral mechanisms, such as the indirect effects on workers of consumers' purchasing decisions. The latter are major but not exclusive determinants of economic class, that is, class in the narrow, abstract sense. Whereas changes in discourses, attitudes and behaviour regarding class in the everyday sense, such as a decline in deference or an increase in contempt for the so-called 'underclass', can make some difference to people's lives, identity-neutral mechanisms associated with market processes tend to reproduce or transform class regardless. By contrast, while patriarchy is also strongly embedded, it can be gradually eroded from within the micro-politics of everyday life by individuals and institutions changing their behaviour in appropriate ways. This is because, unlike class in the narrow economic sense, it is culturally determined in the first instance. If men and women were to disregard gender norms, gender differences would fade, but economic class positions can be reproduced even in the absence of symbolic domination and hostility between classes, and even in the absence of lay awareness of class, though they are often contingently affected by actions which are influenced by perceptions of class. To acknowledge this is in no way to deny that there is symbolic domination in relation to class in the broad sense, or to suggest that it, and the subjective experience of class, are unimportant, only that they are not necessary conditions of the existence of economic class in the narrow sense. A contingent relation is not necessarily an unimportant one – I would hardly have made it the major subject of this book, if it were trivial. It is of central importance to the quality of our lives and what we care about. An interest in the subjective experience of class implies an emphasis on the identity-sensitive mechanisms producing class differences, but the effects of the identity-neutral mechanisms can be felt powerfully too, most obviously through changes in profits, unemployment rates and interest rates. Whereas the latter are experienced as changes happening *to* people, identity-sensitive processes such as class contempt are both felt and enacted by individuals.

A word of warning: in describing classed behaviours I am referring to tendencies, and making generalisations, not blanket claims that are supposed to apply to all cases. Behaviours are influenced by many things, and not even the broadest concepts of class – or indeed class, gender and ethnicity – cover all these influences. In addition, lay reflexivity mediates actors' responses to these influences. In Bourdieuian terms, the behaviour, outlook and habitus of individuals in particular positions, having particular volumes and compositions of capital, and having had particular trajectories through the social field, are also influenced by processes, such as family dynamics, personalities and cultural forms, which are themselves partly independent of these things.

Wanting to be equal or ordinary

Egalitarian sentiments are common in unequal societies. As Myrdal found in *The American Dilemma* and Billig et al. in *Ideological Dilemmas*, scarcely anyone refuses to acknowledge that at some level people should be treated as equals (Myrdal, 1962; Billig et al., 1988). But while such sentiments are common, they are often weak and inconsistently acted upon. Whether actions intended to counter or ignore inequality actually succeed depends on the kind of inequality in question and on how such actions are received by those to whom they are directed. Their impact on class is likely to be much less than on gender and other divisions such as 'race' or sexuality.

In Mike Savage, Louise Bagnall and Brian Longhurst's study of attitudes to class in the Manchester area (Savage et al., 2001a), one of the striking features of many respondents' views was their desire to be *ordinary*. There could be many reasons for this, but one possibility has to do with egalitarianism. It could imply a refusal of pretension and condescension – a wish to remove the barriers of status which impede one's relationships with others – so as neither to feel the embarrassment of being deferred to and resented nor to feel inferior and deferential to others. Interaction and mutual recognition are inhibited and distorted not only by condescension but by deference. The deferential other who refuses to take on the role of equal even when it is offered to them denies the person extending the offer the satisfaction of adequate recognition and sociability.[1]

At the same time, these respondents wanted to be distinctive, but presumably not within a hierarchy. One of the common mistakes critics of egalitarianism make is that egalitarians want to suppress individuality and make everyone the same. Advocates of equality have often responded to this by pointing out that an important justification of equality of recognition of moral standing and distributional equality is that it allows everyone equal opportunity to develop differences, and for abilities, virtues and vices to be valued appropriately, without distortion from morally irrelevant differences of class, gender, race, sexuality or age. If only we could remove morally irrelevant differences such as those of class we could be valued for what we are – different, distinctive individuals. This is why, *pace* Savage (2000, p. 156), it makes perfect sense to want to '"flip" between being ordinary and distinctive at the same time'. As Tawney argued, in order to respect each other for what we are, we must cease to respect each other for what we earn.

---

[1] As we saw in chapter 3, especially where deference seems to be exaggerated it appears sarcastic and contemptuous.

Whatever such views mean, attempts at refusal of class position and equal treatment of class others are likely to fail. Given that class forms a hierarchy and not merely a pattern of differentiation it is clear that class-mixing is itself unequal in that it is easier downwards than upwards. The structural nature of economic class is demonstrated by the fact that while the 'decline of deference' (and condescension?) over the last thirty years might be evidence of a decline of symbolic domination, it has not necessarily been accompanied by any reduction in economic inequalities of class; indeed it may have had the effect of making the latter more acceptable. As Warde et al. argue, the effect of the restriction of increased cultural omnivorousness largely to the elite 'might be to intensify social and cultural inequality under cover of a veneer of universal participation in popular culture' (Warde et al., 2003; see also Skeggs, 2004). Despite this, it is not unusual for individuals, especially those with plenty of economic, cultural and social capital, to imagine that class differences can be neutralised by ignoring them and treating others as equals, as if class were purely a product of misrecognition.[2] As we saw in chapter 3, marked inequalities in economic distribution cannot help but imply unequal recognition or render attempts at equal recognition shallow and illusory. The illusion is encouraged by the kind of vulgar culturalism that assumes that 'culture goes all the way down' and explains class. Of course, that this is an illusion does not reduce the moral case for trying to treat class others as equals, but class in the narrow economic sense is primarily a matter of distribution in which many of the determining processes are indifferent to identity. Its justification or lack of justification is a matter of recognition, but its causal determination is only partly and contingently so. This means that it is harder for individuals 'to strike a blow for equality' with respect to class than to gender. This fact shapes the mixes of shame, guilt and pride that are commonly associated with class. The embedded nature of class differences presents middle class egalitarians with a dilemma: on the one hand, to attempt to ignore the fact that someone has little economic or cultural capital can be highly insensitive; on the other, to acknowledge their lack of such capital can seem patronising, as reinforcing ('rubbing it in') rather than countering inequality. It is also arguably responsible for the failure of equal opportunities policies to address class.

In addition to this structural limit, there are other obstacles to attempts at egalitarian behaviour towards class others which are more similar to those impeding egalitarian actions in relation to gender and 'race'.

---

[2] This view is especially common among middle class students. It typically goes with a belief that they can 'get on with anyone'.

Egalitarian initiatives may be refused by those to whom they are directed because they accept their positions as legitimate and hence not something to be challenged. Just as women who have been socialised into traditional gender roles may be reluctant to let men do housework or to take on jobs conventionally associated with men, so working class people may be reluctant to break out of traditional roles and may refuse opportunities for upward mobility. This conservatism is understandable, since working class culture is a source of support and there are risks involved in deserting it, as upwardly mobile individuals appreciate. As many have noted, moving up involves moving out, and seeming to betray the values of one's class (Lawler, 1999).

Even in the absence of such conservative attitudes, egalitarian behaviour is likely to be regarded with suspicion. It may be sincere: those who have a lot of capital do not necessarily consider themselves superior, even if others assume that they do, and of course it is possible for those who do not have more capital than others to behave in snobbish ways. Egalitarians might wish that, ideally, their class others would just 'take them as they find them' and judge them according to their behaviour, not their position, but this is also naive, given the embedded nature of class and the way that behaviours are subtly differentiated by class. People are judged by where they are coming from even when they are opposed to class and other inequalities. Further, the more those attempting to ignore class boundaries are aware of the suspicion of them, the more difficult it is for them to avoid a self-consciousness that reveals that they are indeed 'out of place', and 'trying to be something they're not'. Downward mixers have simply not 'paid their dues' and can never really understand the situation of the dominated. Hence working class people may be resentful of both middle class outsiders who fail to recognise their situation *and* those who do and claim to understand them (Griswold, 1999, p. 98; see for example Williamson, 2003). Maintaining distance from others one doesn't know, and accepting that one doesn't understand them, is, as Sennett (2003) argues, more respectful than falsely claiming empathy and similarity, for it implies recognition of difference. However, respect from a distance does nothing to challenge the objective inequality even though it may affect its subjective experience.

Attempts at mixing downwards seem to imply a refusal of advantage and symbolic violence, raising the obvious question: 'What's in it for them?' The outsider may merely want to pass as having a different class position from her own out of self-interest, to gain access to the internal goods of other classes, to be a social chameleon in order to get the best of all social worlds (Skeggs, 2004; Warde et al., 2003). This is likely to be an element in the lowering of the divide between high and low culture. Just as racists may enjoy Indian food and despise those who produce it, so middle class people may enjoy football but feel varying degrees of contempt for working class supporters, footballers, and 'footballers' wives'. When they do get access to working class goods and practices* they are unlikely to be accepted by the working class, as we saw in the case of working class ridicule of middle class football supporters. These are rare occasions on which the working class can extract some symbolic profit from the middle classes and experience the pleasure of being able to refuse the privileged something they want, instead of the more common situation of refusing what the privileged refuse them.

However, while these forms of refusal of class mixing are utterly understandable in terms of the struggles of the social field, if the motivation of those who try to mix across class divisions are not selfish then this kind of negative reaction would itself be anti-egalitarian, saying in effect: 'Respect the class system!'[3] Cultural and moral differentiations associated with class can be used to police any transgressions of class, including those of would-be egalitarians, and sometimes doing so is seen as an act of resistance, but it can have conservative effects. There is a danger of this for example, in Beverley Skeggs' hostility to such transgressions (Skeggs, 2004). Ironically, the egalitarian may meet more class resistance from the dominated than do those members of the dominant classes who simply ignore them and respect class differences. Many still expect others to behave in accordance with their position, as long as they show others respect. Being 'what one is' may seem more dignified and easier to respect than trying to be what one is not. Professionals in particular are allowed – indeed expected – to be different. However, the implicit ethic of authenticity is dubious since it naturalises social hierarchies. Similarly, as Bourdieu notes, the working class are likely to be more hostile to one of their own number who tries to be middle class – to be 'something they're not' – than to a middle class person who acts in familiar middle class ways (Bourdieu, 1984).

Condescension is commonly thought of simply as a form of individual behaviour, which may or may not be enacted. This might be the case where someone who is actually an equal of others puts on a condescending manner in her interactions with them, indicating that she imagines herself to be superior. But usually condescension involves relations among unequals. Condescension of this form is commonly ambiguous. The person in the superior position is normally considered condescending if she

---

[3] Similarly with regard to gender, a man trying to be non-sexist and doing feminine things may be under suspicion: is he just trying to gain some advantage (e.g., sleep with feminists)? – or does he have a genuine egalitarian desire to behave in a non-sexist way regardless of whether it brings him advantages?

acts towards those in subordinate positions in a way which indicates her superiority and perhaps distaste but also appears to make concessions to their lowly status ('being gracious enough to talk to them'), and thus draws attention to it.[4] Their words may be contradicted by their deeds and manner, or vice versa. They are likely to be viewed by the subordinate as either simply offensive or uncomfortably ambiguous, though they may be met gratefully, with deference. It is not only that condescension may be perceived even where it is not intended, on account of the suspicions of the interlocutor, but rather that it is inevitable within structural relations of inequality. Alternatively, the treatment of the subordinate as an equal is bound to clash with the objective inequalities of the relationship. Attempts at egalitarian mixing downwards in terms of class are therefore doomed to seem condescending and patronising, even when sincere. (The attempts of egalitarians at mixing upwards without showing deference are likely to be seen as disrespectful by those above them. The latter reaction is of course less troubling for egalitarians than the former, for the dominant should be challenged, not mollified, by egalitarianism.) Thus, condescension within class relations is not merely a kind of individual behaviour but a *structural* feature of the relation, deriving from the objective differences in capitals, especially in cultural and linguistic capital, living conditions and experience.

Qualities such as integrity, warmth and friendliness, however, may sometimes allow people in different class positions to have good relations. This qualification is important precisely insofar as these qualities are valued *across* classes, albeit not to exactly the same degree or in the same form. Again, while we should be aware of class contempt and differences of class habitus we should not underestimate the extent of a desire to treat people fairly and value them for their personal qualities. But such relationships are always likely to be constrained in ways which friendships among class equals are not.[5] For example, it may be easier for them to interact on neutral territory, where their objective inequalities in economic, social and cultural capital are less exposed, rather than in their homes or workplaces where they are glaring and where opportunities for embarrassment loom large.

Hence the structures of feeling about class relations and interactions relate – mostly unknowingly – to the objective nature and structure of those relations as (partial) products of distributive mechanisms, and this

---

[4] It is notable that in older literature, say nineteenth century and earlier, before the rise of egalitarianism, condescension was not seen in negative terms.

[5] It might seem mean-spirited and overly class conscious to dwell on these obstacles (let alone dwell on class for a whole book!), but the problem lies with class inequalities themselves, not their recognition.

continually frustrates egalitarianism at the level of interpersonal inter-actions. The dilemma for egalitarians regarding class is that while they may consider class immoral, the way they interact with class others is unlikely to do more than muddy the waters of the micro-politics of class. It may even ease class tensions by reducing symbolic domination and with it resistance to economic inequality by encouraging the illusion that we are all equally resourced for living as equals. As Nancy Fraser notes, the last thing the working class need is recognition of their difference (Fraser, 1999; see also Coole, 1996), though of course, particular work-ing class people may *want* it, and outsiders may genuinely consider par-ticular goods of working class culture worthy of value. The complexities of inter-class relations and recognition derive from the fact that at the level of the micro-politics of everyday life people of all classes want and need recognition, though not necessarily of their class identity.

Respectability and respect

. . . I began to feel in my flesh that being respectable and getting respect were not one and the same. Anyone listening to Aretha knew that. Respect was about being seen and treated like you matter. (bell hooks, 2000, p. 20)[6]

The pursuit of respectability and of respect both demand recognition of dignity, and perhaps esteem of ability and propriety, but what they imply differs significantly, and their meaning and occurrence vary according to the position of the individual or group within the social field. Respectabil-ity is sought by the dominated but largely eludes their reach. It is par-tially attainable by the middle classes, though precariously. It is taken for granted by the dominant. Respectability is sought somewhat submis-sively and deferentially; respect is claimed or demanded more assertively (though there can of course be intermediate positions). Insofar as respect and respectability differ in terms of assertion and deference they tend to be gendered, respectively, as masculine and feminine. The demand for respect by subordinate groups is more egalitarian, demanding recognition on their own terms, without deference, for what they are[7] (Glover, 2001, p. 23). It is no accident that it comes most often from marginalised but politicised groups such as racialised or ethnic minorities.[8] In such cases,

---

[6] My thanks to Maureen McNeil for drawing this quotation to my attention.

[7] However, the demand is problematic where it is assumed that *all* recognition should be unconditional.

[8] Particularly in youth culture, such non-deferential demands for respect may be picked up and emulated by oppressed and not-so oppressed members of the dominant cul-ture. While a marginalised ethnic minority might demand recognition for its cultural identity, for the white majority working class to do so risks affirming and legitimising their subordinate position.

it usually implies a demand for respect for cultural difference, not merely respect according to dominant norms. In disaffected marginalised young men for whom there are no attainable respectable options because of class or race or gender, it may take the form of seeking respect through intimidation and the celebration of the bad as good (Macleod, 1995). For poor white marginalised young men, this could be a response to the refusal of recognition and goods which would allow them to be equal on majority terms, and the unavailability of an alternative culture whose standards and goods they could achieve. Thus, while the desire for respectability defers to hierarchy and dominant values, the demand for 'respect' from the subordinate does not. Respectability involves being inoffensive, 'not sticking-out' (Southerton, 2000b, p. 196), keeping out of trouble, moderating sexuality, being respectful of and acceptable to the (upper) middle classes, thereby avoiding their moral and aesthetic disapproval. Those who set great store by it may therefore pay a heavy price in terms of self-repression. Respectability's deference to dominant values also allows it to be coupled with snobbery towards those below, so that confirmation of respectability can be obtained both positively from above, and negatively by contrast with the unrespectable below.

One of the main concerns of the young working class women studied by Beverley Skeggs was to be recognised as respect*able*, though this recognition was generally denied to them, not only because of their class but because of their gender and sexuality. This caused them considerable distress (Skeggs, 1997). However, it could be argued that the problem with this is not that respectability was denied to them, but that they wanted respectability rather than respect in the first place. As Skeggs notes, Engels referred to the ideal of respectability as 'a most repulsive thing' and 'a false consciousness bred into the bones of workers' (cited in Skeggs, 1997, p. 3). At the same time, the more challenging nature of the demand for respect does not, of course, necessarily make it any more successful than the pursuit of respectability – indeed, it is likely to be resisted by the dominant as disrespectful, strident, ridiculous and undeserved.

Whatever the strengths of this kind of analysis, it involves a radical reductionism in that it merely inverts the conflation of the posh and the good and the common and the bad, so that the respectable becomes bad and demands for respect automatically valid. As we saw in chapter 5, things are not so simple for the obvious reason that we cannot assume that dominant values are necessarily wholly unworthy of respect, and merely products and devices of symbolic domination. Dominant values – especially moral values – are not necessarily reducible to the values of the dominant. They may include moral values of propriety which are good rather than merely posh. Insofar as recognition involves a conditional element, demands for respect (or respectability) without demonstrable qualities worthy of respect invite rejection as mere foot-stamping. Both the pursuit of respectability and respect and the refusal to acknowledge or grant them typically involve not only conflations of the posh and the good, and the common and the bad, but slides from aesthetic to moral evaluation, so that propriety or impropriety are read off from appearances such as dress and accent. At the same time, there may be more or less implicit distinctions between the desire to be recognised as honest and morally good and the desire to *differ* in other respects. Everyday social interaction rarely allows these issues to be made explicit, and much of the mutual classification and evaluation that goes on is done within a glance – often a glance of class contempt. Nevertheless, the complex ambivalence of working class and lower middle class people about whether to join or refuse the struggle for respectability reflects the complexities of these normative issues, and these in turn derive from the tensions between inequality and the pursuit of recognition.

At one level these are banal points but they can easily be missed if we neglect to explore the normative issues. The detachment of claims for recognition or respect(ability) from qualities that people have is not surprising in a highly unequal, amoral, neoliberal and multicultural society, in which power *per se* demands to be respected regardless of its legitimacy,[9] in which what will sell is more important than what is good or right, and in which judgements of cultural others are likely to be ignorant and ethnocentric. Multiculturalism poses the dilemma of recognising others whose cultures are not known or understood by the majority. While this should not pose a problem for unconditional recognition of humanity, it is likely to do so for conditional recognition, because of the difficulty of making informed, non-ethnocentric judgements of others.[10] For all these reasons, it is not surprising that the demanding and granting of respect have come somewhat adrift from their performative and moral ties, so that respect is demanded without it being clear that it relates to qualities and behaviours worthy of such recognition. In such a context, appearances and impression management are likely to matter all the more.

The fear of refusal of respectability and recognition is particularly evident in encounters with class 'superiors'. For instance, for elderly British lower middle class and working class women, going to see the doctor is

[9] While this is of course a defining feature of domination, echoes of it can be discerned in the threats of violence from marginalised young men, where the performance of masculinity requires the assertion of power.

[10] See also Griswold's discussion of demands for recognition and respect from outsiders while understanding is denied to them (Griswold, 1999, pp. 91ff.).

a major social test, provoking anxieties which may outweigh those they have about their illnesses. Proving themselves to be respectable – not only morally but in terms of social standing – involves particular attention to appearance, bearing and speech so that negative aesthetic and moral evaluations are avoided. Doctors – especially male doctors[11] – may be seen as key figures in their communities, perhaps the only professional, upper middle class people that such women encounter; in fact, with the decline of church attendance and the social standing of priests, they may become the most elevated local people of all to have frequent contact with large numbers of the community.

The doctor would be expected not only to take their symptoms seriously but to grant them recognition as respectable, this being a form of *noblesse oblige*, though one that is not honoured unconditionally, but conditionally upon the respectability and deference of the patient. The confirmation of respectability here is particularly critical given the nature of medical examinations, the cross-gender as well as cross-class nature of the encounter, and the severe embarrassment that many of this generation and class of women have about their bodies, which have to be talked about through metaphors and euphemisms. Respect is more likely to be communicated through carefully modulated distance rather than familiarity, so that through his bearing and gravitas the doctor affirms rather than denies his elevated social position. For the patient, recognition is seen as all the more valuable if it is clearly coming from someone of higher status. He may also be expected to show professional flair, even panache, so that he is seen not merely as an agent or transmitter of impersonal expertise but as something of a virtuoso. He is therefore expected to be able to personalise the performance of the role, so that the patient recognises him as having character, as being, say, Dr Smith, rather than just any doctor – someone who is a figure in the community, someone by whom one should feel proud to be recognised. This, of course, enhances his social capital. Even a little brusqueness and arrogance may, if moderated with some charm and pleasantries, be excused as evidence of his command and standing. (Younger doctors who try to be more familiar and equal may be regarded by these patients as lacking in competence and status and as disrespectful – not only because of their behaviour but because they are not in a position to command – *and hence confer* – respect.) If the doctor does treat them proficiently and with respect, they feel socially elevated and tell their friends and family about the visit with pride. If, however, the doctor fails to listen to them and treat them with respect, the patient

---

[11] It should be remembered that many women of this generation still endorse patriarchy, and therefore do not necessarily prefer to see a woman doctor.

may feel doubly aggrieved because not only has he failed to do his job properly but she feels she has failed the social test.[12]

Thus the doctor is expected not only to be competent but to exhibit appropriately gendered and classed behaviour rather than diverging from such norms. Only then will his behaviour affirm the legitimacy of the naturalised social order. The power relationship derives not only from the asymmetry in medical knowledge between the doctor and the patient but from symbolic domination related to class and gender. (The ability of Dr Harold Shipman, the serial murderer, to get away with killing over two hundred elderly patients, mostly women, for over two decades, no doubt owed something to the deference inspired by his professional confidence and gravitas[13] and to the esteem in which doctors are held in such communities.)

For many such elderly petit bourgeois women, the struggle for respectability is coupled with an intense privatism, and withdrawal from unregulated social interaction. The two became particularly mutually reinforcing in the mid-twentieth century, at the time of their early adulthood, with the growth of a limited economic security and private housing for the upper working and lower middle classes, which made privatism more economically feasible. This was also the period of the ascendancy of the full-time housewife norm. Respect implies a certain distance which allows the other autonomy, so that they are not intruded upon. Thus, lack of need of others can be taken (not necessarily correctly) to imply self-reliance and self-respect. 'They keep themselves to themselves' is still sometimes heard as an expression of respect for such respectful behaviour in neighbours. By contrast, being open and gregarious is threatening because: (a) it reduces this distance, so that there is a risk of being or feeling disrespected by others who are 'too familiar'; and (b) it exposes the seeker of respect to the vicissitudes of social relations through which she might be embarrassed, whether by being 'dragged down' by association with the unrespectable or by exposing her inadequacies to the dominant. Moreover, prolonged isolation could lead to the loss of confidence and social skills, thereby making the loneliness harder to escape. The refusal

[12] Further complexities in these relationships arise where the doctor is black and the patient white or vice versa, producing conflict between deference to class, gender and competence on the one hand, and racist aversion on the other. There is of course a great deal more which could be said about such interactions, particularly regarding gender relations.
[13] The dubious valuation of gravitas and confidence *per se*, regardless of whether they are supported by competence or worth (in other words not only allowing oneself to be 'conned' but celebrating one's gullibility) remains one of the most common problems of the micro-politics of everyday life, particularly organisational life, one which reinforces middle class domination.

of others was self-repressive rather than selfish, though being 'fiercely independent' could easily lead to misanthropic tendencies. Now, in their old age, their loneliness is borne stoically with dignity but their anxiety is intensified by fear of loss of respect in response to their age, physical decline and dependence on carers, so that the concern with respectability may become overriding for them. For such people, the struggle for dignity and respectability is structured through class, gender and age, partly in terms of the norms of earlier cultural formations in which they grew up, producing both visible and hidden injuries.

Class pride

Working class pride takes different forms. It is generally more common amongst men than women, for despite their subordinate class they nevertheless belong to the dominant gender, which provides them with some self-esteem, whose source they may then misread in class terms, though this is likely to be changing now given their deteriorating position in labour markets and the rise of feminism. Among US white working men it is individualistic; among US black working class men, more solidaristic and politicised in relation to race; among French white working class men, more politicised in relation to labourism and its institutions (Lamont, 2000). Working class pride has declined along with the mass collective worker, labourist institutions and the industrial base that supported it, while individualisation has grown – hence the shift from a sense of class based on affiliation to one based on differentiation.[14] This has been coupled with the rise of the rhetoric of meritocracy, which passes off class differences as differences in merit arising from a fair process of individual competition.

Pride in being working class implies very different normative grounds from pride in being middle or upper class. Being proud to be working class has a rationale, in that its members occupy the moral high ground as a consequence of their lack of any undeserved advantage relative to others. Their merits and internal goods cannot be attributed to the accident of birth and inheritance but have been achieved in more difficult circumstances than those enjoyed by the better off, and indeed they could claim to be owed a debt because of their disadvantage and social exclusion and their work in servicing the middle classes. This is also of course why

---

[14] It was probably always less common among fragmented, poorly organised occupations, such as kitchen porters, than among highly organised workers like miners. Deindustrialisation can destroy class pride. The South Wales valleys, which once had the strongest labour organisation and proudest working class culture in Britain, are now known as the heroin capital of Britain.

those who are born into the middle or upper classes are falsely conscious if they imagine this is something to be proud of, for this is a result of an accident, not their efforts. Where middle class people take pride in supposed virtues such as self-reliance and propriety – a sentiment often evident in right-wing newspapers – they typically ignore their privileged circumstances and their dominant relation to and dependence on the working class which facilitate their attainment. They are largely bonuses of their class position, not qualities they can claim credit for. Working class people may also take pride in lacking the pretensions and affectations associated with insulation from the pressure of economic necessity, and in the virtues of self-discipline and hard work that are needed to cope with this, as was the case with the working class men studied by Lamont (Lamont, 2000).[15] There might also be class-specific cultural goods that their holders feel proud to be associated with. More aggressively, the real or imagined question, 'Think you're better than us, do you?', challenges those whose propriety and worth is part of their embodied symbolic capital rather than something they feel any need to prove. To make such a challenge to the assumption of moral superiority of the dominant implies that one has achieved self-respect and has little need to pursue respectability. Yet pride in being working class can also be problematic, if it encourages an acceptance rather than a contestation of class.

Moral boundaries and prejudices

The tendency for class to be experienced through processes of cultural differentiation and distinction has been brilliantly illustrated by Bourdieu (1984). However, as Lamont points out, he 'greatly underestimates the importance of moral boundaries while he exaggerates the importance of cultural and socio-economic boundaries' (Lamont, 1992, p. 5). Often, as Dale Southerton's study of class identity in an English new town shows, people use a mixture of aesthetic, performative and moral criteria to define their own identities over and against others (Southerton, 1999, 2002a and b; see also Kefalas, 2003). Where moral boundary drawing is of major importance to people it tends to be accompanied by self-repression and surveillance to maintain conformity so that their self-image is confirmed. For Southerton's middle class interviewees, tidy gardens and well-kept houses clearly indicated moral superiority. Working class residents regarded the middle classes as pretentious, and merged generalisations about social status with personal characteristics in using

---

[15] There is a danger of romanticisation of working class and moral superiority, as suggested by the title of Lamont's book: *The Dignity of Working Men*.

terms such as 'new money'. In so doing they challenged their others' imputed values regarding the good. Thus, working class criticism of materialism 'allowed respondents to distance themselves from the more affluent, without directly locating themselves in a monetary hierarchy' (Southerton, 1999, p. 168). Working class valuation of down-to-earthness and hatred of pretentiousness could be viewed sceptically as a form of competitive behaviour, a compensatory strategy through which those who lack economic and cultural capital can claim some superiority. At the same time, the moral case for such an attitude is strong, for it amounts to an affirmation of unconditional recognition of others, and a refusal of the pursuit of external goods for their own sake.[16]

Yet the kinds of 'othering' involved in moral boundary drawing can produce strange results, as in the example of the opposition between down-to-earthness and cosmopolitanism. Thus in working class communities, the pursuit and display of cosmopolitanism is read as an attempt to assert cultural and moral superiority. They do not devalue cosmopolitanism simply because they can't afford it or because they are necessarily parochial and xenophobic, but because of its association with snobbery and pretension; in getting closer to other cultures, the cosmopolitans are seen as distancing themselves from the ordinary, the common. As Lamont notes, from the perspective of the working classes, 'cultural sophistication . . . [can be] seen as a superfluous quality in comparison with sincerity or honesty . . .' (Lamont, 1992, p. 125). In the United States such views are justified by positioning intellectualism and cosmopolitanism as being at odds with virtues such as friendliness, generosity towards others, conflict avoidance and cultural egalitarianism. This hostility towards intellectuals is not arbitrary. Intellectuals' vocation is criticism, and their targets include commonsense understandings and practices. They tend to acquire a habitus which maintains this critical front even in situations where others would expect openness and friendliness – an acceptance which passes over differences and flaws; hence they are likely to be seen as cold, prickly, unsociable, and unable to understand the nature of phatic communication (which is often true!). In addition their class position allows them to adopt a contemplative rather than a practical orientation to the world, plus a taste for superfluity. All of these characteristics,

---

[16] These moral attitudes can be affirmed in the most minimal of social interactions. In rural areas of Britain, it is common for people, including strangers, to acknowledge those they pass with greetings such as 'morning', or 'lovely day'. Where they differ in apparent or actual standing, the greetings can be offered deferentially or condescendingly. However, particularly where they are strangers, the greeting can be initiated by the person with lower capital in a way which functions as an assertion of or appeal to moral equality, inviting or guilt-tripping the other to confirm a generous, unconditional recognition of equal status.

together with their acquired skills, can be turned to their advantage, overriding the hostility with which they are often regarded.[17]

These class-differentiated moral dispositions and attitudes are intelligible in the light of objective class structures. Class inequalities give symbolic domination a structural character, as we saw in the case of condescension. In a fundamentally unequal society the celebration of practices such as painting or opera is bound to function as a celebration of cultural and economic advantage, of superiority in aesthetic, performative and perhaps moral worth. This effect operates largely independently of the intentions of those involved in such practices. If there were an egalitarian society, one in which there were no significant differences between social groups in distance from necessity, in which the distribution of practices* and their internal goods across society was equal or random, then the pursuit and celebration of such practices* would not involve any symbolic domination.

Moral boundary drawing has a crucial ambivalence at its heart, which can easily be overlooked: while it provides us with reasons for rejecting and devaluing others, *it also treats the merits claimed for our own group as universally valid*, while refusing to believe that the other could have such merits. Whereas in aesthetic matters, many would be happy to tolerate pluralism, they are less likely to do this with regard to many moral matters. To value down-to-earthness is not merely to say it's only a good thing for one's own group, though we might feel that only our own group has this quality, but that *everyone* ought to be down-to-earth. Likewise with cosmopolitanism. If people did not think these judgements were universally valid there would be no reason for them to think less of groups which did not live up to them. Thus, while middle class valuation of cosmopolitanism could be attributed to mere pursuit of cultural capital for advantage, this is also too cynical. Just as sociologists value foreign food and holidays not only or necessarily in order to gain cultural capital but because they consider those things worthwhile in themselves, regardless of the advantages vis-à-vis others that they bring, so other members of the middle classes can value them for their own sake too.

Moral boundary drawing is also vulnerable to falsification, precisely because members of other communities may be able to demonstrate the qualities they are assumed to lack, or because members of the boundary drawers' own community may fail to meet the standards they claim to monopolise. However, such evidence is likely to be resisted. We can illustrate this by reference to Maria Kefalas's study of the white upper

---

[17] Bourdieu (1993) used the term 'racism of intelligence', and in *Pascalian Meditations* candidly notes, 'I do not like the intellectual in myself' (Bourdieu, 2000, p. 7).

working class/lower middle class residents of 'Beltway' in Chicago's Southwest Side. These people lacked economic security and rightly feared slipping into poverty. They constructed a moral identity based on self-discipline, order, honesty, patriotism, hard work, and pride in home, garden and community. These values were enforced through peer pressure and visibly inscribed into the fabric of their suburb. They defined themselves in contrast to the blacks and poor whites of the inner city, who belonged to what they saw as a dangerous world of disorder, dereliction, fecklessness, ill-discipline, graffiti, filth, drugs and gangs. The fervour with which the residents of Beltway constructed this imagined moral geography and affirmed their identity was proportional to their anxiety about slipping down into this other world, indeed their way of life was a defence against this possibility. Blacks and poor whites were seen as a constant threat to their lives and their property values. Moral boundary drawing on class and race lines helped them create a reassuring world of moral simplicities. This made '. . . it difficult for [Beltway] dwellers to reconcile themselves to the existence of *white* teenage mothers, *white* homeless, *white* drug addicts, *white* gangbangers, *white* single mothers, and poor *whites*' (Kefalas, 2003, p. 155).

The illusory nature of the moral contrasts was forcibly brought home to the community by the murder of two local teenage girls. The trauma of this event was greatly increased by the discovery that their killers were not black or poor white gang members from outside, but two local, white teenage boys, who belonged to a Beltway gang. One was the son of a police officer, the other the son of a firefighter, both archetypically 'respectable' upper working class occupations. Local residents found it enormously difficult to acknowledge these facts or that Beltway had any gangs, and strenuously tried to refuse this threat to their self-identity, for example by suggesting that the boys could not have been normal or proper members of the community. The residents were 'in denial', but their denials had no credibility and merely confirmed the illusory nature of their moral distinctions and the insecurity which drove them to construct such a simplistic worldview.

Conclusion

All these responses to class inequalities – egalitarian actions, the pursuit of respect and respectability, class pride and moral boundary drawing – have a clear moral dimension to them. They all reflect a universal need for recognition, albeit one which is often largely satisfied through other kinds of social relations, within classes, such as among family and friends. The socio-spatial segregation of classes makes living in a class society more bearable not only because it hides material inequalities and symbolic violence but because it facilitates sharing of internal goods (which tend to be class-differentiated too) and provides scope for recognition of worth among equals.

The four responses each resist class inequalities in different ways, but they are all frustrated or turned back into reinforcing class by the durable, structural and embodied character of those inequalities. Even egalitarian actions of individuals trying to interact with members of different classes as equals are likely to have little effect and may be rebuffed as disrespectful and/or condescending. Demands for respect in the context of marked inequalities of distribution are likely to fail; the very pursuit of respect and respectability imply their lack of warrant. Class pride is a source of accommodation to class as much as a defence against it and can function conservatively to reinforce inequality and division. Moral boundary drawing provides a source of self-esteem but hardens class divisions. Yet it also opens itself to challenge by invoking universal criteria which the stigmatised others might actually be able to meet, or which some members of the boundary drawer's own group might fail to meet, as in the case of the Beltway murderers.

Thus at the same time as they are responses to inequalities and divisions, all the moral sentiments and judgements involved have a universalising tendency,[18] which, appeals 'over the head of class', as it were, to criteria that have at least some degree of independence from class. While this is most obvious in the case of egalitarian actions, it is present in the other responses too. The pursuit of respect appeals both for unconditional recognition and conditional recognition of qualities that, while unequally distributed because of class and other inequalities, do not conform totally to them. Demands for respect can also appeal to recognition of the injustice of class, and of fortitude in resisting it. Despite its deferential character, the pursuit of respectability invokes criteria of propriety which are imagined (rightly or wrongly) to be universal or at least common. Occasionally, the dominant may have to acknowledge that those criteria have been met.

In all these ways, moral responses to class both resist and are themselves shaped and frustrated by class. In the next chapter we move beyond such responses and attitudes to actors' more considered evaluations of their own and others' behaviour, and to their views of class itself.

---

[18] Like Smith, we regard this universalisation to derive not from philosophical principles but from the everyday interpersonal dynamics of fellow-feeling and recognition.

8   Responses to class II: explanations, justifications and embarrassment

Introduction

In this chapter we examine how people explain and evaluate behaviour in relation to class, and how they regard class itself. As we noted at the outset, normative evaluation is likely to be more important to people than positive understanding of their situation. Yet these lay normative valuations are also part of their situation, and, while they are often questionable, they usually reveal something about both that context and their holders, and are therefore worth probing for both positive and normative insights. Lay attempts to understand and evaluate the behaviour of members of their own and other classes involve many slippages and blockages but these are themselves instructive. Such reflections could be seen as lay sociologies and philosophies: indeed, some of the problems they run into are not unlike those found in those disciplines – problems of determinism and free will, explaining and justifying, and weighing and relating social causes and individual responsibility. Quite apart from all the likely distortions of judgement produced by entrenched inequalities and the need for self-justification, questions of blaming and praising and attributing responsibility are *inherently* difficult, raising deep metaphysical issues that have been the subject of considerable philosophical debate (Williams, 2003, 2004a). Lay views of class itself are also complex, involving a tendency for normative judgements of class and position within the class structure to override positive assessments of what class *is*. Above all, attitudes to class are characterised by embarrassment, defensiveness, denial and evasion, indicating its morally problematic character. The judgements and responses can be performative or causally efficacious: but as always, just how far, in what ways, and with what effects, depends on the properties of the phenomena – social, psychological and material – they deal with. If we analyse these evaluative responses, drawing upon insights of sociology and moral philosophy, we can develop a better understanding of the visible and hidden injuries of class.

I shall begin with an analysis of how lay actors explain and sometimes justify anti-social behaviour, illustrating it by examples, arguing that while there are elements of refusal and denial in their responses, they are also dealing with problems of explanation which are intrinsically difficult. I shall then address the way in which actors' judgements of their class others sometimes involve fine distinctions between responses to their identities and responses to their behaviour. Again, while there are elements of defensiveness and self-justification in such responses, the difficulties are also inherent in the object of their evaluation itself. Finally, I shall examine the reasons for the common evasiveness and embarrassment about class, arguing that they are a product of class itself and the objective social relations within which people live, and the available discourses through which they can construe them.

Explanation and justification: anti-social behaviour

In going about their daily lives people not only evaluate their own and others' conduct, but sometimes try to explain it, particularly where they find the conduct objectionable. These explanations are a significant element of popular interpretations of class. Although actors may just condemn, they also often attempt to *explain* why people are as they are, why they behave in particular ways; indeed, such explanations are a necessary component of the more considered evaluations that they make. In effect, they sometimes think as lay sociologists or psychologists. Bourdieu would no doubt have objected to such a description, on the grounds that it projects the exceptional circumstances of the contemplative life of academics onto those they study. I have already made it clear that we need to recognise both the scope of unreflective practical action and the role of conscious monitoring and deliberation in everyday life, but again, ironically the strongest answer to those who would marginalise the latter is to be found in the interviews of *The Weight of the World*, where such deliberations are articulated at length, often in ways which reveal folk sociologies (Bourdieu et al., 1999). The interviewees not only condemn others and justify their own conduct, they also try to explain the practices they condemn. Sometimes, being aware of the difficult circumstances in which those responsible for the acts have to live, they express sympathy for them and consider excusing them.

As is typical of everyday understandings of the world, their explanations of character and conduct are over-individualised, that is, they attribute to individuals responsibility for events and circumstances – good as well as bad – which are in varying degrees consequences of wider social forces.

There are difficult philosophical issues here in terms of explanation and attributing responsibility to people, and they arise in lay discourse as well as academic interpretation, causing problems for both.[1] In discussing lay explanations I shall therefore have to digress to comment on the philosophical problems involved. In brief, it is commonly feared that in providing a social explanation for unacceptable behaviour, such as violence, one is also excusing or justifying it. This fear then deters actors from pursuing such explanations any further, so that they then resort to invoking individuals' intrinsic evil as the ultimate cause.

As an illustration we can take an interview from *The Weight of the World*, conducted by Patrick Champagne with four workers living and working on a run-down public housing estate where burglaries and violence and other kinds of anti-social behaviour are common, particularly amongst youths (Bourdieu et al., 1999, pp. 106–22).[2] Three of the interviewees were building superintendents, middle-aged, male, working class, and the fourth a woman with slightly more educational and cultural capital who worked in the housing project office and was married to one of the superintendents. The interviewees not only described and bemoaned the problems of the estate and the anti-social behaviour of the youths but offered and discussed explanations. For example, they were only too aware of the poor state of the buildings and the lack of opportunities, especially for young people, but they also noted, with despair and incomprehension, how, when any effort was put into improving the state of the buildings, the youths immediately vandalised them. They wondered whether the behaviour was a result of their social exclusion. However, they then rejected this explanation on the grounds that exclusion did not *justify* such behaviour, because they (the interviewees) had endured worse poverty when they were young and yet did not respond in this way. Their attempt at explanation then effectively came to an end.

In popular conversation and debate the non-sequitur that what cannot be justified cannot serve as an explanation is often seen as a knockdown argument beyond which one cannot proceed. Social scientists who attempt to explain anti-social behaviour by reference to social conditions are regularly rebuffed by politicians and journalists on the grounds that such conditions do not justify or excuse such behaviour, the implication being that the researchers are doing just that. The same response meets those who try to explain the phenomenon of suicide bombing or terrorism

---

[1] Not least, there is the 'problem' of free will. For a discussion of responsibility in a similar context to that of our discussion, see Midgley, 1984; Williams, 2003, 2004; and Smiley, 1992.

[2] See also his interview of a tenant, ibid., pp. 83ff.

in general by reference to oppression.[3] The idea that 'society is to blame' – the usual reductive description – is regularly lampooned in right-wing media.[4]

Faced with this block, we are invited to resort to the idea that the youngsters on the housing estate are just inherently anti-social. In other words, it as if persons were 'uncaused causes'. If we accept this, then, as former British Prime Minister John Major said, with breathtaking stupidity, we should 'condemn a little more and understand a little less'.[5] This line of reasoning, if it can be called that, wants to refuse explanation and simply identify evil and punish it, that is, respond with reciprocal violence. It implies the absurd idea that localised concentrations of evil just happen to develop at certain times for no reason. Alternatively – or in addition – if a racial identifier can be found for the 'evil-doers', then racist discourses can supply their own 'explanation'.

However, this common block to social explanation is certainly not simply a function of political refusal, a result of people being 'in denial'. It is partly an understandable yet mistaken response[6] to difficult philosophical issues about reasons and causes and free will. While this mistake is common in lay thinking, it is not uncommon in social science, particularly deterministic approaches which reduce actors to dupes – that is, beings which are caused (or 'constructed') but which themselves do no more than relay external forces.[7]

Despite the apparent difficulty of explaining unacceptable behaviour without justifying it, doing so is not only implicit in many familiar situations but in certain conditions is regarded as entirely proper. When an official inquiry is held into why a disaster happened, for example the death of a child subjected to physical abuse despite the knowledge of

[3] Of course, explanation by reference to such conditions can be too simple. It has been frequently pointed out that Osama Bin Laden came from a privileged background. Other influences have therefore to be admitted, in particular the role of discourses, possible sympathy for the oppressed, and the possibility of unoppressed individuals seeking to seize power using those who are genuinely oppressed.

[4] As Garrath Williams points out, withholding all blame and attributing anti-social behaviour wholly to upbringing and social conditions is ultimately insulting in that it fails to acknowledge actors as capable of responsibility – to be *blame* worthy is at least to be *worthy* of blame: 'Blame is actually one of the modes by which we *recognise a human animal as one person among others, capable of entering into and sustaining relationships with other people over the course of her life*' (Williams, 2004a, emphasis in original).

[5] This remark was made in reaction to the murder of James Bulger, a two-year-old, by two ten-year-old boys.

[6] That a belief can be 'understandable yet mistaken' of course already presupposes that to explain something we do not have to approve of it.

[7] As Mary Midgley argues, this determinism, or 'corporatism', tends to generate its opposite, the asocial individual whose realm of responsibility is grossly inflated. The word 'ought' itself presupposes at least some autonomy and responsibility (Midgley, 1984).

the case by social services professionals, its purpose is not primarily to justify the actions which led to the disaster, but to explain them. Unless wholly unforeseeable circumstances are identified as having caused the disaster, it has to be attributed to unacceptable procedures, forms of organisation, character deficiencies and individual decisions. Where the defendants accept the inquiry's descriptions of their behaviour they might respond by citing either external circumstances or diminished responsibility through illness, or they may acknowledge that their behaviour was inexcusable, that they failed to exercise due care, etc.

Explanations can indeed sometimes serve as justifications, and vice versa, if we find the exercise of responsibility to have been reasonable, that is, if we judge the actions taken to have been as good as might reasonably have been expected of someone in that situation, having had the particular constraints and opportunities in life that they had had, and having acted on the basis of good reasons. Sometimes, too, actions which we would normally find unacceptable and unjustifiable are condoned if there were exceptional mitigating circumstances. Thus when, say, a woman is tried for killing a husband who has subjected her to violence for years and made her life intolerable, she may be given a reduced sentence. The explanation is seen as adequate and the behaviour, though not given approval, is condoned. Of course, people can also do things for bad reasons; to deny this would be to imply that lay knowledge and reasoning were infallible. If we identify a bad reason as a cause of an action this helps to explain it but clearly does not justify it.

It is important here to appreciate that explanations of actions do not have to be determinist in the sense of denying actors any autonomy and responsibility. A cause is merely that which produces – or rather co-produces – a change. Everything that happens is caused, invariably by multiple causes. This need not imply a negation of free will, for reasons and choices can be causes, regardless of whether they are good or bad reasons or choices (Bhaskar, 1979; Collier, 1994; Outhwaite, 1987; Sayer, 1992). The world is also open, since many relations between objects are external or contingent, so that whether causal powers are activated and with what effects depends on contingently related contexts. Actors can therefore deliberately intervene in the flow of events and change them. The powers to think, reason and make judgements and decisions are emergent properties whose development depends on a long process of interaction between internal biological and psychological powers, and social, discursive and material processes, during which some of those powers are themselves transformed. The personal is not reducible to the social even though the social is a precondition of the personal (Archer, 2000, 2003). People are determined in the sense of constrained and enabled by various constitutive and limiting forces, but they have powers which are emergent from those forces and which can react back upon them, through interventions in the world. Thus we may become more powerful by replacing unwanted determinations with wanted ones (Bhaskar, 1979; Collier, 1994).[8]

Even the most determinist of social scientists abandon their determinism in their own everyday dealings with others. When others wrong them, they do not simply accept it as one might accept a change in the weather, but demand explanations, justifications and apologies. 'Sorry, but I have no responsibility for my actions' would not be an acceptable response to such demands. There can be no blame or praise or need for apologies in a world where persons are no more than conjunctions of external forces, with no emergent properties. That even the most determinist (like the most relativist) social scientists do criticise, blame, thank and praise others, and give and expect apologies in everyday life, acknowledges the impossibility of determinism.[9]

All events have several causes and enabling conditions; that being the case it rarely makes sense to attribute them to a single cause. But that is what we do when we hold individuals entirely responsible for the outcomes of complex processes. Insofar as we attribute responsibility to them, we acknowledge their own causal powers, including their capability for thinking about actions and their likely consequences. However, even where we do acknowledge social constraints, there is often scope for disagreement over how actors should (have) exercise(d) their limited powers; for example, should they have worked within the existing constraints (i.e., in a reformist way) or challenged some of the constraints (taking a more radical line of action)?

Some forms of social organisation possess – whether by design or by accident – 'fail-safe mechanisms' which make it unlikely that such inevitable, common fallibility will lead to much harm, while others make it highly likely. This is one of the reasons why pathological behaviour is so often localised. Particular kinds of socialisation, providing both

[8] Escaping from causal determinations altogether ('the out-of-gear' conception of freedom) would mean that we could do nothing, for nothing (not even people) would have any determinate properties and powers such that they could be manipulated or manipulate anything else. Freedom and responsibility are only intelligible in a world in which changes are caused but causation is not a matter of regular conjunctions between events but the activation of powers in open systems, that is, systems that are not reducible to fixed regularities, and in which actors have emergent powers which enable them to monitor and intervene in the development of these systems and monitor their own monitorings.

[9] Arguing instead that everything that happens does so by chance is no better, for we would be equally powerless in such a world as in a completely deterministic (i.e., pre-determined) world (Williams, 2004b).

needed material goods and attachments and recognition, are needed to produce 'well-socialised' individuals. Equally, those kinds of socialisation which involve lack of recognition, support and autonomy, and denial of resources held to be desirable and normal, are likely to produce various kinds and degrees of anti-social behaviour. Hence, social conditions are among the causes of both good and bad behaviour, and any adequate social evaluation of behaviour ought not to stop at individuals but should extend to the circumstances co-producing their actions (Midgley, 1984).

Thus, while violent individuals may generally be held responsible for their behaviour, their tendencies owe much to external circumstances. This is acknowledged in Bourdieu's support for a conservation theory of violence; acts of violence by individuals are the more or less delayed and indirect response to violence or other forms of harm done to them, often anonymously, slowly, over long periods and at low levels, which corrodes their sense of self and autonomy.

This is why, if we really want to reduce these forms of visible and visibly reprehensible violence, there is no other way than to reduce the overall quantity of violence which is neither noticed nor punished, the violence exerted every day in families, factories, workshops, banks, offices, police stations, prisons, even hospitals and schools, and which is, in the last analysis, the product of the 'inert violence' of economic structures and social mechanisms relayed by the active violence of people. (Bourdieu, 2000, p. 233)[10]

This is supported by studies of violent criminals in psychotherapy (Gilligan, 2000). To acknowledge the banal point that the kinds of social relations we grow up among influence the kinds of people we grow up to be, is not to deny that anyone can alter those processes or resist their influence, but to recognise that it is difficult, and may sometimes simply be too much to expect. Local concentrations of anarchic, Hobbesian and violent behaviour are invariably induced by severe absolute and relative deprivation and misrecognition, coupled with expectations raised in the wider society regarding levels of consumption and desirable lifestyles, including gender models. Many of these formative processes are highly self-reinforcing and multilateral in character; it becomes difficult for individuals not to behave in a Hobbesian manner if the majority of their community are already doing so.[11] The residents of the Chicago black ghetto

[10] While this avoids restricting evil to individual acts of violence, we don't need to invoke 'structural violence' to explain and/or justify individual violence or other anti-social behaviour. As Mary Midgley comments, 'This seems a tortuous and misleading way of expressing a justification which can stand perfectly well on its own feet. Injustice and oppression can be *worse* forms of wickedness than violence, but they are still distinct from it' (Midgley, 1984, p. 75, emphasis in original).

[11] See Glover's analysis of 'Hobbesian traps' (Glover, 1999).

interviewed by Loic Wacquant make it clear that their world is over-whelmingly Hobbesian (Bourdieu et al., 1999, pp. 130–67), and that if they were not suspicious of others, and continually on their guard and prepared to use force, they would be sure to end up as victims. (Certainly, such behaviour is strongly gendered, but that too is a product of sociali-sation – again not merely as external force or discourse but mediated in and through the long process of formation of selves or subjectification through social interaction in specific material contexts.)

The problem in social research, as in everyday life, is (a) to decide how much autonomy and responsibility individuals have – not only for their actions but for the kinds of people they are,[12] and (b), insofar as they do have some autonomy, to assess how it is exercised, whether their reasons and motives are good. To ignore rationality as an emergent property of human social being and to attribute everything that anyone does wholly to 'social conditions' is an absurdity, which is contradicted every time we reason with people. *The answer to (a) is partly an empirical question about practicalities and partly a normative question about how much responsibility individuals should be expected to exercise.*

These points bring home the need to think about equality and moral-ity in relation not only to a theory of human social being but to concrete societies and their dominant social relations and the typical kinds of indi-viduals they produce. Acknowledgement of the double-sided nature of ethical life implies the need to focus on both internalised dispositions and social circumstances. Moral theory generally abstracts from the lat-ter, as if social life could be represented by a model of already-formed rational moral actors deliberating on how they should behave, situated within uniform, neutral, social conditions. Normative writing on moral-ity frequently has to resort to appeals to what the normal, rational, moral actor would do, without considering that the formation of such beings is itself a contingent social process, dependent on favourable – perhaps widespread but not universal – circumstances. It is as if the existence of individuals who do not conform to the ideal were merely an inexplica-ble aberration, a random quirk of nature, an irritant to the development of ethical theory, rather than something in need of explanation. Ethical theory's overwhelming focus on the good and its marginalisation of evil as simply the absence of the good is wholly inadequate. The costs of moral philosophy's disengagement from social science, particularly soci-ology and psychology, are no more clear than here. A proper analysis of morality would have to examine the concrete circumstances, including

---

[12] Adam Smith seems to have thought this was impossible to determine (Griswold, 1999, p. 251).

the available discourses, that form individuals and their ethical dispositions in particular situations.

Recognition of the social origins of anti-social behaviour diverts attention from individuals to social structures and relations, including not only relations of domination but the many systematically produced unintended consequences of actions, whether harmful or beneficial. It is tempting to say that this involves a switch from moral concern about individuals to a political concern about social relations, but the latter has also to be morally informed if it is not to degenerate to matters of expedience and the rule of might.

Philosophers use the concept of 'moral luck' to draw attention to the fact that the outcomes of our actions, however they be motivated, are often dependent on circumstances which are outside our control, yet we are often judged on the outcomes alone.[13] As Smith notes, to deny approbation to someone for good outcomes that owe much to luck because they do not wholly deserve it may seem mean-spirited (Smith, 1759:1984). Conversely, to appeal to bad luck in one's own defence may seem like whingeing and even reasonable appeals may be suppressed for this reason. In such cases, even if we are aware of the contribution of moral luck, we may be reluctant to acknowledge it explicitly.

While the phenomenon of moral luck is familiar to all, its distribution, whether good or bad, is unlikely to be even or random across the social field; actions that succeed in one social context may fail in another. The 'good works' of the rich and powerful are not only more conspicuous than those of the poor but more likely to produce impressive results. Similarly, we might talk of 'performative luck', concerning the influence of luck on the outcomes of activities which do not have direct moral implications. Thus, the success of schoolchildren's efforts to learn are affected by luck in terms of access to books and computers, trips abroad, etc., all of which vary with class so that an upper middle class child and a working class child may make the same effort at school but with quite different results. Insofar as they receive reward or recognition, this is unlikely to be moderated by discounting for the effects of this luck. Thus the rich are likely to congratulate themselves for what they don't deserve and the poor to blame themselves for what they equally don't deserve. The poor US white and black young men studied by Jay Macleod mainly blamed themselves for their lack of success, even where they had worked hard and kept out of trouble (Macleod, 1995). However, there can also sometimes be awareness of, and hence discounting for, moral

---

[13] These circumstances could include others' responses to the behaviour, for example, whether they are hostile or receptive.

and performative luck, as when people qualify judgements of others by noting that they have 'had it easy' or 'had it hard'. Insofar as we decline to acknowledge instances of the former in our judgements of others for fear of appearing mean-spirited, we help to conceal the unfairness of class.

More fundamentally, insofar as we are shaped by our circumstances, moral luck affects not only the consequences of our actions but our characters. This might be termed *constitutive* moral luck (Griswold, 1999, p. 241); as Martha Nussbaum puts it, 'much that I did not make goes towards making me whatever I shall be praised or blamed for being' (Nussbaum 1986, p. 5). Evaluations can therefore go beyond consideration of responsibility for behaviour to responsibility for character. The individualising tendencies of lay explanations of behaviour and evaluations of character in western culture, which probably derive from the normative significance attached to freedom and autonomy, mean that both constitutive moral luck and social context are overlooked, therefore typically producing flawed moral judgements (Williams, 2003).

Fine distinctions: disapproval of behaviour and disapproval of identity

The youths that so vexed Patrick Champagne's interviewees were mostly of North African immigrant origin. When the building superintendents reprimanded them for their behaviour, the youths would often respond by accusing them of racism. This accusation troubled the interviewees. It is impossible to judge from the interview how far they were racist in their attitudes or whether the youths were just using the term as a convenient weapon. But what I want to draw attention to here is a distinction sometimes made in people's more considered evaluations of others – between judging them for their behaviour and judging them for their identity. Although the building superintendents might have just wanted to play up to the liberal sensibilities of their interviewer, they seemed to want to say that they condemned the youths not for their identity or 'race' but for their anti-social behaviour, these two things being only contingently related, while the youths themselves sought to deflect criticism of their behaviour by saying the superintendents were simply racist.

This form of dispute is extremely common. Equivalents of it can be found with respect to class, gender, sexuality and other kinds of social division: in each case the message is 'I don't have anything against your identity, against you as a person, but I do object to that particular kind of behaviour. Thus in objecting to it I am not being a snob/racist/sexist/homophobe, etc.' This implies that whereas identity is seen as a proper site of difference and pluralism, at least some forms of behaviour – those that supposedly harm or offend others – are not, and are instead subject to universal norms. In some cases, the distinction is simple and unproblematic, but in others, where the behaviour is more strongly associated with the identity, either by choice or by necessity (or through constitutive moral luck), the problems are more intractable. On the one hand it acknowledges and accepts difference, or claims to. On the other hand it makes appeal to standards regarding behaviour that are supposedly shared by those who are being criticised. The accused may reply that the critic is at fault in taking offence at their behaviour. The behaviour in question may indeed be part of the others' identity and seen as legitimate by them. Thus in Northern Ireland the Protestant Orange Order regularly claims the right to stage intimidating marches through Catholic areas on the grounds that doing so has long been part of its identity, to which many observers would reply that this indicates that the identity itself is therefore objectionable. Identities are not inviolable. Difference may be bad. There are also situations where the problematic behaviour of A is a response to oppression – for example, aggression in response to oppression – but is seen by B simply as part of an anti-social identity. In some more difficult cases A may see their behaviour not merely as an effect of oppression but as a positive feature of their identity. Occasionally there are indications of awareness of these problems in actors' evaluations of others.

In some cases the standards regarding behaviour which impacts on others are not shared. Liberals argue that individuals – and by implication groups – should be able to do what they like provided they do not harm others. But harm is difficult to define. John Stuart Mill, who provided a classic defence of this position in his *On Liberty*, distinguished between preventing someone harming others, and expressing disapproval of behaviour which does not cause actual harm but may nevertheless be considered to be bad (Mill, 1859 [1975]). While he argued for both, he did not consider that such disapproval might be unwarranted and could take the form of stigmatising groups and harming them indirectly.

The difficulties of distinguishing between disapproval of behaviour and disapproval of identity go deep because of the social character of behaviour – the fact that behaviours have consequences not only for those responsible for them, but for others. For example, a less remarked feature of Paul Willis's much-cited study of working class boys and schooling in *Learning to Labour* is that in disrupting lessons, the lads were hindering the progress of other children (Willis, 1977). This 'indiscipline' is a prime concern of middle class parents in Britain. Imagine a conversation between two white middle class people, one right-wing (R), the other left-wing (L), both of whom live in middle class residential areas.

R: 'If you're so egalitarian why don't you live in X [a poor area with a large black population]?'
L: 'I'm not against the working class or black people – of course not, but the rate of burglaries and other crime there is much higher than here, and the indiscipline in schools and the risks of bullying for my children are much higher than here. I hate these unnecessary divisions between groups and I despair of the hostility between them, but nor do my children or I want to be victims; the problems are structural, not something I can alter as an individual. Simply desegregating people doesn't change much, indeed it just makes the struggles more overt. Yes, I am in a sense living in bad faith but what can I do about it? At least I'm not in favour of inequalities and racism.'

The argument then degenerates into counter-charges of hypocrisy and racism. Even if L had lived in X one suspects R would have accused her of being a poseur, trying in effect to enhance her cultural and moral capital within her social circle of fellow radicals by living in a working class and black area while retaining the privileges of being middle class in terms of economic and cultural capital, and at the same time selfishly sacrificing her children's future for this moralistic personal project.[14] The accusation of hypocrisy identifies and blames *individuals* for situations, when a deeper analysis shows them to be responses to structural social and economic dilemmas, which are not of the actors' own choosing. The difficulties lie in trying to negotiate such situations, in the short run in which we always live.

We also see in this example the intersection of several themes discussed in earlier chapters: the commitments of parents to their children's welfare; unequal distribution of internal goods; class contempt from R towards those who lose out as a result; and egalitarian sentiments towards them on the part of L. For R, there is no problem, though it involves endorsing inequalities among children for which there is no justification. The usual 'resolution' to such dilemmas is literally built-in to urban development through residential segregation and the localisation of school catchment areas, and reinforced in countries like Britain by allowing schools to select pupils.

These fine distinctions between discriminating against others according to their identity and according to their behaviour or specific

---

[14] Antipathy towards those middle class radicals who, in their every public move and utterance, try to be politically correct is partly a reaction to the use of radical ideas to enhance their holders' cultural capital and increase their social distance from the working classes and from members of rival fractions of the middle classes. (Of course racism and sexism, etc., are far worse.)

characteristics, between social discrimination and 'legitimate discrimination' (Bourdieu, 1993, p. 179), are common among the educated:

It is possible for people to be egalitarian in their views about wealth, both wanting a more equal distribution and resisting the tendency to value people for their wealth, and yet valuing qualities, such as being educated, whose distribution is strongly influenced by wealth, so that they discriminate among others in a highly inegalitarian way, selecting out those who are 'able to talk seriously about things'. (Lamont, 1992, p. 171)

With some justification egalitarian intellectuals may be regarded as hypocritical in this respect, failing to recognise the privilege of being able to adopt a contemplative relation to the world and develop the academic skills known as 'intelligence', and underestimating those forms of intelligence not consecrated by the educational system. It can lead to what Bourdieu terms a 'racism of intelligence', which can be experienced by its victims as being no less exclusive than those 'vulgar' forms of racism which are stigmatised by the intellectual elite, indeed as all the worse for being portrayed as legitimate by those who normally condemn racism (Bourdieu, 1993, pp. 177–9). Though it is unlikely to be intended, it allows 'the children of subproletarians or immigrants [to be referred to] in such a way that social cases become psychological cases, and social deficiencies mental deficiencies, etc.' (ibid., p. 179). The recognition of this displaced or second-order form of legitimation of discrimination creates moral dilemmas for egalitarian intellectuals and is likely to lead to bad consciousness. However, aside from attacking economic inequalities and the educational mechanisms which tend to reinforce class inequalities by legitimising them in terms of educational qualifications, there is no way out of such dilemmas. Merely trying to act more equally towards others does not change these structures and merely intensifies such dilemmas, though of course that is not a good justification for not doing so.

From a normative point of view we need to assess the values and behaviours themselves rather than simply affirming or rejecting them because of their class associations; particular beliefs and behaviours may be unequally distributed by class and gender but they are not good or bad because of such associations but regardless of those associations (Sayer, 2000b). For example, arrogance is more common in the dominant classes than in the subordinate classes, but it is bad in itself, wherever it occurs; while one of the bad things about the dominant classes is the fact that they are often arrogant, arrogance is not bad simply *because* of that class association – though it may be *symptomatic* of that class's relation to others – and it would not become good if it became more common in other classes. (Similarly, class inequality would not be acceptable if only the dominant classes were nicer!)[15] At the same time, given that these behaviours are powerfully socially shaped, we must apportion blame (or credit?) to the forces producing them rather than just to the individuals. Even if we were to conclude that they were almost wholly the product of class, it would not mean rejecting our negative valuation of its effects in terms of behaviour, for the tendency of class inequalities to produce that behaviour would be one of the reasons for condemning class. We should condemn both. In any case, anti-social behaviours are not uniquely the product of class. If class inequalities did not produce suffering and anti-social behaviour (the two being linked in both directions), then there would seem little reason for condemning them. An equivalent argument applies to gender: particular anti-social behaviours associated with men, such as violence, are not bad because of that association: they are bad anyway. One of the bad things – in fact the worst – about masculinity is its monopoly of such behaviour, and it is in virtue of the latter that the former needs to be changed.

We shall return to these matters of evaluation of class behaviour, identity and constitutive luck later and attempt to develop them, but to do that we must now turn more directly to lay views of class itself.

Responses to class itself: ambivalence and unease about class[16]

Asking people what class they belong to tends to prompt complex responses. Answers are often awkward, defensive and evasive, treating the question as if it were a normative one about whether they deserve their class position or whether they consider themselves inferior or superior to others. As Savage et al. put it '. . . they [their interviewees] know that class is not an innocent descriptive term but is a loaded moral signifier' (Savage et al., 2001a, p. 875). Class remains a highly charged issue because of the associations of injustice and moral evaluation. To ask someone what class they are is not simply to ask them to classify their socio-economic

---

[15] Given the pervasiveness of class and gender in inflecting behaviour it is of course extremely difficult to consider how to value behaviours regardless of them.

[16] I am aware that there have been many empirical surveys of people's attitudes to inequalities (see Miller, 1992 and Bowles and Gintis, 1998 for reviews and interpretations of these). While these are interesting they suffer not only from the problem that respondents tend to offer their 'Sunday best' views. As Bourdieu argued (1984, 1993) such surveys offer a poor guide to thoughts and actions: they abstract from the daily contexts in which people act, and their whole history of socialisation: they ignore 'adaptive preferences' or actors' rationalisations and their social reinforcements – symbolic domination and hegemony; they use researchers' categories and frameworks; they fall into the trap of the scholastic fallacy, ignoring practical logic and explaining beliefs and actions wholly in terms of discursive reason and reflection.

position, for it also carries the suggestion of a further unspoken and offensive question: what are you worth? This, in turn, could refer either to wealth or moral worth or other forms of merit. On the one hand, from a normative point of view, one could argue that these are separate matters. This disjunction between economic valuation and ethical valuation can be taken (disingenuously) by the Right to indicate that economic inequalities do not harm people, and are therefore acceptable. However, as we have argued, economic inequalities cannot help but influence recognition.

Tutors who try to get new social science undergraduates to talk about class face similar responses of unease and evasion. As the students gain more experience of sociology they may gradually lose this unease as they learn to objectivise class and disassociate it from their sense of themselves in relation to others; indeed, learning to become a sociologist can seem like a process of learning to bracket out these concerns. While experienced sociologists might put the novices' unease down to naivety about sociology, and feel superior about their own ability to confront class dispassionately, I would suggest there is something to be said for inverting that valuation: while the beginning students have not yet unlearned their very justifiable sense (albeit a scarcely articulated sense) of the moral problems of class, sociologists have unlearned them and become desensitised to them. What is a fraught and highly sensitive issue for many people has all too often become, in the hands of sociologists, a dry academic debate about social classification schema. As Honneth notes, social theory also has difficulty registering struggles arising from the moral experience of disrespect and tends to transform these into categories of interest (such as 'cultural capital' and 'symbolic profit') within a basically Hobbesian model of social conflict (Honneth, 1995, p. 163; see also Thévènot, 2001).

I want to argue that unease and ambivalence about class are reasonable rather than mysterious responses, and that it is sociologists' blasé amoralism which is at fault. We can explain the former responses by probing further into the moral significance of class. My explanation is simple, consisting of three kinds of argument, the first concerned with the injustice of class, the second with its distorting effect on moral sentiments, and the third with the injuries caused by class. There are strong interactions between these, but they are most easily explained separately first.

1.   Defensiveness in response to the arbitrariness and injustice of class

Insofar as actors recognise the arbitrariness and injustice of natal class, and the way it influences individuals' lives – and it is hard for them not to – it can prompt guilt, shame, resentment and defensiveness, and the balance of these feelings and the ways of handling them are likely to vary according to class position. These simple and obvious points often seem to escape the notice of sociologists of class, precisely because they are primarily concerned with what determines the class position of adults, particularly their income and wealth, and hence focus on relationships which are less radically arbitrary (though not necessarily any more just).

Nevertheless, despite the major role of luck, individuals' subsequent fortunes might also be influenced by their own efforts and merits, and so, unsurprisingly, the better off and the upwardly mobile are likely to appeal to these as a defence against any (usually unspoken) accusations of being beneficiaries of luck within an unfair game. Characteristically, the defensiveness takes the form of individuals making exceptions for themselves, acknowledging that while natal class position is a matter of luck, in their own case, and perhaps that of other similar people, their current adult position is a consequence of hard work and talent, and hence justifiable because deserved. In the case of the upwardly mobile, it may even take the form of a heroic narrative in which the individual overcomes the injustice of a lowly class position and moves upwards by her own efforts.

It is nevertheless only a partial defence of class inequalities,[17] as it does not discount that luck is still *also* an influence on class and life chances, and does not deny altogether that these last into adulthood. Some people may try to defend class differences as wholly the product of merit, but it is striking – and pleasing! – to see no such defence in the responses reported by Savage et al. Their respondents' unease about class seems to acknowledge and reflect its injustice. They therefore find themselves wanting both to acknowledge its unfairness as a social structure and to exempt themselves from complicity in it or from having gained unfair advantage due to it, indeed to claim credit for having apparently overcome it. Hence their reluctance to class themselves is *not* usually coupled with a denial of the existence of class or of its arbitrariness with respect to the fortunes of others. The upwardly mobile respondents do not seem to be saying they are good people because they are (now) middle class, but that they have made it into the middle class because they are worthy people, even though not all middle class people are, even though one can also be upwardly mobile through luck, and even though making it into the middle classes is not the only possible fate of the meritorious and worthy. Similarly, there

---

[17] Many moral philosophers would not accept this even as a partial defence (e.g., Baker, 1987).

is at least some recognition among those born into and remaining in the middle classes that they have had undeserved advantages which do not necessarily warrant considering themselves more worthy than others who are less fortunate. In either case, there seems to be an implicit recognition that class is problematic. Their embarrassment about talking about class reflects not so much a denial of the fact of class as an acknowledgement of its lack of justification.[18]

There are further reasons why the appeal to desert is difficult and hence why those who make it do so in rather defensive ways. These are articulated in the corresponding literature on equality in moral philosophy. Here it is common to argue that if talents are innate they are clearly undeserved and therefore warrant no special reward; or, if they are acquired, their acquisition owes much to whether conditions were favourable in early life, which of course reflects class and gender. Even the motivation and the amount of effort people put into their activities may be a product of class and gender background; where there are good prospects (though not too easily gainable) motivation will be encouraged, where there are none, it will not. Although these are somewhat sophisticated arguments against simple justifications of class position in terms of desert,[19] I would suggest that there can sometimes be glimmers of awareness of them in lay thought, and these too are likely to prompt defensiveness.

Not all reactions to class inequalities are so generous. The anger and contempt of the better off (including the more secure working class) for those who are dependent on state welfare is not only a reaction to having to pay taxes towards their upkeep, perceived as supporting those unwilling to work, but also a form of contempt for those in a state of dependence. To be dependent is to lack autonomy and dignity, and to lack these qualities is to invite contempt. Those spectators who fail to realise that the dependent have little control over their fates are likely to despise them for that as well as for having to subsidise them. While natal class is a matter of luck, the poor are typically expected to attempt to strive to escape from their unfortunate position. This is evident in the long history of discourses which distinguish between the deserving and undeserving poor, albeit in increasingly euphemised ways, as in recent 'workfare' discourse. On the one hand these recognise the arbitrariness and unfairness of class, but only for those who supposedly deserve help, while treating class inequalities as justified for those who are undeserving.

---

[18] Compare Parkin's classification of meaning systems of class (Parkin, 1972).

[19] An additional argument made by some philosophers that I have *not* encountered in lay thought, is that while effort and talent are worthy of praise, this does not mean that they need to be rewarded with financial advantages; esteem is all that is warranted (Baker, 1987).

Meanwhile, affluent people who live off the labour of others are rarely seen as undeserving.[20]

One of the common false assumptions that lie behind many of these kinds of reactions to class is 'the belief in a just world' (Lerner, cited in Williams, 2003), that is, a belief in the moral well-orderedness of the world, so that good intentions straightforwardly produce good actions with good effects, which in turn proportionately reward the actor, 'giving them their due'. Hence, the extent to which individuals' lives go well or badly is believed to be a simple reflection of their virtues and vices. It refuses to acknowledge the contingency and moral luck which disrupt such relations arbitrarily.[21] Many things happen to us – good or bad – which we neither deserve nor do not deserve: they happen regardless, driven by forces which have nothing to do with justice or human well-being. While philosophers are apt to portray these as random contingencies impacting on individuals and coming from nowhere in particular, they also include the largely unintended effects of major social structures such as those of capitalism. In other words it is possible to identify structural features of society which add to the lack of moral well-orderedness in the world, and do so not merely randomly but systematically and recurrently, so that the goods and bads tend to fall repeatedly on the same people. Thus there is a great deal of path dependence and cumulative causation in the reproduction of class and geographical inequalities. In explaining these persistent inequalities, the Right tends to appeal to random contingency as the main cause, while the Left appeals to structural causes.[22]

2.   Class and the distortion of moral sentiments

The second source of defensiveness about class has to do with the problem identified by Adam Smith, that moral sentiments about others can

---

[20] The category 'unearned income' is rarely encountered today, having been replaced by the oxymoron 'independently wealthy' (personal communication, Abby Day).

[21] In the terms of critical realist philosophy, it assumes the world is a closed system in which a given action or other cause always produces regular effects. Social institutions typically attempt to create approximations of closed systems around particular activities, but they never control contingency completely. Societies are open systems, structured in various ways by social structures having varying degrees of durability.

[22] This is clear in Hayek's treatment of inequality as primarily a matter of misfortune (Hayek, 1988). He accuses socialists of 'the fatal conceit' of 'constructivism' – the idea that society can be rationally planned. This might be taken to imply a belief in the possibility of constructing a just world. Socialists have indeed exaggerated the possibilities of planning, but then Hayek underestimates them, partly by constructing an individualistic, structureless model of society in which there is only random contingency.

easily be corrupted or distorted by differences in wealth.[23] This distortion results in double standards, so that the same behaviour is judged more favourably when it involves the rich than when it involves the poor.[24] For example, attitudes to young men being drunk and disorderly depend very much on their class; similarly, while workers 'skive off work', managers 'take time off to relax'. Beverley Skeggs's work on young working class women shows their often painful awareness of being judged more severely than middle class women (Skeggs, 1997; see also Reay, 1997a and b, 1998b). It is also evident from the personal narratives in the transcripts in Bourdieu et al.'s *The Weight of the World* that resentment about this is often stronger than resentment about lack of material wealth. Thus, moral stigma and privilege are distributed according to class.

These corrupted moral sentiments work *against* the idea that class is arbitrary and unjust, providing class inequalities with a spurious justification. Whereas, according to the critique of class as an injustice, being working or middle class has little or nothing to do with merit or virtue, the corruption of moral sentiments by wealth insinuates that it does. Of course, these class-distorted moral sentiments are themselves unjust.

Although the use of double standards in moral judgements of the behaviour of people in different classes is common, it is also often opposed and rejected, and indeed refusals of such distortions of moral sentiments and judgements are a common part of lay discourses of class. As one of the working class residents interviewed by Southerton said of middle class residents: 'they think they are a better class of person, simply because their house costs more' (Southerton, 2002a, p. 138), clearly challenging the common elision of economic and ethical worth. Indeed, as we saw earlier, the criticisms of middle class pretension (including pretensions to moral superiority) could be construed as a claim of working class moral superiority.

However, these rejections can sometimes have the counterproductive effect of concealing rather than challenging the injustice of class just noted. Thus a common response, evident in some of Southerton's and Savage et al's interviewees' comments, is simply to refuse such evaluations and assert that 'we are as good as them' (Savage et al., 2001a). While this seems a confident and proper egalitarian reaction, it can sometimes also have quite perverse effects which legitimise or hide inequality because an oppressed person who is nevertheless confident of her own worth may use this to argue that class doesn't make any difference – 'it's what you're

---

[23] This is different from failure to take into account moral luck in that it involves double standards responding to such differences regardless of outcomes.

[24] Similar observations on double standards were made by Tawney (1931, pp. 37–8).

like as a person that matters, not class'. Similarly, while the commonly expressed egalitarian desire to 'take people as we find them' indicates a desire to judge people according to their behaviour and attitudes and avoid the tyranny of stereotyping according to social categories, it can also be used as a way of denying the import of social divisions.

In the same vein, comments such as 'I don't believe in class', often made by middle class sociology undergraduates when embarrassed by having to discuss it, are instructive. Even when the tutor says, 'I'm not asking you whether you think it's a good or bad thing, I'm asking you whether it exists and makes a difference,' the answers often continue to be evasive and blur the distinction between the positive and the normative; 'I believe what matters is who you are, not what your parents did or what school you went to' is a refrain often heard, particularly from relatively privileged students. Its ambiguity is deceptive: it can be taken either as a normative argument against the wrongs of class, or a positive claim that class has little effect – which of course is false, and disguises class privilege, while allowing those with class advantages to take credit for what is actually undeserved. While they claim not to think of themselves as morally superior they see little problem with inequalities in economic, cultural and social capital – these being presumably acceptable because they don't make you a better or worse person. This is a spurious egalitarianism that allows the lowly to say the dominant are their equals and hence which tolerates inequality. It also patronises the disadvantaged. From the point of view of the disadvantaged and harshly judged, as we saw earlier, the distortion of moral sentiments according to class can also produce inner turmoil as a result of the opposing pulls of both wanting to refuse the perceived external judgements and their criteria and wanting to measure up to them.

The embarrassment and evasion indicate an awareness that class differences lack moral justification. The lucky may realise that they are lucky and not want to be seen as claiming superiority because of this, while the unlucky/poor will quite reasonably resist any conclusion that they deserve their disadvantages. Rather than dismissing such sentiments as missing the sociological point, and as an ideology which serves to obscure class, I suggest they should be taken seriously – both sympathetically and critically.

3.   *Injuries of class*

If class position, like gender and 'race', fundamentally affects people's lives, disadvantaging and even injuring some while advantaging and empowering others, then it affects the kind of people individuals become.

The class injuries result both from the material lack and inequalities produced by processes of capitalist uneven development, which result in differences not merely in consumption but in people's ability to develop and realise their skills and commitments, and from the effects upon individuals and groups of class contempt, symbolic domination, or distortion of moral sentiments. It is therefore unsurprising that the most disadvantaged should lack self-respect or be aggressive, or that the rich should be arrogant and patronising. Though both liberal and radical egalitarians often find it difficult to acknowledge, if class damages, then this implies that people themselves are damaged, often in ways which not only limit their potential but may in extreme cases lead to anti-social behaviour. Again, if they are indeed damaged then we cannot escape the negative judgement of their behaviour and character, for if it wasn't a problem then class could not be said to be damaging. Thus Left liberals face the difficulty of being both tough on anti-social behaviour and tough on its causes, when being critical of the processes which generate class and gender differences is often (mistakenly) assumed to imply excusal of the behaviours which they encourage and the suspension of the expectation of others to act responsibly. Perhaps the most obvious example in Britain concerns attitudes towards poor white working class males (Haylett, 2001).

In response to this kind of dilemma it is common for the behaviour of oppressed groups to be either pathologised or patronised. Commenting on this dilemma in relation to working class families, Walkerdine and Lucey write: 'This attempt to rescue, to make working-class families "equal but different", still denies oppression in a liberal endeavour to produce equality out of a misplaced pluralism' (Walkerdine and Lucey, 1989, p. 7; see also p. 192).[25] Bourdieu (2000, pp. 75–6) talks about a similar oscillation regarding popular culture: 'One cannot, in fact, without contradiction, describe (or denounce) the inhuman conditions of existence that are imposed on some, and at the same time credit those who suffer them with the real fulfilment of human potentialities . . .' As we saw in chapter 5, we should also take note of the view from below of these dilemmas, as dominated groups consider their injuries and disadvantages relative to those above them, and often combine a reluctance to believe that there has been anything inferior about the way they have lived (or rather have been allowed to live) with a mixture of envy and resentment of others.

In a commentary on John Steinbeck's great novel *The Grapes of Wrath*, Martha Nussbaum notes that while the impoverished migrants suffer a

[25] As Haylett demonstrates, the idea that 'everyone is different but equal' can also function in the discourse of multiculturalism in a way that renders class as difference – a very congenial transposition for neoliberals (Haylett, 2001).

succession of disasters, injustices and indignities, they retain their dignity and generosity – their moral qualities are undiminished, even strengthened. The story therefore easily wins our sympathy and co-opts our sense of injustice. It is easier to sympathise with the suffering of the good than the bad. But it is also a romantic conceit:

> Steinbeck gives the rich an easy time, really: for he shows that all injustice can produce is unhappiness. If we understand that injustice can strike its roots into the personality itself, producing rage and resentment and the roots of bad character, we have even deeper incentives to commit ourselves to giving each child the material and social support that human dignity requires. (Nussbaum, 2001, p. 414)

This can be hard to acknowledge because it could invite a most odious form of class contempt. I have recoiled from acknowledging it many times in trying to write this chapter. It flies in the face of the relativist tenor of popular (and some parts of academic) culture, and the reluctance to 'be judgemental', which of course is itself a moral sentiment. The dread of *appearing* to regard the most oppressed people as intrinsically of lesser worth – which is not what Nussbaum is arguing – prevents liberals and many self-professed egalitarians from confronting the true shamefulness of the system of which they are ashamed. Despite its good intentions, this is a superficial form of egalitarianism, one which seriously underestimates the injuries of class.[26] Working class pride in moral goodness has some justification, but *extreme* deprivation and inequalities are more likely to inhibit rather than enhance those qualities, as we saw in the case of the young men of the ghetto described by Wacquant (Bourdieu et al., 1999). Nussbaum makes an equivalent point about another fictional character, this time a poor black criminal, noting that his real criminality is a product of his rage and shame, which in turn is a product of racism, not merely 'criminalisation' in the sense of mislabelling and false accusations. Thus qualified, the pathologies of oppression can better be understood by recognising their objective existence and their causes. This is not to deny any responsibility on the part of the oppressed for their actions. People of any class are capable of and indeed do commit crimes or wrongs, but the oppressed are often under additional social pressures and deprivations that make such behaviour more likely. It is the causes – whether social or personal or both – which are the proper object of critical evaluation. Ironically the superficial egalitarianism contradicts sociology's partly well-founded suspicion of notions of intrinsic individual qualities. Pathologies are socially constructed, in a sense, but not only as

---

[26] I am sure that, no matter how much I emphasise that the damage is a social product, someone will accuse me of simple class contempt.

a result of the performative character of the privileged gaze, moral boundary drawing and misrecognition, but by the objective effects of economic insecurity, which are then sometimes *correctly* recognised and represented by others, even though the social causes go unacknowledged. We have to steer a course between exaggerations of such class injuries, which would amount to class contempt, and idealisations of the Steinbeck kind, which can easily become equivalent to 'noble savage' ideologies.

It becomes easier to accept this argument if we realise that the pathologies of class and other inequalities are not limited to the poorest, and there are no good reasons – though plenty of bad ones – for assuming they have a monopoly of anti-social behaviour. At the same time, this does not mean, of course, that life is as bad for the middle classes as for the poor. But there are also deformations produced by positions of dominance: a tendency to treat those below them in the class hierarchy as if they were servants, beings whose feelings and time and autonomy are of lesser importance than their own, indeed beings who are scarcely visible; an inability to understand working class life or to see it as of any importance beyond something which might contain a few cultural goods which might be appropriated; a confusion of wealth and achievement and moral worth (see Lamont, 1992); an inability to understand how their own wealth and ease depend on others or to see how their consumption takes away resources from those who need and deserve them more. Commodity fetishism, to which the capitalist class is more susceptible than any other, involves not so much an unawareness of the social relations of the production, which can seem merely like an ignorance of Marxist economic theory, but an inability to understand the ethical implications of the economic mechanisms of capitalism in terms of the arbitrary and unequal relations between contribution (work), needs, merit and reward, along with the unequal division of suffering and flourishing, insecurity and security that they produce.[27]

Lamont's working class men are critical of what they see as managers' lack of integrity, sincerity and interpersonal skills (Lamont, 2000). This is not merely a prejudice. There are good grounds for assuming this representation has some *justification*: those in managerial positions, especially in capitalist business – where the ultimate imperative is profit rather than what is right or good,[28] and where the competitive struggle against peers is unrelenting and the environment constantly changing – are likely to become habituated to dissembling and opportunism, treating others

---

[27] I know only too well that these points are likely to be contentious: they are the subject of another forthcoming book, on 'moral economy'.

[28] Even where, contingently, the latter is a necessary condition for the former, it cannot be the dominant goal if capitalist businesses are to survive.

purely as means to their ends, as they face continually changing and conflicting demands. As Robert Jackall's outstanding study of the (im)moral lives of corporate managers shows with great force, the Hobbesian pressures facing managers render consistent moral behaviour a recipe for failure (Jackall, 1988). Impression management, instrumentalism, accumulation of external rather than internal goods, avoidance of the weak, ingratiation with the strong, appropriation of credit due to others, evasion of own responsibilities, and willingness to abandon commitments – all of these figure in the lives of the managers studied by Jackall. Obliged to be dominant downwards, compliant upwards and competitive sideways, pragmatism and self-interest invariably overrule ethics, though at personal cost for some: '. . . guilt, a regret at self-abnegation and deprivation . . . alternating anxiety, rage, and self-disgust for willingly submitting oneself to the knowing and not knowing, to the constant containment of anger, to the keeping quiet, to the knuckling under . . .' (Jackall, 1988, p. 204). Meanwhile the petits bourgeois tend to suffer from anxiety and contradictory tendencies of condescension, deference and resistance, and self-repression, as we saw earlier (see also Bourdieu, 1984).[29]

In these and many other ways, class produces not only different access to goods held to be desirable for all, not only incomplete or distorted recognition, but also deformations of character which become part of the habitus. Of course, the match between these characteristics and social position is only approximate, because similar effects can be produced by other mechanisms which do not simply align with class: gender produces its own effects, and all the contingencies of the psychology of interpersonal relations, especially those of family life, can produce virtues and vices independently of class. Classed behaviours and experiences are seamlessly fused with those of gender and other kinds of social divisions. It may be difficult to change these behaviours because gender may be used as a defence against class domination. The young working class women studied by Skeggs saw feminism as threatening because their heavy investments in femininity had won them some respect. If they were to abandon it they had no other forms of cultural capital to compensate for their low class position (Skeggs, 1997). In a different way working class men may use their masculinity to resist middle class domination.

This fusing of class and gender and ethnicity can also pose problems for those who want to distinguish them in making judgements of their own or others' behaviour. Thus laddishness is a working class kind of

---

[29] As Jackall notes, this anxiety of the upwardly mobile can be an asset for managerial work since it encourages conscientiousness and attention to detail (Jackall, 1988, p. 21).

masculinity but it is difficult to separate out the class from the gender elements of it. How we judge people on one of these dimensions may conflict with how we want to judge them on others. Thus a middle class egalitarian may want to object to the sexism of a young working class man but want to avoid snobbery, and indeed even want to act preferentially towards him in relation to his class. Again this highlights the effects of the objective differences between class and gender. But the working class sexist may read this disapproval of his sexism in class terms, as evidence of snobbery rather than as a legitimate criticism of his behaviour. That he might well (mis)interpret it in this way is not surprising given that awareness of sexism and feminism are likely to correlate positively with position in the class hierarchy: one of the effects of class is that it gives unequal access to emancipatory bodies of thought. Similar effects can occur through the crossing of gender and ethnicity, as when feminists worry that their disapproval of the gender relations of a different ethnic group will be seen as racist.

Rather than simply glossing such complexities as evidence of lay 'ambivalence' or confusion about class, gender and ethnicity and leaving it at that, I suggest that we should probe what generates it, for there are good reasons behind it. From a positive point of view, such a strategy may help to identify how people think about class, gender and race (though of course that is also an empirical question), and from a normative point of view, it helps us think about how to go on in the face of such complexities and contradictions.

Conclusion

Actors continually evaluate the behaviour of others, including that of class others. Although, for the most part, they may take its causes for granted, they sometimes try to explain it. Such explanations tend to reflect the relative position of the observer (judge) and observed (judged) but they may also be sincere attempts to understand rather than air prejudices. In so doing they run into difficult issues of explanation and justification, and attribution of responsibility, credit and blame, and fine distinctions between judging behaviour, character and identity.

As regards views of class itself, the mixtures of self-justification, self-deprecation, evasion and embarrassment are not only understandable but partly justifiable responses. Class is morally problematic because of its arbitrary relationship to worth, virtues and status, and this is why it is a highly sensitive subject. Apologists would like to believe that class is a reflection of moral and other virtues, such as effort, merit and achievement (needs tend not come into the picture), though class is likely to figure among the influences *shaping* these.[30] While it is of course important to acknowledge that everyone has some responsibility for their actions and life courses, it is important, first, not to expect too much through inattention to the powerful social forces which enable and constrain everything we do, indeed everything we become. Secondly, it is important to remember that people become classed from birth, and their most formative years are spent under the influence of these social forces when their autonomy is at its most limited. Far too many discussions of class ignore this simple fact.

The defensiveness of the middle classes about class is not necessarily a matter merely of justifying their class position, but of defending their moral worth, regardless of their class position. Attitudes to class itself show *both* a temptation to invoke moral distinctions on class lines *and* unease about the morality of class. Some of the these distinctions can claim some empirical verification – the most oppressed are indeed likely to develop anti-social behaviour, just as the dominant are likely to develop callous and oppressive behaviour. To the extent that there is also any awareness that these moral differences are products of their involuntary occupancy of class positions, it is likely to generate unease.

Class inequalities generate shame among the most disadvantaged. Egalitarians, whatever their class origin, may also feel a less personalised shame about class itself, and quite properly so. As we saw in chapter 6, shame is not merely a product of external disapproval but usually involves the internalisation of and commitment to standards according to which we have failed. Even the advantaged may occasionally recognise instances of their complicity in the reproduction of undeserved inequalities and feel guilty. On the other hand the euphemisms of 'working' and 'middle' class themselves allow complicity between those who acknowledge the existence of class difference but want to deny that people are of unequal worth and those who want to maintain inequalities and unequal treatment and welcome their partial concealment. Class is quite properly an unsettling subject, one that prompts feelings of shame as well as self-justification. We are shamed by class because it is shameful (see also Ehrenreich, 2001).

[30] As a function of simply being human, moral worth might be said to be unconditional and unaffected by class. However, from a positive point of view, as we have argued, moral *character* or virtues and vices are indeed influenced by class and other social relations. This is not an indictment of individuals but of the social structures and discourses shaping them.

9 Conclusions and implications

There are two types of conclusions and implications that I want to discuss. The first concern theoretical and philosophical matters, particularly about valuation, values and the relationship between positive and normative thought. This is warranted because both the subject matter and the approach that I have taken to it have been somewhat unorthodox. I have sought to understand lay normativity in relation to class, attempting to take it seriously and appreciate its internal force, instead of ignoring it or reducing it to a correlate of social position or discursive construction. While it has been a primarily positive analysis of lay normativity, at times it has itself been more openly normative about that subject matter than is usual in social science, and I will add further normative judgements in this last chapter. In the first part I therefore want both to defend the approach to normativity that I have taken and to suggest how normative evaluations such as those I have made might be justified. This involves challenging common views about the assumed 'subjective' nature of valuation, the distinction between positive and normative discourse and the relation between them, and the kinds of grounds that we might appeal to when justifying normative judgements. On all these matters I owe the reader some explanations.

In the second part I address more substantive matters and restate the case for understanding the moral significance of class. In addition, from a normative point of view, I attempt to answer the question which the whole book has begged: can anything be done about class inequalities and the forms of misrecognition and discrimination that go with them? Here we confront one of the possible reasons why so many societies are 'in denial' about class – that many believe that it is inescapable, and that it is a price we have to pay for the alleged benefits of capitalism. I shall argue that we do not have to accept this fatalism.

Philosophical/methodological issues

People look to philosophy for the knockdown argument and the decisive refutation, but ethics, being bound up with people, cannot escape soft-edged psychology, all dispositions and tendencies rather than hard universal laws. (Glover, 2001, p. 27)

... the error of the sceptical opponent of practical reason consists in remaining too much in the grip of the very picture of rational argument that is allegedly being criticized. (Nussbaum, 1993, p. 235)

In chapter 1 I noted how, over the last 200 years, social science has slowly shifted from blending the normative and the positive seamlessly, to a situation where normative thought has been largely expelled from social science, and ghettoised in political and moral philosophy. This process was accompanied by an expulsion of reason (or science) from values, so that values and valuation now tend to be thought of as 'subjective' – at the least as having nothing to do with understanding and explanation, and at worst as a contaminant threatening the objectivity of science. Of course, this has not made social science value-free, but it has successfully marginalised normative thought as a worthy activity in its own right. A side effect of this has been that social science has been ill equipped to understand lay normativity.

A prime concern of this book has been to illuminate the normative, particularly moral or ethical dimensions and implications of beliefs, actions, practices, institutions and social structures. These are without doubt deep and murky waters that one hesitates to enter, but making normative judgements is a condition of being able to live, so social science can only evade these issues at the cost of misunderstanding society. This usually happens through various kinds of identification error or misattribution of causality in which actions that derive from ethical dispositions and decisions are treated as purely interest- or power-determined responses. Alternatively, normativity and 'values' are seen as merely 'subjective', or conventional and habitual, and hence lacking warrant.

Those who see values simply as 'subjective' often slide between three different and contingently related senses of this term. 'Subjective' may mean firstly value-laden, secondly, 'pertaining to subjects', and thirdly, 'untrue' or not necessarily true (Sayer, 2000a; Collier, 2003). There are equivalent, opposite, senses for 'objective'. Not all 'subjective' ideas need be value-laden in a non-trivial sense; we may be indifferent about many things. Values and judgements are clearly subjective in the second sense since they are held and made by knowing subjects. But values and judgements are also *about* something; they pertain to objects – either something independent of the subject or, as in internal conversations, the subject's own thoughts and feelings, which can be treated as objects of reflection. Imagine we have two identical objects, say two copies of this book; it would make no sense to say that one of them was good, while the other was not. How could they be if they were exactly the same? There must be something different about them such that we think they should be valued differently. The simple philosophical point here is that valuation cannot be purely subjective in the second sense, but has also to relate to the properties of its objects. So valuation has both subjective and objective aspects, in fact it involves a relation between the two.

When this objective side is pointed out, some people tend to assume that we are claiming that valuation is objective in the quite different sense of 'involving true statements'. But objectivity in the sense of pertaining to objects does not entail this, indeed the fallibility of knowledge and truth claims derives from the very independence of objects from what we think about them. We can only be mistaken if there is something independent of our thought to be mistaken about. If the objective is collapsed into the subjective, so that there is nothing outside knowledge or discourse, then these must be infallible. So, far from implying privileged access to the truth, the insistence on the objective or object-related dimension of valuation renders fallibility comprehensible (Sayer, 2000a; Collier, 2003). Of course where ethical judgements are concerned, the fuzziness of the objects makes their adequacy particularly difficult to assess, as the quotation above from Jonathan Glover notes. Hence, too, the significance of the quotation from Martha Nussbaum.

We are accustomed to thinking of knowledge in terms of a straightforward distinction between the positive and the normative. In positive thought, we assume that if our ideas fail to fit the world, we should change them to fit the world. By contrast, in normative thought, when we perceive a mismatch between our thinking and how the world seems to be, we assume that the world needs to be changed to fit our ideas (Helm, 2001). So positive thought is 'world-guided', and normative thought 'world-guiding'. But the positive/normative distinction hides an excluded middle, a zone of concepts which are simultaneously positive and normative. Some of the most important phenomena of life are only identifiable from within this zone: 'needs', 'desire', 'lack', 'flourishing' and 'suffering', including their specific forms such as 'fulfilment', 'health', 'illness', 'oppression' and 'disrespect'. Such concepts have both descriptive and evaluative content, indeed the two cannot be separated. Lack, needs and desires are not merely markers of the difference between the ideas of an outside observer and the world, but part of the world which strives to go beyond the state of the world at any given time. In recognising needs I simultaneously adjust my thinking to the world and (*ceteris paribus*) think that the world ought to be changed to meet them. At the same time, remembering Nussbaum's point, we should not expect judgements regarding needs, lack and desire to be infallible. The relationship between what we feel we lack and desire and what will actually satisfy us is something we may struggle to discover. It is not an apodictic relationship and it would be absurd to expect it to be.

Some may want to argue that a separation of positive and normative discourse can and should be achieved by replacing 'value-laden' terms with more neutral, 'positive' language. But if we try to do this two things are likely to happen. One possibility is that the new terminology would take on the same or similar normative 'load' as the old terminology. The other possibility is that in recasting descriptions in neutral terms we would mis-describe the object. This is because the positive and normative content of descriptions are not necessarily inversely related. Consider the following famous example, comparing two statements about the Holocaust: 'thousands died in the Nazi concentration camps' and 'thousands were systematically exterminated in the Nazi concentration camps'. The second is both more value-laden and more factually accurate than the first: the prisoners did not just die naturally, nor were they killed randomly and individually, but according to planned mass executions. Therefore, refraining from using evaluative terms may weaken rather than strengthen the descriptive adequacy or truth status of our accounts.

This tells us something about the relationship between beliefs that are subjective in the sense of value-laden and their objectivity in the sense of their truth status. Value-ladenness and truth are not necessarily inversely related, hence neutrality is not the same thing as objectivity in this sense. This means that it is a mistake to regard values as a contaminant threatening the objectivity (i.e., truth, practical adequacy) of social science, which we must root out or at least minimise. Using terms like 'arrogant', 'condescending', 'vain', 'oppressive' or 'humiliating' in describing social behaviour need not be a problem. We may sometimes use them mistakenly, but then we can also be mistaken in our choice of non-evaluative descriptions.

Many philosophers from Hume onwards have argued that we cannot logically deduce an ought from an is, and that to imagine that we can is to fall foul of the 'naturalistic fallacy'.[1] Even the statement 'X is starving' does not logically entail the statement 'X should be fed'. At one level it is indeed fallacious to imagine that an is statement logically entails an ought statement. But in the realm of practice, in terms of the relation between circumstances and practices, then other things being equal, it would be bizarre to deny X food when we could easily give them it. But then logic is just about the relations between statements, not circumstances and

[1] My thanks to John O'Neill for discussion of these matters.

practices. When I feel hungry my desire to eat does not require a logical warrant.

However, from the point of view of the hazards of social science, the problem is not that of inferring ought from is, but rather the reverse, insofar as we run the risk of wishful thinking (Bhaskar, 1979). But this is a possibility, not an inevitability. We can acknowledge unpalatable facts. Being open in making evaluative judgements does not entail that we will be mistaken in our positive descriptions. If, nevertheless, I have indeed been guilty of wishful thinking I ask critics to point out the instances of this instead of merely complaining about the 'intrusion' of values.

This view of normativity in social science and its objects is clearly at odds with what Habermas termed the 'crypto-normative approach' that has been popular in social science under the influence of post-structuralism. This both implies and yet refuses to provide justifications for critical evaluations of its objects of study; for example, the oppressive nature of certain representations and discourses is implied but just why they are oppressive is not clearly explained, perhaps because of an associated fear that claiming that people are harmed involves imputing 'essential' properties to people, and making claims to truth. It also involves a distanced and deflational view of lay actors' moral concerns. Curiously, normative judgements by social scientists are seen as threatening – as potentially authoritarian rather than merely, as has been intended in this book, as an invitation to others to join in a discussion. The irony is that, as both Hitler and Mussolini declared explicitly, relativism allows tyrants free rein to impose their will on others, come what may (Sayer, 2000a). By contrast, in sticking our necks out and making normative judgements, we expose ourselves to critique.

Crypto-normative approaches are also crypto-positive, in that they sacrifice descriptive richness through their refusal of normative judgements. In evading judging whether something causes suffering or flourishing we miss important positive information. To be told, on the one hand, as is surely correct, that power can be constructive as well as destructive, without attempting to identify in which cases it is one and in which it is the other (in some it may be both, but then we need to know in what ways and respects), is to deny ourselves important information about what is happening. Resistance and transgression are not necessarily good, nor are conservatism and conformity necessarily bad. Their significance depends on whether they contribute to flourishing or suffering, and these are not merely 'boo-hooray words' but descriptions of what happens. Similarly to say, defensively, as Foucault did, that it is not that everything is bad, but that everything is dangerous, is merely another kind of evasion of the unavoidability of the normative in everyday life and social science, and one which may deny us positive knowledge about what happens as well as discriminations between better and worse (Foucault, 1983, pp. 231–2).

I reject also the kind of radical idealism which assumes that the struggle for recognition is purely a matter of representation, projection, othering and power-play, unrelated to the qualities people actually have, or which reduces those qualities to mere discursive constructions. Refusing to distinguish between fair or adequate representations and *mis*representations renders the struggle for respect merely a matter of power-play in which no injustice can ever be done, since representations are simply voluntaristic products of the spectator and are neither fair nor unfair.[2] Projection of undesirable characteristics onto the other is of course an important element of some antagonistic social relations, but what is significant about it is that it produces *mis*representations of the other's actual characteristics. Idealist accounts that treat all pathological behaviours of the dominated as existing in the eye of the prejudiced beholder, as if they could not exist independently of this gaze or 'construction', have a superficial appeal insofar as they avoid blaming the victims of class and other forms of undeserved inequality for their situation. But to some extent the negative qualities attributed by the spectators do exist and to imagine otherwise is to ignore the social mechanisms producing them, as if class were merely a product of prejudice.

A qualified ethical naturalism

Having dealt with the usual way of approaching the relation between social science and normative matters in terms of 'subjectivity' and 'values', I now want to elaborate the approach to ethics that has been implicit in the foregoing chapters. This might be termed a *qualified ethical naturalism*. It is ethically naturalist in that it considers that the very meaning of good or bad cannot be determined without reference to the nature of human social being.[3] As a first cut, we can say that the meaning of good and bad ultimately relates to human[4] needs and to human capacities for flourishing or suffering. This is not merely a matter of 'values' or 'subjective opinion', or of pleasure and pain, for it concerns objective matters – objective in the sense of independent of what particular observers happen to think. Class matters because it creates unequal possibilities for flourishing and suffering.

[2] On the perils of idealism and strong versions of social constructionism, see Sayer, 2000a, chapters 2 and 4.
[3] '[E]thics must be grounded in a knowledge of human beings that enables us to say that some modes of life are suited to our nature, whereas others are not' (Wood, 1990, p. 17).
[4] I accept that we could extend this to other species capable of flourishing and suffering.

It is a *qualified* ethical naturalism because it also acknowledges that these capacities are always culturally mediated and elaborated, in three ways:

(1) Cultural influences upon our environment condition bodies in certain ways – for example, to be tough or soft, violent or passive. While these influences may be discursive they are also enacted physically through action and materials.

(2) Human needs and capacities for flourishing or suffering are always interpreted in various ways by particular cultures, so that the same circumstances will be interpreted differently, though not just any interpretation is likely to be accepted. For example, to some extent socially produced suffering may be legitimised as natural, and perhaps be accepted as fate by the dominated, but not just any suffering can be coped with or legitimised, and therefore resistance is always likely.

(3) Further, some kinds of goods and needs are indeed wholly culturally determined and relative, so that their satisfaction also influences whether members of particular cultures flourish (for example, the need of Muslims to pray). These goods are both defined and valued by particular communities as part of their norms, and they are internalised (to varying degrees) by their members in their commitments so that individuals identify with them and give meaning to their lives through them. Hence some moralities and their associated sentiments apply primarily to those inside a particular community, sharing particular practices and meanings, and not or less so to other communities.

Many will want to say that human flourishing and suffering are 'socially constructed', not merely in the sense that people construe them in different socially available ways, but that there is no human essence, so flourishing and suffering, morality and immorality are no more than what particular cultures happen to construct or 'constitute' them as. This is a blatant form of sociological disciplinary imperialism, leading – as such imperialism always does – to misattributions of causality. It tends to accompany a relativist view of ethics, so that, for example, there are no independent grounds for deeming female genital mutilation to be unethical. (See Nussbaum, 1999 for critiques of such absurdities.)[5] However, even the third kind of culturally specific needs presuppose natural human

---

[5] This also tends to involve an 'upward' reduction of the biological to the social through a denial of ontological stratification and emergence. Another component is a dogmatic anti-essentialism, which typically argues, illogically, that because gender and identity have no essence, nothing has any essence, and which imagines that to impute essences to things is to deny that they can change or assume different contingent forms according to their associated accidental properties (Sayer, 2000a).

qualities not available to most species or objects and so are not entirely independent of any naturalistic preconditions. Socialisation cannot possibly 'go all the way down', as Rorty argued and sociological imperialism implies, for socialisation presupposes an organic body with particular powers and susceptibilities not possessed by objects, like planks of wood, which cannot be socialised (Geras, in Archer, 2000, p. 41). Bodies can be socially modified but always within limits. This qualified ethical naturalism attempts to accommodate both the wondrous variety of human cultural forms and elements which seem to be common to all (Nussbaum, 1993).[6] While there are universal human needs these are always culturally mediated – though within limits – and in addition there are wholly culturally produced (but naturally enabled) needs. This capacity for considerable cultural diversity is an *essential* feature of human beings, involving issues as fundamental as sexual identity, and cosmology. Thus, cultural variety presupposes a kind of universalism, though not one that produces uniformity (Collier, 2003).

Strong versions of social constructionism collapse the difference between understandings and what they are about or of, and hence can make no sense of the fallibility of beliefs, for they assume that what is thought, must be, so that understandings always successfully construct the world as they imagine, and social wishful thinking always works. (The opposite idea – the belief that ideas can be perfect reflections of the world – is little better.) Of course, cultural practices *do* construct or attempt to construct social life in their own image, but how far they are successful depends on how they relate to the properties of the objects they manipulate and address, including people, which are not the product of wishful thinking but are 'other'.

While it might seem easy to accept that cultures can be wrong about human physical capacities for flourishing (for example, promoting foods that cause heart disease), it is perhaps harder to accept this might be true of the more culturally autonomous practices of the kind referred to in (3), which seem to be more self-confirming. Cultural discourses include commentaries on what is good for us, and to the extent that conformity to such beliefs helps one be accepted as a member of a community, their claims have a self-fulfilling character: those who conform may flourish more than those who rebel.[7] But such discourses may be deeply ideological, encouraging the oppressed to embrace their position as worthy, for example, encouraging women to value subservience to men. At the same

---

[6] It is interesting that the beliefs and practices of ancient Greece can, without contradiction, be drawn upon to illustrate both points.

[7] This would be an example of a local optimum position which was inferior to a higher optimum which was more inclusive.

time, discourses, belief systems or cultures are usually rich enough to provide ways of questioning their own beliefs. Thus, one doesn't have to be a non-westerner to see that many western beliefs about what constitutes flourishing are mistaken. The complexity, unevenness and (increasing) openness of real societies invite actors to compare situations of relative flourishing with other situations of oppression and to question why what is possible in one sphere is not in another; for example, why values of equality have not been extended more to gender relations. Again, the fallibility of any discourse, practice or 'social construction' is a product of the independence or otherness of the materials (including personal, social and discursive materials) from the concepts their users may have of them, and this otherness can often be detected.

However, to acknowledge the fallibility of popular conceptions of the good and of morality is not to suppose that there is only one best way of living. There is no inconsistency in arguing both that cultural, including moral, values are fallible, and that different cultures can nevertheless provide different but equally successful forms of flourishing (Nussbaum, 1999; Collier, 2003). While it is difficult to compare different cultures, translation and intercultural communication give the lie to *a priori* assumptions of incommensurability. Such assumptions are as dogmatic as the assumption that there are no significant differences among cultures. Just how much difference and similarity there is among them is an empirical question, and existing evidence suggests both extraordinary differences and overlaps and similarities (Nussbaum, 1993, 1999). The plurality of possible forms of flourishing (and suffering) is likely to go beyond those currently and historically experienced. In developing new ways of living, people can acquire new cultural emergent powers, and discover new ways of flourishing – and suffering. Thus ethics (both descriptive and prescriptive) must allow a creative dimension, albeit not creation out of nothing, as if it meant denying any kind of natural limits and enablements, as seems to be implied in some of Foucault's work (Foucault, 2000), but creation through the use and development of existing materials. There therefore need be no conflict between an ethics of authenticity and an ethics of creativity.[8] We learn as best we can what is objectively possible and what objectively expands human flourishing through social experimentation. That such social experiments, such as those of Talibanism, state socialism or global neoliberalism,

---

[8] It is not only absurd to call, as Foucault does, for an ethic of creativity that is not based on truth about desire, life, nature or body (Foucault, 2000, p. 262), as if these would prevent creativity and new discoveries; it is also dangerous to call for an ethics which disregards the affordances and limits of human social being.

can go horribly wrong is precisely in keeping, rather than in contradiction, with the idea that what constitutes human flourishing is an objective matter in the strong sense, that is, partly independent of 'social construction'.

This is not to underestimate the difficulty of assessing what constitutes flourishing or suffering, but we can make some discriminations between them. Clearly it requires us to assess what human social being involves and what is distinctive about it. Thus, given the human capacity for agency and creativity and the need for stimulation, all people have not only certain basic needs regarding 'beings' (such as being well fed and healthy), but also a need for access to diverse activities or 'doings' (Sen, 1992). As Aristotle argued, flourishing is assisted by full, active use of capacities – which is why the deprivations of prison really do damage people – so that 'the more enjoyable activities and the more desirable pleasures arise in connection with the exercise of greater abilities involving more complex discriminations' (Rawls, 1971, p. 426n). Our class position profoundly influences our access to these kinds of flourishing.

As social beings, the extent to which particular individuals flourish or suffer depends on their relationship to others, on social structures and embedded distributions of power which enable, constrain, and provide interpretations of, their lives. Some individuals or groups may flourish at the expense of others or may suffer in ways that help others flourish. In other words, there may be localised possibilities for flourishing for some, which, though better than some alternatives, are inferior to other social arrangements that allow flourishing to be more of a positive-sum game. The ideal would be a society in which the flourishing of all is the condition of the flourishing of each individual. However, the very existence of local secondary optima, and material conditions such as the spatial segregation of the dominant and the oppressed, reduce pressures to work towards more inclusively beneficial forms of social organisation. One of the impediments to better forms of society is the fact that the eudaimonistic impulse can be met tolerably well from the point of view of people's well-being locally, and sometimes at the expense of others who are, or are imagined to be, remote.

While people can flourish or suffer and have a strong sense of the difference, the possibilities for living well depend less on the practical-adequacy of their beliefs and dispositions and more on social structure and the distribution of power. Similarly, the likelihood of their acting virtuously depends on whether the institutional contexts in which they live encourage or discourage this. In generally abstracting from these structures moral philosophy shares with commonsense thinking an individualistic cast so that the force of its normative arguments is addressed more to individuals' characteristics and behaviour than to forms of social organisation.[9] A final qualification to our ethical naturalism would therefore be that it should evaluate institutions and social structures as well as individual behaviour.

In order to grasp the moral significance of class it is necessary to reject various forms of conventionalism and subjectivism, which treat normativity, including morality, as purely a matter of convention, as nothing more than 'what we do round here', or as 'merely subjective'. These treat the relative success of various norms or arguments in a sociologically reductionist way, as being wholly attributable to matters of social positioning, socially granted authority, performance and confidence, and power and luck, and as having nothing to do with reason (including emotional reason) regarding flourishing and suffering; indeed, the latter are also seen as merely conventionally or subjectively defined. Such approaches run into four related problems. First, they cannot articulate why anything is progressive rather than regressive – why, for example, racism is not progressive while anti-racism is (each, after all, involves different ideas about 'what we do round here'). Secondly, arguments for conventionalism and subjectivism involve a performative contradiction (why argue or reason so carefully for a position which denies argument or reason any force?). Thirdly, they conceal theory/practice contradictions: when advocates of such views are wronged in everyday life, they don't complain by merely appealing to 'what we do round here' or 'what is socially constructed as wrong', or by pulling rank, or by saying it's against their subjective beliefs. They usually *explain* to the person who has wronged them why their actions were wrong or unfair, by pointing out damage, harm, insult or injury that has been done, and hence they appeal to reason, not merely authority or power. These three problems all derive from a more basic one in social science: a common but often unnoticed inconsistency between third person accounts of behaviour which explain it wholly in sociological terms ('they would say/do that, given their social position'), and first person accounts of behaviour which use *justification* ('I do X not because of my social position but because I believe – and am willing to argue – that it is the best thing to do, given the nature of the situation'). Fourthly, in denying emotions any cognitive power as evaluative judgements on matters affecting our well-being, and hence as a source of insights into flourishing and suffering, conventionalism and subjectivism produce an alienated conception of morality as an external system of regulation having no connection to our concerns and needs. One reason for drawing upon the work of Adam Smith is that his view of morality or ethics is

---

[9] For example, see Peter Singer's discussion of ethical responses to poverty (Singer, 1993).

grounded in an empirical analysis of moral sentiments or emotions. This both takes note of their relation to social phenomena that bear upon our well-being and provides at least a rudimentary moral psychology. Another reason is that the spectator's view of morality lends itself to evaluations of self and other and class, and acknowledges the importance of recognition (Griswold, 1999, p. 180; Sayer, 2004).

This qualified ethical naturalism is not as robust as I would like it to be, but the alternatives of subjectivism, conventionalism and relativism are so much worse, even though they are tempting. They are easy to invoke in discussion but difficult or impossible to live by. What is proposed here is not easy to defend through argument, but it would be hard to avoid living other than in ways which are consistent with it.

The continuing significance of class

Though an ideal of an equal distribution of material wealth may continue to elude us, it is necessary, nevertheless, to make haste towards it, not because such wealth is the most important of man's treasures, but to prove that it is not. (Tawney, 1931, p. 291)

Class in the broad sense used in everyday life, and in the sense used by Bourdieu, is reproduced through a wide range of relations and processes: economic, cultural, social, including more specific educational and linguistic processes. While the economic mechanisms of capitalism *per se* are not, in practice, the sole generators of class, they could reproduce class inequalities even without the contributions of other (non-capitalist) economic mechanisms, or cultural and social mechanisms, such as those of gender and status. Class is therefore both 'structural' to capitalism, yet contingently co-determined by many non-capitalist influences, as explained in chapter 4.

Having once been the fundamental source and subject of conflict in the political culture of capitalism, class inequality is now the problem that dare not speak its name.[10] Whereas racism and increasingly sexism

---

[10] 'Radical Egalitarianism is now the orphan of a defunct socialism. The unruly and abandoned child of the liberal enlightenment had been taken in by socialism in the mid-nineteenth century. Protected and overshadowed by its new foster parent, radical egalitarianism was relieved of the burden of arguing its own case: as socialism's foster child, equality would be the by-product of an unprecedented post-capitalist order, not something to be defended morally and promoted politically on its own terms in the world as it is . . . It thus fell to reformists, be they laborist, social democratic, Eurocommunist or New Deal, to make capitalism liveable for workers and the less well off, a task they accomplished with remarkable success in the advanced economies. But in the process the egalitarian project was purged of its utopian yearnings for a world of equal freedom and dignity, and narrowed to the pursuit of a more equal distribution of goods.' (Bowles and Gintis, 1998, p. 361.)

are rightly seen as objects of official disapproval, class is either ignored or euphemised as 'social exclusion'.[11] This allows class contempt and other forms of symbolic domination and misrecognition to pass unnoticed. Differences in the distribution of respect, contempt, envy, resentment or condescension and deference are partly a product of inequalities in economic distribution, not merely because wealth is often taken as an index of worth, but because economic inequalities make objective differences to people in terms of their chances of achieving things that are likely to win conditional recognition.

Sociology may not have given up on class altogether, but it often tracks and represents class in ways that miss its normative significance. We will understand class better if we stop reducing people to occupants of positions, or bearers or performers of class, etc., and attend also to their normative dispositions and beliefs, even though these only contingently affect the reproduction of class. Lay normativity is not reducible to habit or the pursuit of self-interest and power, but has a crucial moral dimension, relating, as we have seen, to a feel for how actions, events and circumstances affect well-being. Certainly most behaviour is 'classed' but this only has normative significance insofar as it affects people's capacity for flourishing. Feelings about class are suffused with tensions: between ethical evaluation and economic valuation; between status and worth; between judgements of moral luck in terms of deserved and undeserved advantages and disadvantages; between acknowledgement of injustice and defensive rationalisation and evasion; and between recognising class as ethically problematic yet being able to do little or nothing about it at the level of interpersonal or even institutional action. The intractability of these tensions derives from the structural inequalities in which they are rooted.

Our moral sensibilities have a discursive aspect to them, which Smith and many other philosophers took for granted, but discourses must have some degree of practical adequacy in relation to what they are about and what they are attempting to do in order to gain any acceptance; while they influence what we become, we cannot just become anything, for we have particular, selective susceptibilities and powers. To have any influence on the kinds of people we become, discourses must, in a sense, be 'psychologically adequate'. Thus different cultures or discourses may colour and direct moral sentiments so that the specific things we feel ashamed or proud about vary culturally and historically: but the capacities for

---

[11] This is not to say this term has no use: it is more appropriate for the situation of ethnic minorities, for instance. As regards class, social exclusion is more of a response than a cause.

sentiments such as joy, pride and shame are universal. Subjective experience in general, and that of class in particular, makes little sense in
abstraction from moral sentiments, from individuals' monitoring of their
own and others' behaviour, and from the approval or disapproval they
receive. Dispositions and motives relating to others are typically mixed,
combining self-interest and 'othering' with more moral sentiments of
benevolence, compassion and justice. It is in virtue of the latter that anyone cares about 'othering' and inequality. Inequalities are experienced
not merely as matters of differences in tastes or forms of aversion towards
others (though these are important), but in the pursuit of goods, including valued ways of life and recognition. The struggles of the social field
are about not only the distribution of power, rights and responsibilities,
resources and recognition, and goods and bads, but their very definition
and evaluation.

Equality of recognition is now a prominent theme in mainstream
politics, at least at the level of rhetoric. According to Britain's New
Labour, everyone is recognised as of equal worth, yet New Labour policies
have achieved little in countering the inequalities in distribution which
make such claims ring hollow. Like many governments New Labour has
exploited the illusion that the politics of recognition can replace, instead
of complementing, the politics of distribution. It is as if, at least at the
level of rhetoric and style, rejecting snobbery, sexism, homophobia and
racism will be sufficient to bring about a fairer society. It is also tempting
for the comfortably-off to go along with the idea – one that has taken
root in popular 'feelgood' culture – that the dominated can be helped
by encouraging them to have more self-esteem, as if, by an act of social
levitation, they can free themselves from their lowly position, and without any redistribution of resources to them. At the level of style, New
Labour avoids the upper class, elitist associations of Conservatism, but
its economic policies are primarily a continuation of neoliberalism rather
than a rejection (Jessop, 2002).

The evasion of class and the illusion of meritocracy encourage moral-
ising policies such as government workfare programmes which effectively
pathologise individuals by holding them responsible for class disadvantages, hardening resentment in the process. Thus, New Labour's pre-
ferred discourse of 'social exclusion' has a moral element, one whose
superficial compassionate tone barely conceals an attribution of responsibility for their situation to the excluded themselves (Fairclough, 2000,
pp. 51–65). Similarly, the popularity of policies calling upon 'communities' (itself a telling euphemism for class and 'race') to mobilise their
'social capital' stems partly from the fact that they involve 'bootstrap-
ping' rather than redistribution of economic capital. In an interesting

discussion of class, gender and New Labour, Cora Kaplan argues that New Labour wants to make 'class' an obsolete category, not by attacking inequality, but by personifying class in terms of the working class associated with old Labour and Britain's disappearing industrial history, and its imagery of old, male manual workers imbued with solidaristic rather than individualistic values. Class has become 'a censored term . . . not to be mentioned lest it call up or produce old antagonisms' (Kaplan, 2003, p. 3). An open and critical approach to class is feared as it would imply alliances with groups New Labour has helped to pathologise, and risks alienating 'middle England'.[12] Instead of challenging class, it diplomatically accommodates to it.

As with other social divisions like that of gender, one of the most revealing questions about class is 'What should we do about it?' This forces us beyond a vague, unfocused, negative feeling about the subject, which is what so-called critical social science typically produces, and makes us identify what exactly is problematic about it. Greater equality would be a significant improvement in itself, but as we have argued earlier equalisation is not enough. We have sooner or later to ask: equality with respect to what reference point?; the lifestyles of a particular class, or by reference to some other conception of the good?

Regarding gender, I argued that the simple association of a particular characteristic or behaviour with men or women did not in itself make it good or bad. To argue otherwise would be to appeal to dual standards (Annas, 1993). Thus an anti-social, repressive form of behaviour would not become less bad if it was differently gendered, or distributed in gender-neutral fashion. The appropriate response to situations in which goods (whether objects, behaviours or institutions) are monopolised by particular groups is to enable equal access to them. The appropriate response to situations in which 'bads' are unequally distributed is to eliminate them, not distribute them more equally. There may also be 'necessary evils' – bads unavoidably connected to goods; these should obviously be more equally distributed. To be sure, we can never expect to create a world in which access to goods and exposure to necessary evils is perfectly equalised, but there is no good reason why a particular class or group should shoulder the burden of necessary evils such as unpleasant kinds of work. This simple rule regarding the universalisation of the good need not imply lack of attention to difference; it is compatible with recognising different needs – for example, those of the disabled – and different forms of flourishing – for example, different sexualities – as

---

[12] The term 'middle England' not only excludes the rest of the UK but is a euphemism for middle class.

part of the good, but we cannot evade the question of the legitimacy of differences. We can pursue this question not in order to stamp out difference but rather to embrace good or innocuous differences. We have to make at least some judgements on what is good regardless of its social distribution in order to make decisions on the politics of distribution and recognition. This is now recognised as regards gender (Fraser, 1997).[13] However, the equivalent message has yet to be grasped as regards class, perhaps because of an inability to distinguish the posh from the good, which results in middle class lifestyles being taken as the norm.[14]

I appreciate that it is tempting to evade questions of the good and merely argue for a 'levelling up' to the position of the better-off. Left-leaning liberal responses tend to do this. It seems an attractive proposal for it offers the promise of eliminating poverty apparently without others having to make significant sacrifices. New Labour has had its own version, in which getting the poor into work through the workfare state is imagined to be sufficient to solve the problems of 'social exclusion' (Marquand, 1998). There are many possible arguments against this, both in terms of its feasibility and its desirability. Here are just three regarding its desirability.

First, it could be argued that some of the goods enjoyed by the dominant were too expensive in terms of the sacrifices made by others to produce them. The rich do not merely have more goods than the poor, they command vastly more of others' labour in the production of the goods and services they consume than do other contributors to the division of labour. And as even the neoliberal Hayek acknowledges, differences in incomes in market economies have more to do with luck than merit. To question their wealth is partly to question their disproportionate dependence on the labour of others, and hence whether society can afford the rich. A policy of reducing inequality would imply a shift in the division of labour towards servicing the consumption of hitherto poorer groups, so that fewer workers would produce luxury goods and more would produce basic and middling goods. Second, studies of happiness in relation to wealth show that above a basic level, increases in wealth make little difference to happiness. Friendships, recognition, love and satisfying work are

---

[13] The need to go beyond simple notions of equality in terms of resources and address questions of the good is also recognised in the capabilities and functionings approaches pioneered in development studies by Sen and Nussbaum (Sen, 1992, 1999; Nussbaum, 2000; *Feminist Economics*, 2003).

[14] As Julia Annas notes, it's hard to imagine complete de-gendering in the pursuit of the good, but that should not stop us pursuing piecemeal changes in that direction (Annas, 1993). In principle, I don't find complete abolition of class differences so hard to imagine, though for practical reasons, as I explain below, it is hard to imagine.

more important (Lane, 1991). The pursuit of wealth as a source of happiness is illusory. Third, given current unsustainable levels of consumption, there are ecological grounds for choosing a moderate level of wealth to equalise around. The rich are the least ecologically sound social group. And combining the second and third points, it can be further argued that frugality (not poverty) need not mean compromising happiness.

These arguments do *not* amount to an agenda of levelling down or equalising misery, as opponents of egalitarianism are wont to argue. On the contrary, the approach of this book implies a 'levelling up', only not by reference to the rich and powerful but by reference to the good. As we have noted, there are many conceptions of the good, and many ways of flourishing, but not just any form of social organisation promotes them or enables equal access to them, and there are still more ways of suffering or incomplete, uneven flourishing. Refusing the liberal priority of the right over the good need not be a recipe for authoritarian imposition of a particular conception of the good, but rather a challenge to make the question of the good central to public deliberation.

There is a different and more fundamental objection to a radical egalitarian politics of distribution and recognition as regards class, namely that class is structural to capitalism, and in the demonstrable absence of superior alternatives to capitalism, we therefore have to accept class inequality. One rather tired response is to acknowledge that state socialism indeed failed, but claim that real socialism has still not been tried. Although I respect the aspirations, this is a feeble response because of the repeated failure to institute such a system: if it is so superior, why has it not been put into practice successfully? As I have argued elsewhere (Sayer, 1995), the principal problem of 'real' socialism/communism is that, however much we might wish it were not so, neither democracy nor central planning nor networking can cope with the intractability of the kind of complex division of labour that an advanced economy requires. Markets – though not on the same scale as at present, and with greater regulation – are required to coordinate at least significant parts of this division of labour. This might be compatible with a significant role for worker-owned enterprises producing for markets, though, as yet, forms of organisation and support for such enterprises (and complementary regulation of capitalist enterprises) which can make them successful on an extensive scale have not been developed (Bardhan and Roemer, 1993).

Many will argue that globalisation makes an egalitarian politics of distribution within single countries more difficult, by increasing the linkages between rich and poor globally, and producing de-industrialisation. However, whether this leads to widening or narrowing inequalities on a global scale depends on the form of globalisation and the way it is regulated.

The neoliberal version encourages a 'race to the bottom' as regards labour remuneration and working conditions, and continued rich country dominance of global trade, but as critics have repeatedly pointed out, this is not a natural, inevitable process nor one of laissez-faire but just one possible form of globalisation, one produced by neoliberal regulation. Other forms are possible.

Although class is structural to capitalism, capitalism can function successfully with a good deal less economic inequality than occurs in societies such as the USA or UK, and with fewer barriers of symbolic domination than in countries such as the UK and France. Inequalities within capitalist countries have varied considerably over time. In Britain in 1976 the incomes at the 90th percentile were 2.9 times those at the 10th percentile. Twenty-five years later, the ratio had risen to 4:1. The percentage of people in households with incomes less than 60 per cent of the median has risen from 13 per cent in 1979 to 23 per cent in 2000 (Aldridge, 2004). As in many other countries, the increase in income inequality in Britain has widened primarily as a result of rapid increases in earnings at the top. The pay gap between men and women contributes to income inequalities: the overwhelming majority of low-paid workers are women, and the gap is wider in Britain than in any other member state of the European Union fifteen, with women's average gross hourly earnings 76 per cent of average male gross hourly earnings, compared to an EU average of 84 per cent (Aldridge, 2004). A combined assault on low pay and gender inequalities in employment is therefore needed.

There are further differences among capitalist countries. While Swedish CEOs earn less than three times average earnings, US CEOs earn over ten times average earnings. In 1990 American physicians earned more than three times those in Britain, France, Sweden and Japan. These differences are not explicable simply in terms of demand and supply differences, for the markets in which they work are differently structured and regulated, and the groups in question have been able to build up different power bases and strategies of closure (Verba et al., 1997). Normative (moral economic) influences also vary between these societies.

While the overall tendency in the last twenty-five years has been increasing inequality in many advanced capitalist countries, this is not the only possible direction. Capitalism has gone through boom periods in which levels of direct taxation in many successful economies were considerably higher than at present. Reductions of working hours can help reduce unemployment and, depending on its level, minimum wage legislation can boost low incomes. Educational systems vary considerably in the extent to which they help to reproduce inequality: allowing selection and parental choice (in practice always limited, unequal and liable to produce perverse effects) exacerbates the tendency for educational achievement to be dependent on cultural capital.[15]

Neoliberals might argue that inequality is a price worth paying for alleged benefits in terms of economic growth and success. However, empirical research shows that there is little or no relationship between the economic performance of nations and the degree of income inequality within them (Glyn and Miliband, 1994). They might also say that very high incomes are necessary for motivating the most talented people who will supposedly make companies successful. But this is to rationalise what is no more than the exercise of power. They pay themselves such incomes not because it is justified or necessary but because they can. Companies have succeeded in the past and still do in other countries with lower executive pay, and there is no reason why they could not do so in the future. The extent to which pay premiums motivate people to work harder and better varies according to cultural as well as economic differences: it is both an empirical question and a normative one. Again, research on happiness analysed by Lane (1991) suggests that while many are indeed motivated by pay, it fails to bring them the benefits they imagine.

It would of course be naive to suppose that ethical arguments are ever sufficient to bring about political change, but politics without ethical guidance is directionless and prone to repression rather than emancipation. Cases need to be made for progressive income tax, for greater inheritance tax, for limits on the mobility of capital, for a liveable minimum wage, for reduced working hours, for equality between men and women and different ethnic groups, for approaching education in terms of better systems rather than individual choice, and for many other policies bearing upon mechanisms that reproduce class and other inequalities. There are difficult moral economic arguments to be made here which demonstrate that, often, what allows us apparently to pursue our self-interest is not actually in our interests or favourable to social well-being. Clearly the cases need to be made at international levels as well as national, for many such policies cannot hope to be successful without international economic and social policy agreements to stop them being undermined by competition from more liberalised economies. I do not underestimate the difficulties of such a strategy, but it could substantially reduce class inequalities and

---

[15] Aldridge (2004) reports that the odds of a child from a middle class background making it into the middle class in adulthood – as opposed to the working class – relative to the same odds for a working class child are of the order of 15:1 across modern societies.

their associated injustices. While it would not completely eliminate them, the impossibility of achieving perfection has never been a good argument for not pursuing achievable improvements.[16]

Recently, the British children's charity, Barnardo's, published some advertisements containing striking and disturbing photomontages of four newborn babies, one with a syringe in its mouth, one with a bottle of methylated spirits, one with a cockroach, and one with a silver spoon. Presumably the idea was to indicate the diversity of fates that await them. Newborns are unquestionably of equal moral worth, equally needy, equally deserving of a good life, yet class inequalities quickly ensure that their life-chances are decidedly unequal.[17] Of course adults have some responsibility for their own life-chances, but their chances are already strongly shaped by class (and other sources of inequality) long before they achieve the maturity to exercise that responsibility, and class itself shapes just how capable they are of doing so. We need not only a politics of recognition but a rejuvenated egalitarian politics of distribution that confronts the injustice of class inequalities openly, one that does not treat class as if it were merely the outcome of competition amongst adults on a level playing field, but which recognises its profound effects on people from birth. In fact, redistribution in itself would be an advance in terms of the politics of recognition. I hope this book has contributed to making the case for such a politics.

[16] As Anne Phillips argues, while there might be arguments against complete inequality among individuals, there are no good grounds for inequalities between men and women (Phillips, 1999).

[17] Even if it were to be argued that they had different genetic endowments, this in itself would provide no justification for the differential treatment that results from class inequalities.

Bibliography

Aboulafia, M. 1999, 'A (neo)American in Paris: Bourdieu, Mead, and pragmatism', in Shusterman, R. (ed.), *Bourdieu: A Critical Reader*, Oxford: Blackwell, pp. 153–74

Aldridge, S. 2004, *Life Chances and Social Mobility: An Overview of the Evidence*, Prime Minister's Strategy Unit, Cabinet Office

Alexander, J. C. 1995, *Fin de Siècle Social Theory*, London: Verso

Alexander, J. C. 2003, *The Meanings of Social Life*, Oxford: Oxford University Press

Alexander, J. C. and Lara, M. P. 1996, 'Honneth's new critical theory of recognition', *New Left Review*, 220, pp. 126–36

Anderson, E. S. 1993, *Value in Ethics and Economics*, Cambridge, MA: Harvard University Press

Anderson, E. S. 1999, 'What is the point of equality?', *Ethics*, 109, pp. 287–337

Annas, J. 1993, 'Women and the quality of life: two norms or one?', in Nussbaum, M. C. and Sen, A. (eds.), *The Quality of Life*, Oxford: Clarendon, pp. 279–96

Appadurai, A. (ed.) 1986, *The Social Life of Things: Commodities in Cultural Perspective*, Cambridge: Cambridge University Press

Archer, M. S. 2000, *Being Human*, Cambridge: Cambridge University Press

Archer, M. S. 2003, *Structure, Agency and the Internal Conversation*, Cambridge: Cambridge University Press

Arendt, H. 1965, *Eichmann in Jerusalem*, revised edn., Harmondsworth: Penguin

Aristotle, 1980, *The Nicomachean Ethics*, trans. D. Ross, Oxford: Oxford University Press

Baier, A. 1994, *Moral Prejudices*, London: Routledge

Baker, J. 1987, *Arguments for Equality*, London: Verso

Barbalet, J. M. 2001, *Emotions, Social Theory and Social Structure*, Cambridge: Cambridge University Press

Bardhan, P. K. and Roemer, J. E. (eds.) 1993, *Market Socialism: The Current Debate*, New York: Oxford University Press

Barrett, M. and Phillips, A. (eds.) 1992, *Destabilising Theory*, Cambridge: Polity

Bartky, S. L. 1990, *Femininity and Domination: Studies in the Phenomenology of Class*, London: Routledge

Bauman, Z. 1993, *Postmodern Ethics*, Oxford: Blackwell

Bauman, Z. 2001, *Thinking Sociologically*, Basingstoke: Macmillan

Beck, U. and Beck-Gernsheim, E. 2002, *Individualization*, London: Sage

Benhabib, S. 1992, *Situating the Self*, Cambridge: Polity

Benton, T. 1993, *Natural Rights: Ecology, Animal Rights and Social Justice*, London: Verso

Bhaskar, R. 1975, *A Realist Theory of Science*, Leeds: Leeds Books; 2nd edn 1979, Brighton: Harvester

Bhaskar, R. 1979, *The Possibility of Naturalism*, Brighton: Harvester

Billig, M., Condor, S., Edwards, D., Cane, M., Middleton, D. and Radley, A. 1988, *Ideological Dilemmas*, Beverly Hills, CA, Sage

Booth, W. J. 1993, *Households: On the Moral Architecture of the Economy*, Ithaca, NY: Cornell University Press

Bourdieu, P. 1977, *Outline of a Theory of Practice*, Cambridge: Cambridge University Press

Bourdieu, P. 1984, *Distinction: A Social Critique of the Judgement of Taste*, London: Routledge

Bourdieu, P. 1986, 'The forms of capital', in Richardson, J. G. (ed.), *Handbook of Theory and Research for the Sociology of Education*, London: Greenwood Press, pp. 241–58

Bourdieu, P. 1987, '"What makes a class?": on the theoretical and practical existence of groups', *Berkeley Journal of Sociology*, 32, pp. 1–17

Bourdieu, P. 1988, *Homo Academicus*, Cambridge: Polity

Bourdieu, P. 1990a, *In Other Words: Towards a Reflexive Sociology*, Cambridge, Polity

Bourdieu, P. 1990b, 'The scholastic point of view', trans. L. Wacquant, *Cultural Anthropology*, 5, pp. 380–91

Bourdieu, P. 1990c, *The Logic of Practice*, Cambridge: Polity

Bourdieu, P. 1991, *Language and Symbolic Power*, Cambridge: Polity

Bourdieu, P. 1993, *Sociology in Question*, London: Sage

Bourdieu, P. 1996a, *The State Nobility: Elite Schools in the Field of Power*, Cambridge, Polity

Bourdieu, P. 1996b, 'On the family as a realized category', *Theory, Culture and Society*, 13 (3), pp. 19–26

Bourdieu, P. 1998, *Practical Reason*, Cambridge: Polity

Bourdieu, P. 2000, *Pascalian Meditations*, Cambridge: Polity

Bourdieu, P. 2001, *Masculine Domination*, Cambridge: Polity

Bourdieu, P. et al. 1999, *The Weight of the World*, Cambridge: Polity

Bowles, S. and Gintis, H., 1998, 'Efficient redistribution: new rules for markets, states and communities', in Wright, E. O. (ed.), *Recasting Egalitarianism*, London: Verso, pp. 3–74

Butler, J. 1997, 'Merely cultural', *Social Text*, 52/53, pp. 265–77 and (1998) *New Left Review*, 227, pp. 33–44

Calhoun, C. 2003, 'An apology for moral shame', *The Journal of Political Philosophy*, 11 (2), pp. 1–20

Charlesworth, S. 2000, *A Phenomenology of Working Class Experience*, Cambridge: Cambridge University Press

Cockburn, C. 1985, *Machinery of Male Dominance*, London: Pluto Press

Cohen, G. A. 1995, *Self-Ownership, Freedom and Equality*, Oxford: Oxford University Press

Collier, A. 1994, *Critical Realism*, London: Verso

Collier, A. 1999, *Being and Worth*, London: Routledge

Collier, A. 2003, *In Defence of Objectivity*, London: Routledge

Coole, D. 1996, 'Is class a difference that makes a difference?', *Radical Philosophy*, 77, pp. 17–25

Craib, I. 1997, 'Social constructionism as a social psychosis', *Sociology*, 31 (1), pp. 1–18

Craib, I. 1998, *Experiencing Identity*, London: Sage

Crompton, R. 1993, *Class and Stratification: An Introduction to Current Debates*, Oxford: Blackwell

Crompton, R. 1996, 'Gender and class analysis', in Lee, D. J. and Turner, B. S. (eds.), *Conflicts about Class: Debating Inequality in Late Industrialism*, London: Longman, pp. 115–26

Crompton, R. 1998, *Class and Stratification*, 2nd edn, Cambridge: Polity

Crossley, N. 2001, 'The phenomenological habitus and its construction', *Theory and Society*, 30, pp. 81–120

Day, G. 2001, *Class*, London: Routledge

Donnison, D. 1998, *Policies for a Just Society*, London: Macmillan

Durkheim, E. 1951, *Suicide*, New York: Free Press

Durkheim, E. 1984, *The Division of Labour in Society*, Basingstoke: Macmillan

Ehrenreich, B. 2001, *Nickel and Dimed: On (Not) Getting By in America*, New York: Metropolitan Books

Fairclough, N. 2000, *New Labour, New Language*, London: Routledge

Fairclough, N., Jessop, B. and Sayer, A. 2001, 'Critical Realism and semiosis', *Journal of Critical Realism*, 5 (1), pp. 2–10

Feminist Economics, 2003, special double issue on 'Amartya Sen's Work and Ideas: A Gender Perspective', 9 (2 and 3)

Fevre, R. 2000, *The Demoralization of Western Culture*, London and New York: Continuum

Fielding, A. J. 1995, 'Inter-regional migration and intra-generational social class mobility 1971–1991', in Savage, M. and Butler, T. (eds.), *Social Change and the Middle Classes*, London: University College Press

Finch, J. 1989, *Family Obligations and Social Change*, Cambridge: Polity

Finch, L. 1993, *The Classing Gaze: Sexuality, Class and Surveillance*, St. Leonards, Australia: Allen and Unwin

Foucault, M. 1983, 'On the genealogy of ethics', in *Michel Foucault: Beyond Structuralism and Hermeneutics*, ed. Hubert L. Dreyfus and Paul Rabinow, 2nd edn, Chicago: University of Chicago Press, 1983

Foucault, M. 2000, *Michel Foucault: Ethics*, ed. P. Rabinow, London: Penguin

Fowler, B. 1997, *Pierre Bourdieu and Cultural Theory*, London: Sage

Frankfurt, H. G. 1998, *The Importance of What We Care About*, Cambridge: Cambridge University Press

Fraser, N. 1995, 'From redistribution to recognition? Dilemmas of a "postsocialist" age', *New Left Review*, 212, pp. 68–93

Fraser, N. 1997, *Justice Interruptus: Critical Reflections on the 'Postsocialist' Condition*, New York: Routledge

Fraser, N. 1998, 'Heterosexism, misrecognition, and capitalism: a response to Judith Butler', *Social Text*, 53/54, pp. 278–89 and *New Left Review*, 228, pp. 140–50

Fraser, N. 1999, 'Social justice in the age of identity politics: redistribution, recognition and participation', in Ray, L. J. and Sayer, A. (eds.), *Culture and Economy after the Cultural Turn*, London: Sage, pp. 53–75

Fraser, N. 2003, 'Distorted beyond recognition', in Fraser, N. and Honneth, A., *Redistribution or Recognition?: A Political-Philosophical Exchange*, London: Verso, pp. 198–236

Fraser, N. and Honneth, A. 2003, *Redistribution or Recognition?: A Political-Philosophical Exchange*, London: Verso

Frow, J. 1995, *Cultural Studies and Cultural Value*, Oxford: Clarendon

Geras, N. 1995, *Solidarity in the Conversation of Humankind: The Ungroundable Liberalism of Richard Rorty*, London: Verso

Geras, N. 1998, *The Contract of Mutual Indifference*, London: Verso

Gerhardi, S. 1995, *Gender Symbolism and Organizational Cultures*, London: Sage

Giddens, A. 1991, *Modernity and Self-identity: Self and Other in the Late Modern Age*, Cambridge: Polity

Gilligan, J. 2000, *Violence: Reflections on Our Deadliest Epidemic*, London: Jessica Kingsley Publishers

Glover, J. 1999, *Humanity: A Moral History of the Twentieth Century*, London: Jonathan Cape

Glyn, A. and Miliband, D. (eds.) 1994, *Paying for Inequality: The Economic Cost of Social Injustice*, London: IPPR/Rivers Oram Press

Goldthorpe, J. H. and Marshall, G. 1992, 'The promising future of class analysis', *Sociology*, 26, pp. 381–400

Goodin, R. E. 1985, *Protecting the Vulnerable: A Reanalysis of our Social Responsibilities*, Chicago: University of Chicago Press

Gouldner, A. 1971, *The Coming Crisis of Sociology*, London: Heinemann

Griswold, C. L. Jr. 1999, *Adam Smith and the Virtues of Enlightenment*, Cambridge: Cambridge University Press

Gross, E. 1986, 'What is feminist theory?', in Pateman, C. and Gross, E. (eds.), *Feminist Challenges: Social and Political Theory*, Boston, MA: Northeastern University Press, pp. 125–43

Habermas, J. 1990, *Moral Consciousness and Communication*, Cambridge: Polity

Harré, R. 1979, *Social Being*, Oxford: Blackwell

Harré, R. and Madden, E. H. 1975, *Causal Powers*, Oxford: Blackwell

Hayek, F. A. 1960, *The Constitution of Liberty*, London: Routledge

Hayek, F. A. 1988, *The Fatal Conceit: The Errors of Socialism*, London: Routledge

Haylett, C. 2001, 'Illegitimate subjects?: abject whites, neoliberal modernisation, and middle class multiculturalism', *Environment and Planning D: Society and Space*, 19, pp. 351–70

Helm, B. W. 2001, *Emotional Reason: Deliberation, Motivation and the Nature of Value*, Cambridge: Cambridge University Press

Holmwood, J. 2001, 'Gender and critical realism: a critique of Sayer', *Sociology*, 35 (4), pp. 947–65

Honneth, A. 1986, 'The fragmented world of symbolic forms: reflections on Pierre Bourdieu's sociology of culture', *Theory, Culture and Society*, 3 (3), pp. 55–66

Honneth, A. 1995, *The Struggle for Recognition: The Moral Grammar of Social Conflicts*, Cambridge: Polity

Honneth, A. 2001, 'Recognition or redistribution? Changing perspectives on the moral order of society', *Theory, Culture and Society*, 18 (2–3), pp. 43–55

Honneth, A. 2003, 'Redistribution as recognition', in Fraser, N. and Honneth, A., *Redistribution or Recognition?: A Political-Philosophical Exchange*, London: Verso, pp. 110–97

hooks, b. 2000, *Where We Stand: Class Matters*, New York: Routledge

Irwin, S. 1995, *Rights of Passage*, London: University College Press

Jackall, R. 1988, *The Moral Maze*, Oxford: Oxford University Press

Jessop, B. 2002, *The Future of the Capitalist State*, Cambridge: Polity

Jordan, B. 1996, *A Theory of Poverty and Social Exclusion*, Cambridge: Polity

Jordan, B. 1998, *The New Politics of Welfare*, London: Sage

Kaplan, C. 2003, 'The death of the working class hero', *Social and Cultural Review*, 4, pp. 1–8

Keat, R. 2000, *Cultural Goods and the Limits of the Market*, Basingstoke: Palgrave

Kefalas, M. 2003, *Working-Class Heroes: Protecting Home, Community and Nation in a Chicago Neighbourhood*, Berkeley, CA: University of California Press

Kuhn, A. 1995, *Family Secrets: Acts of Memory and Imagination*, London, Verso

Kymlicka. W. 2002, *Contemporary Political Philosophy*, 2nd edn, Oxford: Oxford University Press

Lamont, M. 1992, *Money, Morals and Manners: The Culture of the French and American Upper-Middle Class*, Chicago: Chicago University Press

Lamont, M. 2000, *The Dignity of Working Men: Morality and the Boundaries of Race, Class and Imagination*, New York: Russell Sage Foundation and Harvard University Press

Lane, R. E. 1991, *The Market Experience*, Cambridge: Cambridge University Press

Lane, R. E. 1998, 'The road not taken: friendship. consumerism, and happiness', in Crocker, D. A. and Linden, T. (eds.), *Ethics of Consumption*, Lanham, MA: Rowman and Littlefield, pp. 218–48

Lareau, A. 2003, *Unequal Childhoods: Class, Race and Family Life*, Berkeley, CA: University of California Press

Lawler, S. 1999, 'Getting out and getting away': women's narratives of class mobility', *Feminist Review*, 63, pp. 3–24

Lawler, S. 2000, *Mothering the Self: Mothers, Daughters, Subjects*, London: Routledge

Lichtenberg, J. 1998, 'Consuming because others consume', in Crocker, D. A. and Linden, T. (eds.), *Ethics of Consumption*, Lanham, MA: Rowman and Littlefield, pp. 155–75

Lovell, T. 2000, 'Thinking feminism with and against Bourdieu', *Feminist Theory*, 1 (1), pp. 11–32

Lynch, K. and Lodge, A. 2002, *Equality and Power in Schools*, London: Routledge

McCall, L. 1992, 'Does gender *fit*? Bourdieu, feminism and conceptions of social order', *Theory and Society*, 21, pp. 837–62

MacIntyre, A. 1981, *After Virtue*, London: Duckworth

Macleod, J. 1995, *Ain't No Makin' It: Aspirations and Attainment in a Low Income Neighborhood*, 2nd edn, Boulder, CO: Westview Press

McMylor, P. 1994, *Alasdair MacIntyre: Critic of Modernity*, London: Routledge

McNay, L. 2001, 'Meditations on *Pascalian Meditations*', *Economy and Society*, 30 (1), pp. 139–54

McRobbie, A. 2002, 'A mixed bag of misfortunes?', *Theory, Culture and Society*, 19 (3), pp. 129–38

Manent, P. 1998, *The City of Man*, trans. Marc A. LePain, Princeton: Princeton University Press

Marquand, D. 1998, *The Unprincipled Society: New Demands and Old Politics*, London: Fontana

Marshall, G., Swift, A. and Roberts, S. 1997, *Against the Odds*, Oxford: Clarendon

Marx, K. 1975, *Early Writings*, London: Pelican

Marx, K. 1867:1976, *Capital: Vol. 1*, London: New Left Review/Penguin

Midgley, M. 1972, 'Is "moral" a dirty word?', *Philosophy*, 47 (181), pp. 206–28

Midgley, M. 1984, *Wickedness*, Routledge and Kegan Paul

Mill, J. S. 1859, 'On Liberty', in *John Stuart Mill: Three Essays, with an Introduction* by Richard Wollheim, 1975, Oxford: Oxford University Press, pp. 5–141

Mill, J. S. 1869, 'The Subjection of Women', in *John Stuart Mill: Three Essays, with an Introduction* by Richard Wollheim, 1975, Oxford: Oxford University Press, pp. 427–548

Miller, D. 1992, 'Distributive justice: what the people think', *Ethics*, 102, pp. 555–93

Murphy, J. B. 1993, *The Moral Economy of Labor*, New Haven: Yale University Press

Myrdal, G. 1962, *An American Dilemma*, 20th anniversary edn, New York: Harper and Row

New, C. 2004, 'Sex and gender: a critical realist approach', *New Formations*, forthcoming

Norman, R. 1998, *The Moral Philosophers*, 2nd edn, Oxford: Oxford University Press

Nussbaum, M. C. 1986, *The Fragility of Goodness*, Cambridge: Cambridge University Press

Nussbaum, M. C. 1993, 'Charles Taylor: explanation and practical reason', in Sen, A. and Nussbaum, M. C. (eds.), *The Quality of Life*, Oxford: Clarendon, pp. 232–41

Nussbaum, M. C. 1996, 'Compassion: the basic emotion', *Social Philosophy and Policy*, 13 (1), pp. 27–58

Nussbaum, M. C. 1999, *Sex and Social Justice*, Oxford: Oxford University Press

Nussbaum, M. C. 2000, *Women and Human Development: The Capabilities Approach*, Cambridge: Cambridge University Press

Nussbaum, M. C. 2001, *Upheavals of Thought: The Intelligence of Emotions*, Cambridge: Cambridge University Press

Offe, C. 1985, *Disorganized Capitalism*, ed. J. Keane, Cambridge: Polity

O'Neill, J. 1998, *The Market: Ethics, Knowledge and Politics*, London: Routledge

O'Neill, J. 1999, 'Economy, equality and recognition', in Ray, L. J. and Sayer, A. (eds.), *Culture and Economy after the Cultural Turn*, London: Sage, pp. 76–91

Outhwaite, W. 1987, *New Philosophies of Social Science*, London: Macmillan

Parkin, F. 1972, *Class Inequality and Political Order*, London: Granada

Phillips, A. 1997, 'From inequality to difference: a severe case of displacement?' *New Left Review*, 224, pp. 143–53

Phillips, A. 1999, *Which Equalities Matter?* Cambridge: Polity

Polanyi, K. 1944, *The Great Transformation*, 2nd edn 1957, New York: Basic Books

Pringle, R. 1988, *Secretaries Talk: Sexuality, Power and Work*, London: Allen and Unwin

Probyn, E. 2002, 'Shame in the habitus', paper delivered to the Feminism and Bourdieu conference, Department of Sociology, Manchester University, UK

Rawls, J. 1971, *A Theory of Justice*, Oxford: Oxford University Press

Reay, D. 1997a, 'The double-bind of the "working class" feminist academic: the success of failure or the failure of success', in Mahoney, P. and Zmroczek, C. (eds.), *Class Matters: Working-Class Women's Perspectives on Social Class*, London: Taylor and Francis, pp. 18–29

Reay, D. 1997b, 'Feminist theory, habitus, and social class: disrupting notions of classlessness', *Women's Studies International Forum*, 20 (2), pp. 225–33

Reay, D. 1998a, 'Re-thinking social class: qualitative perspectives on class and gender', *Sociology*, 32 (2), pp. 259–75

Reay, D. 1998b, *Class Work: Mothers' Involvement in Their Children's Primary Schooling*, London: University College Press

Reay, D. 2002, 'Shaun's story', *Gender and Education*, 14 (2), pp. 221–34

Ribbens McCarthy, J., Edwards, R. and Gillies, V. 2003, *Making Families: Moral Tales of Parenting and Step-Parenting*, Durham: Sociologypress

Robbins, D. 1999, *Bourdieu and Culture*, London: Sage

Rosaldo, R. 1993, *Culture and Truth: The Re-Making of Social Analysis*, London: Routledge

Runciman, W. G. 1966, *Relative Deprivation and Social Justice*, London, Routledge and Kegan Paul

Savage, M. 2000, *Class Analysis and Social Transformation*, Buckingham: Open University Press

Savage, M., Bagnall, G. and Longhurst, B. 2001a, 'Ordinary, ambivalent and defensive: class differentiation in the Northwest of England', *Sociology*, 35, pp. 875–92

Savage, M., Crompton, R., Devine, F. and Scott, J. (eds.) 2001b, *Renewing Class Analysis*, Oxford: Blackwell

Sayer, A. 1992, *Method in Social Science: A Realist Approach*, 2nd edn, London: Routledge

Sayer, A. 1995, *Radical Political Economy: A Critique*, Oxford: Blackwell

Sayer, A. 1999, 'Bourdieu, Smith and disinterested judgement', *The Sociological Review*, 47 (3), pp. 403–31

Sayer, A. 2000a, *Realism and Social Science*, London: Sage

Sayer, A. 2000b, 'System, lifeworld and gender: associational versus counterfactual thinking', *Sociology*, 34 (4), pp. 707–25

Sayer, A. 2000c, 'For postdisciplinary studies: sociology and the curse of disciplinary parochialism/imperialism', in Eldridge, J., MacInnes, J., Scott, S., Warhurst, C. and Witz, A. (eds.), *Sociology: Legacies and Prospects*, Durham: Sociologypress, pp. 85–91

Sayer, A. 2001, 'For a critical cultural political economy', *Antipode*, 33 (4), pp. 687–708

Sayer, A. 2002a, 'Reply to Holmwood', *Sociology*, 35 (4), pp. 967–84

Sayer, A. 2002b, 'What are you worth?': Why class is an embarrassing subject', *Sociological Research Online*, 7 (3) http://www.socresonline.org.uk/7/3/sayer.html

Sayer, A. 2003, '(De-)Commodification, consumer culture and moral economy', *Environment and Planning D: Society and Space*, 21, pp. 341–57

Sayer, A. 2004, 'Restoring the moral dimension in social scientific accounts: a qualified ethical naturalist approach', in Archer, M. S. and Outhwaite, W. (eds.), *Defending Objectivity: Essays in Honour of Andrew Collier*, London: Routledge, pp. 93–114

Scheff, T. J. 1990, *Microsociology: Discourse, Emotions and Social Structure*, Chicago: Chicago University Press

Scott, J. C. 1990, *Domination and the Arts of Resistance: Hidden Transcripts*, New Haven: Yale University Press

Sedgwick, E. K. and Frank, A. (eds.), 1995, *Shame and Its Sisters: A Silvan Tomkins Reader*, Durham, NC: Duke University Press

Segal, L. 1999, *Why Feminism?*, Cambridge: Polity

Sen, A. 1990, 'Rational fools: a critique of the behavioural foundations of economic theory', in Mansbridge, J. (ed.), *Beyond Self-Interest*, Chicago: Chicago University Press, pp. 24–33

Sen, A. 1992, *Inequality Re-examined*, Oxford: Oxford University Press

Sen, A. 1999, *Development as Freedom*, Oxford: Oxford University Press

Sennett, R. 2003, *Respect: The Formation of Character in a World of Inequalities*, London: Allen Lane

Sennett, R. and Cobb, J. 1972, *The Hidden Injuries of Class*, New York: Knopf; London: Fontana

Sevenhuijsen, S. 1998, *Citizenship and the Ethic of Care*, London: Routledge

Shusterman, R. (ed.) 1999, *Bourdieu: A Critical Reader*, Oxford: Blackwell

Simmel, G. 1990, *The Philosophy of Money*, 2nd edn, trans. T. Bottomore and D. Frisby, London: Routledge

Singer, P. 1993, *Practical Ethics*, Cambridge: Cambridge University Press

Singer, P. 1997, *How Are We to Live?*, Oxford: Oxford University Press

Skeggs, B. 1997, *Formations of Class and Gender: Becoming Respectable*, London: Sage

Skeggs, B. 2004, *Class, Self, Culture*, London: Routledge

Smart, C. and Neale, B. 1999, *Family Fragments?*, Cambridge: Polity

Smiley, M. 1992, *Moral Responsibility and the Boundaries of Community*, Chicago: University of Chicago Press

Smith, A. 1759:1984, *The Theory of Moral Sentiments*, Indianapolis: Liberty Fund

Smith, A. 1776:1976, *An Inquiry into the Nature and Causes of the Wealth of Nations*, ed. E. Cannan, Chicago: University of Chicago Press

Soper, K. 1995, *What is Nature?*, Oxford: Blackwell

Southerton, D. K. 1999, 'Capital Resources and Geographical Mobility: Consumption and Identification in a New Town', PhD thesis, Lancaster University, Lancaster, UK

Southerton, D. K. 2002a, '"Us" and "them": identification and class boundaries.' *Soundings*, 21, pp. 133–47

Southerton, D. K. 2002b, 'Boundaries of "Us" and "Them": class, mobility and identification in a new town', *Sociology*, 36 (1), pp. 171–93

Staveren, I. van 2001, *The Values of Economics: An Aristotelian Perspective*, London: Routledge

Steedman, C. 1985, *Landscape for a Good Woman*, London: Virago

Tawney, R. H. 1931, *Equality*, 4th edn 1952, London: George Allen and Unwin

Taylor, C. 1994, 'The politics of recognition', in Gutmann, A. (ed.), *Multi-culturalism: Examining the Politics of Recognition*, Princeton, NJ: Princeton University Press

Thévènot, L. 2001, 'Organized complexity: conventions of coordination and the composition of economic arrangements', *European Journal of Social Theory*, 4 (4), pp. 405–25

Thompson, E. P. 1963, *The Making of the English Working Class*, Harmondsworth: Penguin

Thompson, E. P. 1991, *Customs in Common*, New York: New Press

Thomson, R. and Holland, J. 2003, 'Making the most of what you've got: resources, values and inequalities in young people's transitions to adulthood', *Educational Review* 55 (1), pp. 33–46

Tilly, C. 1998, *Durable Inequality*, Berkeley, CA: University of California Press

Tronto, J. 1993, *Moral Boundaries*, London: Routledge

Turnbull, C. M. 1972, *The Mountain People*, New York: Simon and Schuster

Unger, P. 1996, *Living High and Letting Die*, Oxford: Oxford University Press

Verba, S., Kelman, S., Orren, G. R., Miyake, I. and Watanuki, J. 1997, *Elites and the Idea of Equality: A Comparison of Japan, Sweden and the U.S.*, Cambridge, MA: Harvard University Press

Walby, S. 1986, *Patriarchy at Work*, Cambridge: Polity

Walby, S. 1990, *Theorizing Patriarchy*, Cambridge: Polity

Walby, S. 2001, 'From community to coalition: the politics of recognition as the handmaiden of the politics of redistribution', *Theory, Culture and Society*, 18 (2–3), pp. 113–35

Walby, S. 2004, 'The European Union and gender inequality', *Social Politics*, 11 (1), pp. 4–29

Walker, M. A. 1998, *Moral Understandings: A Feminist Study in Ethics*, London: Routledge

Walkerdine, V. and Lucey, H. 1989, *Democracy in the Kitchen*, London: Virago

Walkerdine, V., Lucey, H. and Melody, J. 2001, *Growing Up Girl: Psychosocial Explorations of Gender and Class*, Basingstoke: Palgrave

Warde, A., Tomlinson, M. and McMeekin, A. 2003, 'Expanding tastes and cultural omnivorousness in the UK', Centre for Research on Innovation and Competitiveness, University of Manchester and UMIST, UK, mimeo.

Werbner, P. 1999, 'What colour "success"? Distorting value in studies of ethnic entrepreneurship', *The Sociological Review*, 47 (3), pp. 548–79

Williams, B. 1993, *Shame and Necessity*, Berkeley, CA: University of California Press

Williams, G. 2003, 'Blame and responsibility', *Ethical Theory and Moral Practice*, 6, pp. 427–45

Williams, G. 2004a, 'Praise and blame', *Internet Encyclopedia of Philosophy*: http://www.utm.edu/research/iep

Williams, G. 2004b, 'Responsibility as a virtue', Institute for Environment, Philosophy and Public Policy, Lancaster University, Lancaster, UK. www.lancs.ac.uk/staff/williagd/papers.htm

Williams, R. 1977, *Marxism and Literature*, Oxford: Oxford University Press

Williamson, J. 2003, 'Lady bountiful tries life in the slums', *New Statesman*, 20.1.2003, pp. 25–6

Willis, P. 1977, *Learning to Labour*, Aldershot: Gower

Winch, P. 1958, *The Idea of Social Science*, London: Routledge Kegan and Paul

Wolff, J. 2003, 'The message of redistribution: disadvantage, public policy and the human good', *Catalyst Working Paper*, London, http://www.catalystforum.org.uk

Wood, A. W. 1990, *Hegel's Ethical Thought*, Cambridge: Cambridge University Press

Wynne, B., Waterton, C. and Grove-White, R. 1993, *Public Perceptions and the Nuclear Industry in West Cumbria*, Lancaster: Centre for the Study of Environmental Change, Lancaster University

Yar, M. 1999, 'Community and Recognition', PhD thesis, Lancaster University, Lancaster, UK

Yar, M. 2001a, 'Recognition and the politics of human(e) desire', *Theory, Culture and Society*, 18 (2–3), pp. 57–76

Yar, M. 2001b, 'Beyond Nancy Fraser's "perspectival dualism"', *Economy and Society*, 30 (3), pp. 288–303

Young, I. M. 1990, *Justice and the Politics of Difference*, Princeton, NJ: Princeton University Press

Index